Acts of Narrative Resistance

ACTS OF NARRATIVE RESISTANCE

Women's Autobiographical Writings in the Americas

LAURA J. BEARD

University of Virginia Press

CHARLOTTESVILLE AND LONDON

University of Virginia Press

© 2009 by the Rector and Visitors of the University of Virginia
Printed in the United States of America on acid-free paper

First published 2009

9 8 7 6 5 4 3 2 1

LIBRARY OF CONGRESS CATALOGING-IN-PUBLICATION DATA

Beard, Laura J., 1962–
   Acts of narrative resistance : women's autobiographical writings in the Americas /
Laura J. Beard.
      p.   cm.—(American literatures initiative)
   Includes bibliographical references and index.
   ISBN 978-0-8139-2862-3 (cloth : alk. paper)
   ISBN 978-0-8139-2863-0 (pbk. : alk. paper)
   1. Autobiography—Women authors.   2. Autobiography—Political aspects.   3. Latin
American prose literature—Women authors—History and criticism.   4. Latin American
prose literature—20th century—History and criticism.   5. Canadian prose literature—
Women authors—History and criticism.   6. Canadian prose literature—20th century—
History and criticism.   7. Women—America—Biography—History and criticism.
8. Women in literature.   9. Biography as a literary form.   I. Title.
PQ7081.5.B43   2009
809'.93592—dc22

                                                                                    2009020563

THE
AMERICAN
LITERATURES
INITIATIVE

A book in the American Literatures Initiative (ALI), a collaborative
publishing project of NYU Press, Fordham University Press, Rutgers
University Press, Temple University Press, and the University of Virginia
Press. The Initiative is supported by The Andrew W. Mellon Foundation.
For more information, please visit www.americanliteratures.org.

For my mother, Barbara Lucy Moss Beard,
and in loving memory of my father, John S. Beard,
who taught me about ethical acts of resistance

CONTENTS

Illustrations

Acknowledgments

This book has been a long time brewing on the back burners, bubbling up in conference papers presented, articles published, classes taught, grant proposals written, and many conversations with colleagues, family, and friends. It has been brewing long enough that it is hard to say exactly when it started, or what went into the pot first, but I have many people, organizations, and funding sources to thank in this space.

I first wrote on Luisa Futoransky and Helena Parente Cunha as part of my doctoral dissertation in the Department of Hispanic and Italian Studies at Johns Hopkins University, and I gratefully acknowledge the American Association of University Women for the American Fellowship that allowed me to devote my last year at Hopkins to writing full-time. My dissertation director, Dr. Sara Castro-Klarén, remains a remarkable mentor and friend; I cannot begin to express here all that she has meant to me. I also thank Noel Valis, for her careful reading of that long-ago dissertation.

For opportunities to share conversations with Nélida Piñon, Helena Parente Cunha, Luisa Futoransky, and Ana María Shua, in Baltimore, Washington, D.C., Rio de Janeiro, Buenos Aires, and Louisville, Kentucky, I thank the generous support of the Department of Hispanic and Italian Studies, the Latin American Studies Program, and the Women Studies Program at Johns Hopkins University and the Office of the Vice President for Research, the Office of the Provost, and the Department of Classical and Modern Languages and Literatures at Texas Tech University. My greatest thanks and admiration go to the wonderful authors themselves, for their works, their warmth, and their wisdom, their generosity and their humor. I thank my former colleagues in the Department of Women's Studies at the University of Victoria, for introducing me to Lee Maracle's *Bobbi Lee: Indian Rebel* and encouraging me to include it in my course there on testimonial literature.

A faculty development leave, supported by the Office of the Provost at Texas Tech University, in the spring of 2006 gave me the time needed to complete this book manuscript. Generous support from the Fulbright Program has also given me time to devote to research and writing. My first article on *Bobbi Lee: Indian Rebel* and Shirley Sterling's *My Name Is Seepeetza* was written while I was a Fulbright Senior Scholar in Mexico in 1999–2000, working on a different project; and the final revisions of this manuscript were completed while I was occupying the University of Alberta Research Chair in Native Studies, doing research for a book on autobiographical narratives on the Indian residential schools.

A 2002 Newberry Library Summer Institute entitled "American Indian Autobiography as Personal and Tribal History: Who Gets to Tell the Story?" helped form the way I approach Native autobiographies. I am grateful to the Lannan Institute, the Newberry Library, all my colleagues in the Institute, and, most particularly, to Kate Shanley for her amazing wisdom and grace in creating that space and that experience. In 1995, a National Endowment for the Humanities Summer Seminar, "Issues in the Rhetorical Theory of Narrative," with James Phelan at Ohio State University, sharpened my readings of narrative texts, and I similarly thank Jim for his wisdom and grace and my colleagues in that wonderful seminar for all the conversations in and out of class. I continue to learn from colleagues in the Society for the Study of Narrative Literature, the Association for the Study of American Indian Literatures, Feministas Unidas, the Latin American Studies Association, the Brazilian Studies Association, the International Auto/Biography Association, and the Modern Languages Association.

My appreciation also goes to audience members for insightful comments and questions at the following conferences and venues where I have presented bits of this work: the International Auto/Biography Association; various International Conferences on Narrative, sponsored by the International Society for the Study of Narrative; Latin American Studies Association Conference; Modern Languages Association; the Exile in the Hispanic & Italian World Colloquium at the University of Victoria; the Fourth International Congress of the Americas, Universidad de las Américas, Puebla, Mexico; Seminario Nacional de

Professores Universitarios de Literaturas en Lingua Inglesa, São Paolo, Brazil; Asociación de Literatura Femenina Hispánica Conference; the Mid-America International Conference on Hispanic Literature, and as a guest lecturer in the graduate program in English at the Universidad Federal de Santa Catarina, in Florianópolis, Brazil.

Part of chapter 1 appeared in an earlier form in *College Literature*, while parts of chapter 2 were published first in an article in *Intertexts* and later as a chapter in *Luisa Futoransky y su palabra itinerante*, edited by Ester González Gimbernat. Traces of those chapters can be found in an article in Spanish in *Revista iberoamericana*. Some of chapter 3 appears in an earlier form in *Hispanófila*; what became part 3 of this book, with chapters 5 and 6, appeared in a much earlier form in an article in *Studies in American Indian Literatures*. I thank all for the permission to reprint here. I am particularly grateful to Ana María Shua for permission to include the photos from *The Book of Memories*, to Luisa Futoransky for permission to include illustrations from *De Pe a Pa*, and to Groundwood Press for permission to include illustrations from *My Name Is Seepeetza*.

For their willingness to read parts of this work in draft form with patience and grace I thank Sara Castro-Klarén, Marcy Schwartz, Kathryn Shanley, Sharon Nell, David Larmour, Marjean Purinton, Bruce Clarke, Hafid Gafaiti, Genaro Pérez, Fred Suppe, Susan Stein, Allen Miller, Thomas Barker, and Ellen Beard. I owe great thanks to the outside readers for the University of Virginia Press, whose careful critical attention and generous commentary were enormously helpful. I thank the staff at the University of Virginia Press, especially my terrific editor, Cathie Brettschneider, and the excellent editors who worked with me at the American Literatures Initiative, Tim Roberts and Susan Murray.

My deepest thanks go to my family—my mother, Barbara Beard; my sister, Ellen Beard; my brothers, Donald Beard, Bruce Beard, and Brian Beard—for always believing in me, for always being there, for trips to the airport and walks in the woods, for long-distance conversations, for laughter and love. My own autobiographical narrative and my own lessons in resistance start with you and with Dad. And my deepest thanks go to my husband, Tommy, and to our son, Murray John—your love and support are amazing and your awesome storytelling abilities showcase the power of narrative in our lives every day.

ACTS OF NARRATIVE RESISTANCE

Introduction

> *For many women, access to autobiography means access to the identity it constructs. Therefore, the distinction between self-representation as a political discourse and self-representation as an artistic practice is less important than their simultaneity of function in a particular culture and for specific audiences.*
>
> —LEIGH GILMORE, *AUTOBIOGRAPHICS*

Theorists of autobiography have struggled for decades to define what autobiography is and what it is not, to mark out the distinctions between autobiography and fiction, and to decide to what extent we can commit to the referentiality of an autobiographical text or to what extent every autobiographical subject is a fictive subject, just a pleasing illusion. Regardless of all the discussion and theoretical debate, autobiographical texts remain popular with readers, with presses, with critics, with moviegoers, with all sorts of audiences and publics. Turning lives into stories seems irresistible. We turn to life narratives in part to see what they might teach us about how individuals in different cultures experience their sense of being an "I" (Eakin, *How* 4). The autobiographical texts chosen for this study are written by and about individuals whose experiences of being an "I" have not always been valued either in the dominant cultures of their nations or in the dominant literary cultures of autobiographical studies. These writers have chosen autobiographical genres in order to claim spaces in which they might write an "I," or sometimes a "we," that can work to uncover mechanisms of oppression and lay out paths toward political and social change.

I examine autobiographical genres created at the nexus of political discourse and artistic practice, taking as my examples texts written out of diverse but particular cultures of the Americas. I discuss three specific autobiographical practices of contemporary women of the Americas, practices that can be read as forms of narrative resistance. In naming their own identities as part of their struggles to challenge domination, the women employing these genres create autobiographical acts of political and narrative resistance. Their texts resist easy classification into traditional generic categories; many of them demonstrate narrative resistance in their form of construction as those who tell their life stories resist the conventions and language of the traditional, male-authored, Euro-American autobiography.

I focus on these works as acts of narrative resistance. Barbara Harlow asserts that the term "resistance" was first used in a 1966 study that makes an important distinction between literature written under occupation and that written in exile, noting:

> [S]uch a distinction presupposes a people's collective relationship to a common land, a common identity, or a common cause on the basis of which it becomes possible to articulate the difference between the two modes of historical and political existence, between, that is, "occupation" and "exile." The distinction presupposes furthermore an "occupying power" which has either exiled or subjugated, in this case both exiled and subjugated, a given population and has in addition significantly intervened in the literary and cultural development of the people it has dispossessed and whose land it has occupied. Literature, in other words, is presented by the critic as an arena of *struggle*. (2)

Harlow's discussion of the term "resistance" resonates with literature produced by Indigenous peoples and with testimonial literature in Latin America—a literature frequently identified with resistance movements in Latin American countries as the witnesses who are moved to narrate are often involved in proposing revolutionary solutions for the problems in their nations. Narrative works of resistance literature directly confront both the critic and the artist with the responsibilities of involvement in the political context in which the works are constructed (Harlow 78). The autobiographical genres and works by women writers of the Americas I explore here can be read as resistance literature. While the related pedagogical arguments lie beyond the scope of this book, I would also, in a broader context, argue for teaching many of these autobiographical works as acts of narrative resistance in order to confront scholars and students with the responsibilities of involvement in the political contexts in which these texts are constructed.[1]

In an effort to generate new readings with this book, I pair works by women writers from different nations, in most cases writing in different languages. Each pair is chosen for its exemplification of a particular genre or tradition in women's autobiographical writings in the Americas. In offering this series of contextualized paired readings of autobiographical works written by women, all published in the 1980s and 1990s, I examine how subjectivity "has been produced, imagined, scripted and resisted" (Whitlock 2) by women writing in different locations, each marked by her own sexuality, nationality, ethnicity, social and economic class, native language, etc. Ana María Shua and Luisa Futoransky are Argentine Jews, one writing from her native Buenos Aires, the other from exile in China, Japan, and France. Nélida Piñon and Helena Parente Cunha are authors who locate themselves differently in the racial, ethnic, and cultural intersections of Brazil. Lee Maracle and Shirley Sterling are Aboriginal women from British Columbia who write out of different Indigenous traditions and life experiences but whose autobiographical writings underscore many of the same problems present in the Canadian mosaic.[2] While the voices of these women (and the other women whose texts appear as intertexts here) are ones not often heard in critical discussions of women's autobiography, a greater appreciation of how they take up different autobiographical genres, and how they put them to work to construct their own identities while resisting the imposition of other identities, can deepen our understanding of women's writings in the Americas and of contemporary autobiographical traditions in general.

By looking at these provocative texts from Argentina, Brazil, and Indigenous Canada, I seek to broaden our discussions of women's autobiographical voices. It has been proclaimed that "[w]omen's autobiography is now a privileged site for thinking about issues of writing at the intersection of feminist, postcolonial, and postmodern critical theories" (Smith and Watson, *Women, Autobiography, Theory* 5), but not all women's autobiographical texts have been equally privileged. Comparative literary studies often delegate works by Latin American women to a secondary status while texts by Native women of Canada are usually not considered at all. Clearly, women of the world do not speak in one voice nor share one common experience; studies of women's autobiography that center on writings by women of one race, one culture, or one nation can suggest a more monolithic sense of women's lives or women's writings than is warranted. As Françoise Lionnet writes in *Autobiographical Voices: Race, Gender, Self-Portraiture*: "We women are so diverse and live in such varied cultural, racial, and economic circumstances that we cannot possibly pretend to speak in a single voice. It is by listening to a plurality of voices from various corners of the planet and across centuries that we will strengthen our ability to resist demeaning power structures" (xi). By placing the study of women's autobiographical genres in the context of a plurality of women's voices from various corners of the Americas, I hope to contribute to the discussion Lionnet suggests. The women studied here use their voices to resist demeaning power structures at work in their countries. By paying close attention to those voices, to how these women use their autobiographical writings to uncover mechanisms of oppression and to discover their own sources of strength and power, we gain a greater understanding of how autobiography and testimony can function as political tools.

I am interested in examining how these authors use these texts to "reveal their troubles with the old 'I' at the same time that they make trouble with that generic 'I'" (Smith, *Subjectivity* 4–5). As Leigh Gilmore reminds us, autobiography works "within discourses that construct truth, identity, and power, and these discourses produce a gendered subject" (*Autobiographics* xiv). Reading these autobiographical texts provides insight into how women of disparate races, cultures, countries, and classes have negotiated those discourses and resisted the ideologies at work behind them. Autobiographical studies that are focused too narrowly on Eurocentric texts give us too limited an understanding of those discourses and of the ways in which gendered subjects are produced in our societies.

The texts I have selected were all published in the 1980s and early 1990s. These years mark out important political, historical, social, and literary moments in the Americas: brutal dictatorships (and their aftermaths) in Latin America, the increasing awareness of Native peoples and issues around the 1992 "celebration" of the "discovery" of the Americas, growing women's movements throughout the Americas, the incorporation of poststructuralist theory, and more. The texts I have chosen from this period are provocative examples of the autobiographical genres I highlight, examples that give us greater insight into what Smith has called "the complex ways in which histories of the subject, discourses of identity, cultural inscriptions of the body, and laws of genre coalesce in the autobiographical 'I'" (*Subjectivity* 4). I am interested in how these authors negotiate the discourses of personal, cultural, ethnic, national, sexual, gender, and, in some cases, Indigenous identities in order to inscribe their own stories and their own life experiences. I explore how each author negotiates the dominant discourses at work in her country in order to carve out a textual space for her own identity, one that resists the prescribed identities and dominant ideologies.

My reading of these various life narratives demonstrates how these authors "operate along the moveable boundaries of genres" (Zamora, *Contemporary American Women Writers* 6) at the same time that their characters seek to define and embrace a selfhood created at the inter-sections of different discourses of identity. These are women who write beyond the endings, along the margins, and across boundaries of genre and gender. The anthropologist Michael Fischer has asserted that be-cause "ethnicity is something reinvented and reinterpreted in each generation," autobiographical writing is as necessary as it is inevitable (195).[3] Lee Maracle and Shirley Sterling have to reinterpret what it is to be Nlakapamux, Stó:lô, Salish, or Cree after generations of enforced resi-dential schooling; Ana María Shua and Luisa Futoransky reinvent and reinterpret what it is to be both Argentine and Jewish, as descendants of Eastern European immigrants; Nélida Piñon explores what it is to be Brazilian and Galician; and Helena Parente Cunha, what it is to be Brazilian, particularly Bahian, with the possibility of African ancestors. In the works of these authors, autobiography and fiction overlap quite naturally as the writers and their protagonists record and imagine in creative ways.

Autobiographical writing has always played an important role in emancipatory politics. Sidonie Smith refers to texts by women that par-ticipate in self-consciously political autobiographical acts as autobio-graphical manifestos ("Autobiographical Manifesto" 189). She refers to these texts as purposeful, bold, contentious, working to dislodge the old Eurocentric, phallocentric "I" "through an expressly political collocation of a new 'I'" in service to a new reality, a new emancipatory politics— something the women writers I discuss are all doing, albeit in sometimes different ways.

The constituent aspects of the autobiographical manifesto are clearly visible in the autobiographical works discussed in the following chapters. Each of these texts appropriates and contests sovereignty, but their strat-egies are different as their moments and places of creation differ. Indeed, the autobiographical genres discussed here signal crucial moments in the project of women's autobiography in the Americas. The works of Helena Parente Cunha and Luisa Futoransky represent a critical step in the feminist project of autobiography in the late 1980s in the Americas. While metafiction may be seen as a dated genre by some literary critics today (other critics trace out the meta- at work in television, film, com-ics and other pop-culture genres), at the time that Parente Cunha and Futoransky were writing their autobiographical metatexts, the context was different. As the self-consciousness of metafictional works arises from within each specific discourse, we must read the critical importance of Helena Parente Cunha's texts within the social, political, and cultural context of Salvador, Bahia, in the 1980s. Parente Cunha's work was scandalous in her native Salvador, and she shocked many of her colleagues and compatriots by publishing it. Her work was severely censured in many quarters, yet other critics noted the bravery of her work, the violence of her critique against masculine oppression, and the courage of her positions (Parente Cunha, *Com a palavra* 157).

Lee Maracle and Shirley Sterling also appropriate and contest sovereignty, not via the self-consciously theoretical and playfully metafictional discourse of Parente Cunha or Futoransky but rather via the straightforward, passionately political discourse of Indigenous women committed to uncovering mechanisms of oppression and discovering strategies for healing and strength in their communities and their nations. Sterling uses the journal format and the focalization of the young schoolgirl to compel her readers to ask, "How can we best combat the type of racist thinking which put together the residential schools? ("Seepeetza Revisited" 12–13).

All of these authors are committed, with their texts, "to bring to light, to make manifest," most specifically to make manifest new perspectives on identity, experience, and ways of knowledge. The family sagas written by Ana María Shua and Nélida Piñon bring to light the experiences and perspectives of citizens of the Argentine and Brazilian nations not always considered in the official histories of those nations, just as the *testimonios* of Maracle and Sterling make manifest accounts of the Canadian state that can expose the falseness of the views offered from the center of white power.

Perhaps one of the most important aspects of the autobiographical manifesto, an aspect shared with the genre of *testimonio*, is that it looks toward the future, toward positive change, for the self and for society. The "I" writes under the sign of hope and the possibility of change, as "the manifesto attempts to actively position the subject in a potentially liberated future distanced from the constraining and oppressive identifications inherent in the everyday practices of the *ancien régime*" (Smith, "Autobiographical Manifesto" 194). These texts look back critically, but they also look forward with hope to a new set of possibilities, a new set of spaces.

For, as Gloria Bird (Spokane) asserts, writing, "at its liberating best, . . . is a political act. Through writing we can undo the damaging stereotypes that are continually perpetuated about Native peoples. We can rewrite our history, and we can mobilize our future" (30). All the authors I study here, at their "liberating best," write as a political act. They write to undo damaging stereotypes, to rewrite their histories, and to mobilize their futures. The texts chosen for this study are all ones that foreground the relationship of identities to power. As autobiographical manifestos, they insist on "new interpretations, new positionings of the subject as a means of wresting power, resisting universalizing repetitions that essentialize, naturalize, totalize the subject" (Smith, "Autobiographical Manifesto" 195). These are authors writing texts that have a political purpose, texts that call for a transformation in the society surrounding the self that writes.

While there is much that unites the authors I discuss, they are also very different authors, coming from different countries and cultures, writing out of different languages and locations in the Americas. In bringing their texts together here, I do not wish to erase important differences between these books and authors and the living webs of the peoples and traditions from which they arise (Allen, *Studies* xi). Thus I find it crucial to take my critical approaches from the texts themselves. In her introduction to *Latin American Women's Narrative: Practices and Theoretical Perspectives*, Sara Castro-Klarén affirms that for many feminist critics today, there "emerges a rising tide that enables critics to theorize on women's writing from the very texts at hand. It is the text's work of disordering, creation of alternate voices, disobedience and transgressions, silences and testimonial strategies that flex, question, contest and even break metropolitan theory, feminist or otherwise" (33). The texts I discuss do that work, enriching our discussions of autobiographical genres and women's writing. Metafiction often embodies within itself its own critical frame of reference, and I exemplify how the autobiographical metafiction by Helena Parente Cunha and Luisa Futoransky questions traditional theories of autobiography as the authors inscribe new textual spaces at the intersections of fictional autobiography and autobiographical fiction. The narratives by Nélida Piñon and Ana María Shua use a variety of voices to create a story of the family and of the nation that resists and disorders the official discourses of nation and history proffered by the governments of Brazil and Argentina. The autobiographical texts by Lee Maracle and Shirley Sterling employ silences and testimonial strategies to contest the ideological stronghold of Canadian discourses on multiculturalism and the Canadian mosaic.

In "The Usable Past: The Idea of History in Modern U.S. and Latin

American Fiction," Lois Parkinson Zamora addresses the move to enlarge the term "American" in comparative literary studies from the national context (United States) to the hemispheric context. As she notes, "It is a significant expansion, since 'America' encompasses thirty-five countries and fifteen territories or protectorates, four principal Indo-European languages and countless indigenous languages, 676 million inhabitants, and more than sixteen million square miles of land" (11). While her comment is intended to help us realize the challenges in discussing American (in the hemispheric context) literature, another challenge lies in her statement that is perhaps not always fully appreciated by readers. The "Indo-European languages" are prioritized both by placement in the sentence and by the fact that they are counted. The Indigenous languages are labeled as "countless." Her use of the word "countless" implies a large number, certainly more than four, but it can also imply that they are not worth counting. Most scholars working in comparative literary studies in the Americas have focused only on those literary works produced within Indo-European traditions, ignoring the languages, literatures, cultures, and tribal traditions of Indigenous peoples. I bring Native voices into the discussion by focusing, in part 3, on works by Indigenous authors. The citations from the Native-authored primary texts, as well as the many citations from Native scholars, bring a broad spectrum of Indigenous wisdom and knowledge to the issues of self, identity, memory, and narration that are so vital to the discussion of autobiography.

My purpose here is ambitious, interweaving discussions of texts that are not normally considered together. But by bringing together authors, texts, and locations not normally foregrounded in literary studies, by attending to writers and narrative forms that are often left out in a more narrow construction of the autobiographical, we begin to discern other textual weaves at work in the vibrant pattern and project of women's autobiography in the Americas. By bringing to the critical table women's writings from Argentina, Brazil, and Native North America, I shift the focus away from Eurocentric texts in order to deepen and strengthen our understanding of women's autobiographical writings. The women whose texts I study here merit a wider audience in comparative literary studies; their autobiographical texts elaborate on the resistance of these women to the controls that others would exercise over their lives and their life stories. The lives they narrate and the social and political issues they raise in their resistance narratives are, to repeat Lee Maracle's words in *Bobbi Lee*, "about why we must talk" (ii).

A final note, on languages and translations: Because I hope that this work will be useful to scholars working in various fields—autobiography studies, Latin American studies, Native studies, women's studies, Inter-American studies, and comparative literature—I have used English translations of the texts originally written in Spanish and Portuguese. In the case of narratives that are available in English translation, like Nélida Piñon's *The Republic of Dreams*, Ana María Shua's *The Book of Memories*, and Helena Parente Cunha's *Woman between Mirrors*, I cite the published English translations. In the cases of works not published in English (both primary texts and interviews or articles in Spanish or Portuguese), I use my own English translations. Due to space constraints, I cannot include all the original quotations, but when the crucial wordplay in Spanish or Portuguese will be obvious even to nonspeakers, I sometimes provide quotations in the original language.

PART ONE

ADDRESSING THE SELF: AUTOBIOGRAPHICAL METAFICTION

. . . I'm going to begin my story. Here, where my body intersects with the space of my images. I have something to say because I'm going to say myself to myself, like anyone face to face with memory or a mirror. No, I'm not going to write my memoirs, or my biography or paint my portrait. I'm a made-up character. I exist only in my imagination and in the imagination of my reader. And of course, I exist for the woman who is putting me on paper.

—HELENA PARENTE CUNHA, *WOMAN BETWEEN MIRRORS*

In *On Autobiography*, Phillipe Lejeune defines autobiography as a "retrospective prose narrative written by a real person concerning his own existence, where the focus is his individual life, in particular the story of his personality" (4). With a self called to witness "his" own being, the traditional view of autobiography is grounded in authority, the unique authority of the autobiographer over "his" life story.

Acknowledging the difficulty of distinguishing autobiography from the autobiographical novel, Lejeune develops the idea of the autobiographical pact, a form of contract between author and reader in which the autobiographer explicitly commits her/himself to a sincere effort to come to terms with and understand her/his own life, knowing that a complete historical exactitude is impossible. Lejeune stresses that texts are written for readers and it is readers who make them function (4). Autobiography, then, is as much a mode of reading as it is a mode of writing, a statement echoed by numerous critics of autobiography.

The acknowledgment that autobiography is a kind of fiction, its self and its truth as much created as (re)discovered realities has contributed to the boom in studies of autobiography, in particular to the recent proliferation of studies of women's autobiographies. In this section, I examine a particular genre within women's autobiographical traditions in the Americas: metafictional novels written on the borders between autobiographical fiction and fictional autobiography. Luisa Futoransky and Helena Parente Cunha use their fictionalized life narratives to challenge the concepts inherent in auto/bio/graphy, employing a variety of narrative and linguistic devices to explore the possibility and impossibility of writing a coherent self, a coherent life, a coherent text. Their texts foreground the representation of identity, entering in dialogue with autobiography without following obediently the conventions of that genre. These are examples of texts that invoke certain conventions and expectations of autobiography in order to produce and highlight forms of dissonance; texts that "allow reading effects implied by autobiography to remain lively even as they press beyond autobiography's formal boundaries" (Gilmore, "Anatomy" 227). As narratives more interested in proliferating questions than in providing answers, these autobiographical metafictions are critical to a study of women's autobiographical writings in the Americas.

Metafiction, like autobiography, has been seen as "less a property of the primary text than a function of reading" (Currie 5). Also like autobiography, metafiction is a type of borderline discourse, "a kind of writing which places itself on the border between fiction and criticism, and which takes that border as its subject" (Currie 2). The assimilation of critical perspectives into the fictional narrative, a fixation with language and its relationship with the world, and a self-consciousness of the artificiality of the narrative's constructions are all metafictional elements that can be traced in these feminist autobiographical metafictions. Since metafiction concerns itself so centrally with the issues of meaning construction, metafictional texts were a vital tool for feminist challenges to the traditional construction of (gendered) meanings in Latin America in the 1980s. The metafictional autobiographical novel allowed feminist authors the space, and gave them the power, to explore not only their own lives, but also conditions of literary production, questions of representation, and constructions of gender and identity. Through the practice of writing autobiographical metafiction, Helena Parente Cunha, Luisa Futoransky, and their counterparts explored theories of autobiography and fiction. Their autobiographical narratives help us to understand the ideological function of autobiographical storytelling.

Pressing beyond autobiography's formal boundaries, Parente Cunha and Futoransky problematize the authority of the signature as that which is crucial to the identity of autobiography. Rather than having an authorial signature that matches the name of the protagonist/narrator in the text, Parente Cunha inscribes a nameless protagonist and Futoransky writes a modified version of her name. Their play with names exemplifies Gilmore's assertion that for men, the mythology of the signature involves either the empowerment or the anxiety of influence, but for women, the title page is often a site of evasion, presenting itself "not as fact but as an extension of the fiction of identity, and it is frequently more comprehensible as a corollary to laws regarding women's noninheritance of property. For women, the fiction that our names signify our true identities obscures the extent to which our names are thought of not as our own but as the legal signifier of a man's property" (*Autobiographics* 81).

Futoransky and Parente Cunha employ their autobiographical fictions, in part, to contest the fiction that our names signify our true identities. Reading against each other two works that are written in different languages, from different countries, and out of different cultures yet are narratively analogous, we trace out one autobiographical tradition chosen by women writers of the Americas to frame novelistically and autobiographically the fiction of identity. Parente Cunha and Futoransky create autobiographical and self-conscious protagonists who are aware of the precarious nature of their lives and their subject positions, whose subjectivity is in transit, "no longer one, whole, unified and in control, but rather fluid, in process and hybrid" (Braidotti 9). The texts in which they inscribe those protagonists might be also called "transpositions," echoing Rosi Braidotti's use of the term as "an in-between space of zigzagging and of crossing: non-linear, but not chaotic; nomadic, yet accountable and committed; creative but also cognitively valid; discursive and also materially embedded—it is coherent without falling into instrumental rationality" (5). In their meta-autobiographical texts, we see the process of creating autobiography, the decisions that precede the writing of an autobiography but that are usually suppressed in the actual writing of the text. By creating these transpositional texts, Parente Cunha and Futoransky create autobiographical texts that are less a reflection of life and more a reflection of their own processes of making meaning out of life.

Parente Cunha and Futoransky both write autobiographical fiction that defies any concept that "identities are self-identical, persisting through time as the same, unified and internally coherent" (Butler, *Gender Trouble* 16–17). From the very first page of her award-winning first novel, *Mulher no espelho* (1983; *Woman between Mirrors*, 1989), Parente Cunha challenges the idea that identities are self-identical, employing the metaphor of the mirror to grapple with the problem of the self that does not coincide. In her trilogy of novels, *Son cuentos chinos* (1986; They Are Chinese Tales), *De Pe a Pa: De Pekín a París* (1986; From Pe to Pa: From Peking to Paris), and *Urracas* (1992; Magpies), Futoransky similarly employs autobiographical fiction to explore the inconsistencies and multiplicities of identities. By choosing to write their novels as fictional autobiographies, Parente Cunha and Futoransky immediately establish an irreconcilable tension between a form that traditionally relied upon the constitution of a sovereign "I" and a narrative that posits the impossibility of such a construction. Throughout their narratives, the authors and their narrator/protagonists both evoke and contest the conventions of autobiographical writings as they search for other ways of writing the self.

These metafictional novels foreground the representation of identity, entering in dialogue with autobiography without following obediently the conventions of the genre. These life narratives resist easy categorization into literary genres, dancing always at the borders between metafiction and autobiography, between autobiographical fiction and fictional autobiography, just as the women who write themselves into and out of these texts resist easy categorization by the societies and cultures that would seek to place them into restrictive roles and limit both their mobility and their subjectivity.

1 /   The Mirrored Self: Helena Parente Cunha's *Women between Mirrors*

In autobiography we are always asked to go through the looking glass from both sides.

—TIMOTHY DOW ADAMS, *LIGHT WRITING AND LIFE WRITING: PHOTOGRAPHY IN AUTOBIOGRAPHY*

Helena Parente Cunha's *Mulher no espelho* (1983; *Woman between Mirrors* 1989) has been called "the heterogeneous and theoretically self-conscious sort of work that is typical of the best feminist novelistic production in Latin America today" (Williams 15). Parente Cunha responds to Hélène Cixous's admonition to "write yourself. Your body must be heard," writing her self and her body into a feminist autobiographical text that packs a powerful punch against patriarchy.

While both Luisa Futoransky and Helena Parente Cunha write from their bodies, Parente Cunha's autobiographical texts reveal a more theoretical stance of self-reflectivity. Eneida Leal Cunha sees in Helena Parente Cunha's text a solution to a common dichotomy present in other authors, "a confluence and a dialogue between creating literature and reflecting on literature, the ambiguity of the texts written by those who study and make literature" (*Com a palavra* 154). Parente Cunha is an author who both studies and creates literature. Holding Ph.D.s in literary theory and Italian literature, she is a professor of literature and literary theory at the Federal University of Rio de Janeiro. She has published more than a dozen works, including poetry, essays, short stories, and novels, and edited collections on Brazilian writers. She is part of a community of Latin American writers working within universities "who make obvious in their writings their use of literary devices" (Eneida Leal Cunha 155). Parente Cunha is exemplary for the ways in which she makes visible the tensions between author, narrator, and protagonist as she foregrounds the process and construction of her autobiographical text.

While Parente Cunha was a critically acclaimed author in Brazil prior to the publication of *Women between Mirrors*, this text brought her wider recognition and international acclaim. *Women between Mirrors* won the 1982 Prêmio Cruz e Sousa and the 1984 Prêmio Luíza Cláudio de Sousa, both from the Brazilian PEN Club. The novel was translated into English and German, and articles about Parente Cunha's work began appearing in U.S. literary journals. *Woman between Mirrors* continues to exemplify the formal experimentation and theoretical concerns Parente Cunha showed in earlier works, but it also attracts readers with its story of a female character in crisis and its critical portrayal of Brazil's patriarchal society. *Woman between Mirrors* plays with the conventions of both autobiography and fiction, marking an important moment in metafictional autobiography in Brazil, indeed, in the Americas. In his review of the English translation, Luis Fernando Valente asserts that "*Woman between Mirrors* bears unquestionable evidence that post-modern self-consciousness does not have to yield a cold and cerebral text, as is the case with so many North American metafictionists, but can be used, rather, to generate a fictional text in which innermost feelings and powerful emotions play a central role" (697). Powerful emotions played a role in both the creation and the reception of this autobiographical narrative. Feminist critics and women's studies students in the U.S. often react in strongly positive ways to the book. On the other hand, conservative sectors in Salvador, Bahia, considered the text shocking, scandalous, even pornographic, and Parente Cunha herself admits that she would not have published it when her father was still alive.[1] Her admission is an indication that this text is no theoretical exercise in literary form but rather an autobiographical exploration and a societal critique.

In this life narrative, the protagonist is a nameless woman, her identity thus not "resolved" at the lexical level by the recognition of a proper name. The namelessness of the female protagonist problematizes the autobiographical act. For, as Lejeune affirms in "The Autobiographical Pact," "What defines autobiography for the one who is reading is above all a contract of identity that is sealed by the proper name. And this is also true for the one that is writing the text" (19). By not assigning a name to her protagonist, Parente Cunha rejects Lejeune's contract of identity. Her narrative is instead an example of that "extended inquiry into the claims to knowledge made by the presence and absence of the names around and through which the body is made to cohere" (Gilmore, "Anatomy" 229). I propose that we read Parente Cunha's text as a refusal of the patriarchal regime of names and the identities it compels (230). I also propose that we read the namelessness of the protagonist as an act of narrative and political resistance.[2]

Parente Cunha's nameless protagonist is born into an upper-middle-class Brazilian family with its traditional family roles—the domineering father, the submissive wife/indulgent mother, the daughter whose innocence has been carefully prolonged, and the spoiled son. The old roles cannot be easily reproduced in the family created by the protagonist's marriage. The marriage breaks up, as do the relations between the parents and the children. At age forty-five, the protagonist has to redefine her life.

The metaphor chosen for such a redefinition is that of the protagonist standing in front of a three-way mirror, determined to see herself from every angle. Jenijoy La Belle argues that female characters, "when they are most concerned with their self-identities, or when crises in their lives throw them back on their sole selves," frequently turn to mirrors to contemplate their images in the glass (2). Ironically, while the protagonist of *Woman between Mirrors* stands looking at the numerous faces reflected in the mirrors, she is, for the reader, faceless. There is no conventional nineteenth-century narrative description of her features, her hair, her clothing. That scene no longer yields signification; the body has lost the ability to represent the self. That loss is itself significant, for the failure of the mimetic function has political uses. Authors write texts in part to reconfigure what counts as the world as literary texts enter "a field of reading as partial provocations, . . . initiating a set of appropriations and criticisms that call into question their fundamental premises" (Butler, *Bodies* 19). Parente Cunha's postmodern text works to reconfigure what will count as the world, provoking a set of criticisms of the roles traditionally assigned to women in Brazilian society.

The scene of the protagonist facing her image in the mirror and telling her life story is the primordial scene compelling the autobiographical voice: "one speaks across a gulf to address an inanimate face, one's own, and urges it to speak" (Gilmore, "Anatomy" 225). The protagonist of Parente Cunha's text speaks across a gulf, addressing an inanimate face(s) in the mirror and urging it (them) to speak. Parente Cunha toys with the issues at play in this attribution of face to voice and voice to face throughout her metafictional narratives.

The protagonist addresses herself to the multiple reflections in the mirror, telling her story (stories) to those endless images of her person that symbolize the various identities she could choose to adopt. Yet her story will not be a memoir or biography, because "I am a made-up character. I exist only in my imagination and in the imagination of my reader. . . . At home or on the street, people don't know me" (1). Her statement that her existence is limited to the pages of the text, that she would not be recognized on the street or even at home, leads her to question whether anyone can ever recognize another person. Her use of the verb *saber* instead of the *conhecer* that would be more commonly used with people is significant. The choice of *saber* emphasizes the depth of knowledge she stresses when she asks whether anyone really knows anyone else:

> Por acaso, alguém sabe alguém, carne e grito sob a capa do rosto, ordenado e composto em carapaça? Quando falo, as pessoas pensam que pensam que falam conmigo. Isto porque se confundem com as imagens exteriores, sempre iguais ou semelhantes e, de alguma forma, fixas, se levarmos em conta o correr de um dia, ou até mesmo de um ano. (7)

> [Does anyone really know anyone else, flesh crying out from beneath the mask of the face, this polished, proper shell? When I speak, people think they think they're speaking to me. What throws them off is always going by the outside, always identical or similar, to some extent fixed, and we're going by the outside if we mean the length of a day, or even of a year. (1)]

While other people may believe that she is the same person each time they see her, the protagonist argues that people rely too much on what happens on the outside of the skin, allowing the changes that take place on the inside to pass unnoticed. Just as questionable as the presumption in autobiographical referentiality that the reader can move from the knowledge of the text to knowledge of the self is the leap made from seeing a unified body to assuming a unified self.

Indeed, the protagonist argues there is often no connection between the exterior and the interior of a person. When tears run down her face, she is not crying, for the truth is "on the outside, I have no connection with myself. I am not even speaking, when I speak" (1). The exterior appearance is but a simulacrum. The story of portraiture that *Woman between Mirrors* narrates challenges the reliance on the visual at the same time that it challenges the assumption that the outside and the inside of a person not only are the same, but are even knowable.

The protagonist also stresses that identities change over time. People are not the same each day, each year. The self is always in transition because it is always in dialogue with other personalities and social forces.

These statements at the beginning are borne out over the course of a narrative in which the protagonist's self is seen as emergent, in process, always changing. Her desire to create this autobiographical performance is a response to the flux of self-experience, an instinctive gravitation "to identity-supporting structures" (Eakin, *How* 20).

The Self in Dialogue: I, the Woman Who Writes Me, and the Author

Like the autobiographer who, in making the text, creates a self that would not otherwise exist, the protagonist of Parente Cunha's fictional autobiography is conscious that she would not exist without the written text. But even in her own fiction she does not claim an unproblematic sense of identity. She resists participation in the masquerade of autobiographical writing that necessitates "an iconic representation of continuous identity" (Smith, *Poetics* 47), choosing instead to problematize the "I" of autobiographical writing. For, "when I say I, I'm not the woman who is writing this page. When I say I, I'm merely imagining myself. She is the one who is writing" (2). Almost as soon as the protagonist speaks as *eu* (I) she introduces *ela* (she)—"a mulher que me escreve" (the woman who writes me). The traditionally strong autobiographical "I" is missing from this fictional autobiography, its space only partially and problematically filled by a postmodern "I" that is anonymous, ambiguous, and multiple. The "I" seems never to stand alone. Debra Castillo's reading of a sentence of Julieta Campos's 1978 novel *Tiene los cabellos rojizos y se llama Sabina* (*She Has Reddish Hair and Her Name Is Sabina*, 1993) could be applied here as well (without, perhaps, the "he"): "'I' refracts into 'you' . . . and into 'he' and 'she.' The 'I,' 'you,' 'he,' 'she,' and intermittent 'we' and 'they' in turn serve as nodes organizing a proliferation of other characters, or character-positions, some of whom carry on dialogues with each other, some of whom ignore each other's existence, some of whom contradict each other or logically cancel each other out, some of whom occupy the space of the subject in near simultaneity" (153). Parente Cunha's protagonist speaks as *eu* (I), refers to the woman who writes her as *ela* (she), and is addressed by that woman as *você* (you). They carry on dialogues with each other, ignore each other, contradict each other, cancel each other out, and occupy the space of the subject in near simultaneity.

Raymond Leslie Williams asserts that "the most interesting technical device" in *Woman between Mirrors* "is the constant presence of a voice identified as 'the woman who writes me'" (15). Within the text, the protagonist explains this "woman who writes me": "Who is the woman who writes me? I know, because I made her up. Meanwhile, she doesn't know me. She thinks that she has me in her hands to write as she wishes" (2). From this first introduction of "the woman who writes me," the protagonist asserts her superior position, "*I* know, because *I* invented her." At the same time, "the woman who writes me" thinks that she controls the protagonist. Their struggle for control over the story, the text, the truth, continues throughout the text. "The woman who writes me" thinks she can write the protagonist as she wishes, but the protagonist claims to be "an irresistible presence that keeps getting away from her" (2).

At times "the woman who writes me" tries to banish the protagonist from her mind, but the protagonist knows that "the woman who writes me" cannot refuse her life: "For years I've been waiting for her to be ready to face me. Me, I'm a character built into her life" (2). There are times when "the woman who writes me" avoids the protagonist, and goes months without writing, but the protagonist knows that she will have to return for it is to write the protagonist's story that "the woman who writes me" exists, it is for that which the protagonist invented her.

But "the woman who writes me" has trouble writing the protagonist because the protagonist moves to her own rhythms, not to those of the woman who writes her. "The woman who writes me" tries to impose her own interpretations on the protagonist's actions, causing the protagonist to complain, "She can't follow me without trying to irritate me with explanations" (7). "The woman who writes me" mixes up her emotions with those of the protagonist, but the protagonist insists they keep things straight, using dramatically short, simple sentences to affirm her assertions: "She is she. I am I. She has her problems. I have mine. If I exist in her imagination, she wasn't the one who created me. I have made myself. Afterward I invented her. . . . She wants to get a hold on me. She can't. I escape from her words. Her anxiety" (2). The protagonist makes a strong statement about her autonomy and self-creation, "I made myself," but nevertheless had to create the other woman to write her story. They both struggle against their mutual dependence, with one or the other of them frequently asserting independence and control over the other only to have that independence and control undercut in the next sentence. The repetition and reiteration of the subject pronouns *eu* and *ela* are sustained throughout the narrative as the protagonist reasserts her control over her own story and her careful demarcation of the boundaries between "I" and "she," "mine" and "hers."

The question of the identity of "the woman who writes me" is continually addressed by the protagonist: "If some of my experiences went the
same way for the woman who writes me and seem also to have gone just
the opposite way, it's because we love to cancel each other out. Reverse
images face-to-face in the mirror. The other side. Reverse is the same as
the opposite side" (6). As reverse images of each other, "the woman who
writes me" is the woman the protagonist sees in the mirror. Like many
autobiographers, Parente Cunha "create[s] several, sometimes competing
stories about or versions of herself as her subjectivity is displaced by one
of multiple textual representations" (Smith, *Poetics* 47). Competing stories about and versions of "the woman who writes me" and the protagonist drive the plot. The two are presented by a dialectic of oppositions:
"Outgoing and happy, that's her. Sober and serious, that's me. She opens
up, I close up" (6). Parente Cunha's narration takes the form of a dialogue; becoming interactive, autobiographical identification "becomes
reciprocal, adaptive, corrective, affirmative" (Egan 7). The protagonist's
perceptions of her self and her life are continually contested and "cor-
rected" by the woman who writes her. Parente Cunha's metafictional autobiography (or meta-autobiography) seems to bear out Susanna Egan's
suggestion that "if the ontological self, as author/autobiography and as
object of reference, has been theorized out of existence, it is forced into
reappearance by interacting with another" (9).

Not only their personalities but the actions and life decisions of the
protagonist and the woman who writes her are diametrically opposed.
"The woman who writes me" is remembered as the child who walked to
school alone, ran away to the beach when her father beat her, disobeyed
her father's orders. The protagonist had to walk to school with her nana,
accepted her guilt when her father beat her, accepted a number of injustices: "I accepted my father's liking my brother better. I accepted my
husband's not letting me go out alone. I accepted living at the beck and
call of my three children. I accepted, I accepted, the risk and the loss,
and alone with myself came out the better. She used to run away from
her parents' home, never got married, went out with a lot of men. The
triumph and the danger, but alone by herself, she came out the loser" (7).
The protagonist's endless submission and patient acceptance are drawn
out in the text—I accepted, I accepted, I accepted—a litany evocative
of a catechism lesson in church. Parallel construction and oppositional
terms are again used to describe the two women: "risco e perda, solitário
ganho. . . . Triunfo e perigo, solitária perda."

The protagonist questions which of the two paths is better, more authentic. Readers might question which of the two stories is the "true" story of the self. But Parente Cunha consistently frustrates any desire for truth or settled meaning. Her text eludes any interpretation that would achieve meaning by the assigning of identity of agency, as in a paragraph that discusses the father(s) of the two women: "Her father. Her authoritarian father whom I adored and she despised. *In truth*, each has her own father. According to her, the difference is all in our reactions. Rebellion and submission. She doesn't know that the difference is in the identity of the two fathers. Absolutely the same, only different. One shouting is not the other one shouting. Each heard the shouting at different times, though it was the same shouting, the same fight. I loved, and she hated, our father. Our fathers" (7, emphasis added). Parallel but oppositional verb forms are used here to describe the emotional involvement of the two women, "eu superamei e ela superodiou" (I superloved and she superhated). This oppositional pull is present throughout the paragraph. The identity of the two fathers is absolutely the same, yet not the same. It was one shout, but heard at distinct times and in dissimilar ways. These passages are examples of Parente Cunha the writer putting into play the theories of deconstruction that Parente Cunha the professor of literary theory has read and taught.

"The woman who writes me" emerges as an antagonist or "other" of the protagonist as they enter into a kind of dialogue during the course of the narrative. "The woman who writes me" interrupts the narration at times to speak to the protagonist, addressing the protagonist as *você* (you)—thus the woman not only writes her but writes *to* her.

The protagonist is conscious of "the woman who writes me" and of their differences. The protagonist eventually rebels against the restrictions placed on her: "I like to put on my forbidden dresses, the ones my husband called indecent. I smile, I'm in on this with myself. . . . Who is that sultry provocative woman in the mirror? It's not me. She looks like her, the woman who writes me. I keep on dancing, in my red dress, clinging, plunging, slit up the side, I hardly recognize the image that jumps out at me from the mirror. Is it she? Is it me? Which one is for real?" (25). Just as readers may question which is the "true" story of the protagonist's life, the protagonist herself questions "qual é a verdadeira?"

For in asking this question, Parente Cunha is questioning the authenticity of the roles imposed on women in patriarchal societies. When the protagonist wonders who she is when she smiles at the image in the mirror, the brazen woman in the tight red dress or the good housewife and mother, discretely dressed and without any makeup, she is questioning those prescriptive roles and any "truth" that might be found in them. As she asks, "Where's the mask? On the scrubbed clean face or on the one daubed with false colors? While I pile on the makeup, am I taking off my mask? Or am I putting on my mask, when I wash my face?" (25–26), Parente Cunha asks her readers to see the masks women are forced to wear in patriarchal systems, to question whether there are masks to uncover or whether, paradoxically, there are only masks, only roles women are expected to play. She challenges the patriarchal system in which women are always seen in relation to others, with a woman's "individuality sacrificed to the 'constitutive definitions' of her identity as member of a family, as someone's daughter, someone's wife and someone's mother" (Benhabib and Cornell 12).

To add to the multiplicity of voices and perspectives created by the protagonist and the woman who writes her, there is an author expressly mentioned in the text. In traditional autobiography, the author, narrator, and protagonist all share the same proper name. In this fictional autobiography, the author, narrator, and protagonist all share the lack of a proper name. Giving a definitive name is a gesture of control, but here control of the text is dispersed among the three women. This multiplicity evokes Lejeune's claim for autobiography that "[e]verything happens as if . . . no combination of the system of persons in enunciation could satisfactorily 'totally express' the person" (35). The singular, sacrosanct "I" of autobiography is no longer satisfactory.

In a long passage of the text, the protagonist explains the interrelationship of the three women, claiming that it is indispensable to delineate the boundaries between the character, the narrator, and the author. As she explains: "I am the character here. The narrator is herself, the woman who writes me. The author has nothing to do with the story. The authoress, that is. These are the three entities which, as it so happens, have come together" (52). While the protagonist earlier claimed she knew "the woman who writes me" because she invented her, the protagonist does not know who the author is. Furthermore, she claims, the author does not enter into the story. That this statement is immediately followed by the question—"Or does she? Are we projections of her fantasies?"—again shows the strong dialectic quality of the protagonist's consciousness. But these questions are ultimately not important, for the protagonist is the one who plans the terms of the discourse here. Although the author would not want to become fictionalized by participating in this story, the protagonist explains that if she wanted the author to enter the story, the author would. However, the protagonist dismisses the author, claiming

"[n]ão estou interessada no desinteresse da sua vida" ("I am not interested in her lack of interest in her life" [52]). She goes on to explain that
if she depends on the woman who writes her, the author depends on her.
Without the protagonist, there would be no book; without the woman
who writes her, she herself would not take shape. The author would not
exist without the other two.[3] The protagonist's supposed control over the
author is undercut by her dependence on the other woman.

Although the protagonist claims it is crucial to keep straight who is
the character, the narrator, and the author, she blurs those distinctions
at every possible opportunity, interweaving the three identities. Each
invents the others, depends on the others, resists the others. Their interdependence, and the impossibility of any one of them standing alone,
create a vivid demonstration of the self that does not coincide.

Just as at times "the woman who writes me" avoids the protagonist,
and goes months without writing, so too does the inscribed author get
frustrated, wondering when the protagonist will work out her life so that
this book can be finished:

> A minha autora me espreita com medo e cansaço. Quer saber por
> onde irei agora, no passe do impasse. Poderia escolher o suicí-
> dio. . . . Não, não escolhi o suicídio. Nem para mim, nem para a
> mulher que me escreve. Nem tampouco para a autora. (107)

> [My authoress peers at me in fear and exhaustion. She wonders how
> I'll go about it now, to break through the impasse. I might choose
> suicide. . . . No, I didn't choose suicide. Not for me and not for the
> woman who writes me. Not for the authoress either. (80)]

By its word choice, this passage in which the inscribed author wonders
where the protagonist will go "no passe do impasse" recalls the earlier
passage in which the protagonist, in speaking of the author, proclaims
"[n]ão estou interessada no desinteresse da sua vida." The "passe do impasse" and "interessada no desinteresse" wordplay brings the two passages into juxtaposition so that inscribed author and protagonist are
brought into association in the reader's mind, again blurring the lines of
demarcation between the two.

By playing with the idea of suicide, a conventional fate for unmarried
heroines in nineteenth-century narrative endings, the protagonist reminds us again of her status as a fictional character. As the "heroine" of a
postmodern novel, she not only rejects that traditional ending for herself
but also reemphasizes the question of who has the plotting prerogative

by claiming the power to choose suicide for the woman who writes her or for the inscribed author. The protagonist thus claims narrative power, the authority to write their life stories, to author their deaths.

She rejects suicide in favor of a reevaluation of life: "These months were worth something for taking stock. For me, for her. My slavery, useless. Her freedom, also useless. Nothing led to anything. The mirrors are more and more being cleared of images. Useless reflections that go skimming coldly over the smooth glass, vacuously" (77–78). Just as the repetition of "aceitei, aceitei, aceitei" emphasized the submission of the protagonist, here the repetition of "inútil" reinforces a sense of the pointlessness of her lifestyle and gives her the impetus to make a change.

Proclaiming the Union of Opposites

The slavery/liberty dichotomy is a recurrent motif in *Woman between Mirrors*, a text that contests certain aspects of Brazilian ideology on race. Debra Rosenthal asserts that race mixture "was formative in the history of the Americas primarily in terms of cultural constitution, political organization, nation building, civil identity, and . . . literary expression" (1). Rosenthal situates racial hybridity at the heart of the literature of the Americas. Earl Fitz makes a similar claim about Brazilian literature, declaring that the "theme of racial intermingling, in fact, is a defining motif of Brazilian literature" (13). Parente Cunha's text is set in Salvador, Bahia, the capital of colonial Brazil and the center of the former slave trade.[4] By 1803, Salvador had a population of 100,000, with 40,000 blacks, 30,000 Europeans, and 30,000 mulattos (Fitz 12), numbers that suggest that many Brazilians can claim some African ancestry; and Salvador remains the heart of Afro-Brazilian culture in Brazil. References to Afro-Brazilian images and beliefs (particularly *candomblé*)[5] form a part of the rich textual weave of *Woman between Mirrors*.

Slavery/liberty is used as another of the diametric oppositions describing the protagonist and the woman who writes her. The protagonist's enslavement to her family and the freedom of the woman who writes her are both dismissed as useless. Both lifestyles result in empty images in the mirrors.

Having rejected her previous enslavement for a new freedom, the protagonist of Parente Cunha's text looks at herself naked in the mirror.

Sinto o arrepio bom que estremece o meu sexo e me sobe até às narinapalpitantes. Nua diante dos meus espelhos. Mas por que nunca eu me havia posto assim? Nua, nuíssma, absolutamente nua, sem medo, sem pudores. Sou eu, eu, muitíssimo eu, gritam infinitamente as imagens assomadas em todas as direções. (108)

[I feel the cool thrill in my sex with a shiver running clear up to my quivering nostrils. Naked in front of my mirrors. But why didn't I ever do that before? Naked, stark naked, absolutely naked, with no fear, with no fake modesty. It's me, me over and over again, comes the unending cry of the images looking out in all directions. (80)]

Parente Cunha again uses repetition for effect in this passage. The words *nua* (naked) and *eu* (I) are each repeated in quick succession and put into superlative form, shouted out in orgasmic celebration and affirmation. Having discarded the exterior trappings of clothing, the protagonist feels that, naked, she has finally found her "I." But it is not "I" as unique subject of discourse, for, unexpectedly, the verb is in the third person plural: "gritam"—they shout. Rather than a unique "I," we encounter an infinite number of "I"s. The unusual circumstance of an infinite number of images shouting out "I am I" can be interpreted variously: as undercutting the strength of the statement "I am I" by taking away its singularity; or as affirming a greater strength by virtue of the solidarity of each "I" with the others (with the second interpretation recalling the spirit of the Latin American testimonialists discussed in part 3).

When the naked protagonist sees a lewd smile in the mirrors, she thinks at first it is the woman who writes her, but then realizes it is her own smile, "without fear" (80). Touching her own body, running her hands along "a lovely body not young, ready to claim its birthright of pleasure" (81), she invents her own body.[6] Her breasts that have only known the fat, sweaty hands of one man, now know the pleasure of her own touch. She discovers a body ready for sexual pleasure and assumes an active subjectivity, appropriating that sexual experience for herself. Regarding herself and her body as valuable, she now inhabits her own body with a sense of ownership. Running her hands and her gaze down her own body, she reassembles the body as whole and takes control of it.

The protagonist's proclamation that she will create her own independence the way she had created her submission reasserts the slavery/freedom motif.[7] At first she finds the creation of independence difficult as neither she, the woman who writes her, nor the author knows what should be the first step. They realize that they need to maintain a certain amount of coherence and verisimilitude, a difficult task when the author is no more verisimilar or coherent than the protagonist.[8] The protagonist's vow not to be limited by considerations of verisimilitude in fiction shows her intense awareness of her existence as a literary character:[9] "I refuse to consider myself tied to a total psychological coherence and I proclaim the union of opposites. Although the union of opposites can't be said to be illogical. Reality is the sum total of opposites. . . . I repress all the opposites that have characterized me thus far" (83). The notion that reality is the sum of all the oppositional parts echoes the earlier statements about the need to hear all the voices and feel all the silences in order to know a person. Admitting that her selflessness in the past was really fear rather than selflessness, she determines to set free all her emotions and desires, all the contradictions within her. The protagonist, after years of abject servitude to her husband and sons, withdraws into her consciousness after the breakup of the marriage. Thinking through her life, arguing with the woman who writes her, the protagonist turns from her servitude to a new life of freedom.

But while she celebrates her freedom as a fictional character, she has trouble putting that freedom to use. In spite of her desire to be independent and to resist the traditional gender script of objectivity and passivity, the social signifying practices are so entrenched as to be difficult to overcome: "Why can't I make full use of the freedom I could get from my privileged situation as a character? On the level of imagination, possibilities are infinitely, irresistibly multiplied" (83). The level of the imaginary is like her mirrors, providing endless possibilities, irresistible multiplicities.

A phone call from a friend of her husband, one whose gaze had always made her uncomfortable, allows her to start off on a new path. In a narrative cliché, she enters into an affair first with her husband's friend, then with other men, meets artists (or would-be artists), starts to write, gets published, leads a very different life: "For the first time in my life, I've come to feel freely, wholly, fully female. And eager. This sensation gives me a dizzy rush, a joy I never felt before or even suspected" (87). The string of three adverbs, "livremente, integralmente, plenamente," recalls an earlier adverbial trio when the protagonist said she lived "exclusivamente, totalmente, exaustivamente" for her husband (16). The two passages in juxtaposition again offer the slavery/freedom opposition.

When she looks in the mirror, her body is whole, her feet no longer gnawed away by rats. Now it is the feet of "the woman who writes me" that are gnawed by rats, the rats that the protagonist now denies, the rats that "exist only in her mind. And in her feet, of course. The guilt of her rats. The rats of her guilt" (107). The rats inhibit the freedom and mobility, first of the protagonist, then of the woman who writes her. The image of the female body without the feet serves to make visible the wounds that restrictive social control mechanisms inflict on the female body.

Once the protagonist is free of the rats, she is able to see that they are caused by guilt. Trying to escape from *her* guilt, "the woman who writes me" marries her high school biology teacher. She stays home, prepares his meals, dresses in prim clothes, and scolds the protagonist for the damage the latter's immoral ways are doing to her sons. The protagonist claims that "the woman who writes me" talks about her (the protagonist's) sons because the protagonist wants her to want to talk about them: "because I don't want to talk about them. Or think. They made their bed. I made mine. Consciously or unconsciously, each of us sets out an individual course. Choose your own path. Choose it or is it chosen for you?" (118). Again the protagonist speaks emphatically—"Each person chooses her/his own road"—then immediately questions her own statement. Her monologue is always a dialogue.

A reading of this passage suggests that "the woman who writes me" exists to do the thinking and worrying that the protagonist no longer is willing to do. Their roles and attitudes have changed dramatically, as though the two women had switched personalities, or perhaps switched places, walking through the looking glass to take up the position on the other side. The protagonist has given up living exclusively for her husband and sons, while "the woman who writes me" now holds the protagonist responsible for the lives of her sons, each affecting an absolute transition into the opposite. That the protagonist can play two such opposing roles—submissive, obedient wife and sexually liberated woman—to the full, switching from one to the other at will, demonstrates the interchangeability (and thus the invalidity) of these overdetermined versions of woman made available in Western patriarchal culture. In her ability to move from one role to the other at will, she is curiously both inside and outside the male-centered semiotic systems that codify women. The protagonist's supposed fulfillment of these stereotypes actually demonstrates Parente Cunha's resistance to the stereotypes.

In the end, "the woman who writes me" finds that her attempt at marriage is no more successful than was the protagonist's. The Hegelian reversal did not work, for, as deconstruction has shown, binary oppositions must inevitably collapse upon themselves when forced to extremes. A simple switching of places does not indicate progress. Both women end up back at the mirror, looking at each other, seeing their feet gnawed by rats. As the mirrors multiply their images to infinity, the women are united by their remorse. At this point, "My face in the mirror is her face. I'm her. She's me" (132). The emphatic distinction between the protagonist and the woman who writes her—"Eu sou eu. Ela é ela" ("I am I. She is she.")—is gone. The singular, unique, self-identical "I" of autobiographical writings is not possible.

The back cover of the English edition of *Woman between Mirrors* proclaims that, the work's protagonist "moves toward full self-realization, reincorporating all those exotic and erotic elements that both she and 'the woman who writes me' had denied." But to claim "full self-realization" is to fall back into the belief in the self as fully constituted subject, into the belief in wholeness and completion that Parente Cunha is writing against throughout the text. An assertion of reincorporation is also difficult to sustain in light of the fact that the face is now missing the body, the corpus or corps that is the root of rein*corp*oration.

To claim the closure of a full self-realization is also to impose a conventionally acceptable reading to the ending of a narrative that has been challenging conventional narrative forms. Parente Cunha, in *Woman between Mirrors*, is "writing beyond the ending," what Rachel Blau DuPlessis defines as "[t]he invention of strategies that sever the narrative from conventional structures of fiction and consciousness about women" (x). Parente Cunha employs strategies that express critical dissent from dominant narrative patterns; she writes differently in order to engender authority differently in her autobiographical texts.

Whose Truth to Be Told?

For the question of authority (and author-ity) thus becomes an overt theme of *Woman between Mirrors*. If this text relies—in its own fictional way—on autobiographical authority, how can it honor the obligation to referential truth without determining first whose truth is to be told? Readers feel compelled to ask who is in charge of the text: the protagonist, the woman who writes her, the author, or, perhaps, the reader?

The protagonist would appear to have the position of greatest power in this narrative, because she is the only one of the three—protagonist, woman who writes her, inscribed author—who can speak in the first person or address the reader directly. The protagonist asserts: "She, the woman who writes me, can't speak of herself here. Only I have the right to speak of her. With the freedom that comes from my fiction. . . . The moment she says I, she isn't any more. Here, I can only mean me, I'm the only me" (24). For "the woman who writes me" to say "I," the protagonist explains, she would have to invent herself the way the protagonist has invented herself. Presumably, were "the woman who writes me" to do that, it would result in another book. For this book is to tell the story of the protagonist, and it is she who gets to set the boundaries, both of the text and of her own self.

It is left then to the readers of this complex text to decipher the relationship between the protagonist and the woman who writes her. If "the woman who writes me" is an alternate self of the protagonist, which of the two selves is the more reliable narrator? Can there be a "reliable narrator" in an autobiographical text? The questions raised by *Woman between Mirrors* underscore important issues in the study of autobiographical genres.

Although "the woman who writes me" cannot address the reader directly, she does speak to the protagonist, in the italicized sections of the text. The protagonist often reiterates her own control, remarking that the woman who writes her "spoke because I let her. In the game of I-she, I do all the deciding" (18). That the inscribed author never speaks at all in the text seems to prove the protagonist's point that the author would not want to participate in the story because she would not want to become a fictional character. The inscribed author enters the novel only when the protagonist talks about her, bearing out the protagonist's claim that the author enters the text not at her own will, but at that of the protagonist.

That multiple voices participate in the structuring of the narrative helps deconstruct the notion of a character's identity as a fixed, unified subject. The interdependency of the three women—protagonist, woman who writes her, inscribed author—is Derrida's play of differences put to work. Parente Cunha plays with poststructuralist theories in her narrative in the same way that she plays with psychoanalytic theories and autobiographical conventions.

Indeed, Carmen Chaves Tesser reads *Woman between Mirrors* as Parente Cunha "'working through' the maze of post-structuralist thought," arguing that in Brazil, theory has been driving literature rather than analyzing it (594). Chaves Tesser traces Parente Cunha's readings of Foucault, Derrida, and Lacan. She points out how, in Derrida's notion of the decentering of ideas, "[m]eaning blurs, as in a foggy mirror image—one makes out the image only through prior knowledge of what it is supposed to be" (595).

For Foucault, language, death, and the mirror are all intertwined. He sees language as rushing forth before the imminence of death: "Headed toward death, language turns back upon itself; it encounters something like a mirror; and to stop this death which would stop it, it possesses but a single power: that of giving birth to its own image in a play of mirrors that has no limits" (54). If, as Chaves Tesser suggests, the protagonist of *Woman between Mirrors* is language itself, it is precisely this power that it wields in the text—giving birth to its own image in a play of mirrors that has no limits.

In *Woman between Mirrors*, the protagonist's story is reflected in Parente Cunha's narrative—with its persistent, insistent discussion of which of the three (character, narrator, or author) *knows* what will happen, *determines* what will happen, *determines the existence of the others*—a narrative that challenges all notions of fiction and authority as it foregrounds the process of construction of an autobiographical narrative. The multiple reflections of the protagonist's body in the mirrors challenge the single-lens optics through which woman is traditionally viewed. The pluralized presentation of her body is an act of creative resistance, evading a single source of identity. Sheila Rowbotham has argued that a woman cannot experience herself as a single unique entity because she is always aware of how she is defined as *woman* by the dominant male culture. Rowbotham uses the metaphor of the mirror to stand for the reflecting surface of cultural representation into which a woman stares to form an identity: "The prevailing social order stands as a great and resplendent hall of mirrors. It owns and occupies the world as it is and the world as it is seen and heard" (27). Rather than reflecting a unique, individual image back to each woman, those multiple mirrors project an image of *Woman*, the fixed identity society imposes on women. Because women do not recognize themselves in that hall of mirrors, they develop a dual consciousness. Split between the self as defined by the dominant culture and the self as different from that prescription, women are "never all together in one place, . . . always in transit, immigrants into alien territory" (31). Feminist critics of autobiography have seen writing the self as a way to shatter that cultural hall of mirrors and break the silence imposed by male speech and authority.

Sylvia Molloy also employs the image of the mirror to discuss the space of the woman writer, asserting that "socially conventional forms of female inscription function for these women writers like mirrors: they provide them with specular others that are both familiar and alien, images that do, and do not, signify them, images whose fixity they alternately yearn for and deride. Impossible to breach, this representational gap . . . constitutes the space of the woman writer; and the ambiguous trace she leaves there, as a counterinscription, is, indeed, her only possible signature" (Castro-Klarén, Molloy, and Sarlo, 111). Throughout *Woman between Mirrors*, we can see how the specular others the protagonist sees reflected in her mirrors are both familiar and alien.

What we see in Parente Cunha's text is an example of what Teresa de Lauretis describes as "a subject constituted in gender, to be sure, though not by sexual difference alone, but rather across languages and cultural representations; a subject engendered in the experience of race and class, as well as sexual relations; a subject, therefore, not unified but rather multiple, and not so much divided as contradicted" (2). In Parente Cunha's self-conscious narrative, the protagonist recognizes that she only exists in the words of the text, that she is indeed a subject constituted by language: "I will live only if she writes me" (8).

Throughout this fictional autobiography, we can see how the protagonist's identity is constituted in large part by reading and writing, such that the practices of reading and writing are exercises in subjectivity. She remembers that, "Ever since I was a little girl, I've liked reading immensely. . . . My open space of freedom and fantasy. When I read, I cut all bonds and break through my limitations" (48). Reading brings her freedom—the language of enslavement and liberty is evoked here again. The protagonist frequently identifies with characters from children's stories like Rapunzel (94) and Snow White (77–78); for both Parente Cunha and Luisa Futoransky and the selves they inscribe in their autobiographical metafictions, meaning is narrative meaning.

For Parente Cunha's protagonist, writing is also a sexual act, secret and transgressive. At seventeen, she writes in a secret diary named "Franky" and dubs her pillow "Johnny."[10] With the sexual language she uses in her diary, she converts these objects into lovers, "Every night I give Johnny my rose bud that opens up for him, for him alone and no one else. . . . I also give myself to you, my darling Franky" [54]). When her father finds her diary, he becomes furious. The language he employs—"you tramp, you whore, you bitch" (55)—shows that for her authoritarian father, writing and pleasure (in particular the self-pleasure of masturbation) are forbidden for women.[11]

In *This Sex Which Is Not One*, Luce Irigaray affirms that what continues to be the most forbidden for women is any expression of her own sexual pleasure: "For in fact feminine pleasure signifies the greatest threat of all to masculine discourse, represents its most irreducible 'exteriority,' or 'exterritoriality'" (157). Irigaray questions if the multiplicity of female desire and female language can only be understood as shards of a violated sexuality. She asserts that the "rejection, the exclusion of a female imaginary certainly puts woman in a position of experiencing herself only fragmentarily, in the little-structured margins of a dominant ideology, as waste, or excess, what is left of a mirror invested by the (masculine) 'subject' to reflect himself, to copy himself" (30). As we have seen, not only do the readers of *Woman between Mirrors* experience the protagonist as always already fragmented into three parts—the protagonist, the woman who writes her, and the author—but the protagonist can only experience herself in a fragmented manner.

In "The Power of Discourse," Irigaray affirms that if a woman wants to express her own pleasure, she confronts a difficult path: "That 'elsewhere' of feminine pleasure can be found only at the price of *crossing back through the mirror that subtends all speculation*" (77). The autobiographical fiction of Parente Cunha pushes at the limits of narration, language, passion, and the imagination, crossing back through the mirror that subtends all speculation in order to enter into a space where female desire can be articulated.

By celebrating female sexuality and female pleasure in its various forms in *Woman between Mirrors*, Parente Cunha transgresses the norms of bourgeois Bahian society, as brilliantly embodied in her authoritarian father: "My father was overwhelming, he crushed everyone around him. . . . We were all insignificant around him, all powerful, commanding or countermanding, and there we were, down at his feet, submissive, subjugated, subdued, submerged, subtracted" (14). Her father's ways were learned from his father: "My father was the son of a powerful landowner from the interior, used to ordering people around, whip and spur at the ready, and he was by training and temperament a man who knew how to make himself obeyed. My father pretty much kept to my grandfather's dogmatic ways" (36). Her father did not allow any freedom of expression nor any expression of sexuality. He believed that dancing was indecent (46), that a woman who wears makeup is a prostitute (36) and he took the lipstick off his daughter's lips with such violent force that her lips bled.

Also repressed in this bourgeois family is any discussion of mulatto origins. "Naquele tempo, na casa de meu pai, era feio se falar, era feio se pensar em candomblé, coisa em que branco não se mete. Mas painho, eu não sou branca, sou morena. Cale esta boca, menina" (145). "In those days, at my father's house, it was nasty to talk about, nasty to think about *candomblé*, something a white person should steer clear of. But Daddy, I'm not all that white, I'm dark. Hush up, girl" (110). She is not allowed to recognize even the possibility of African ancestors and is instead to model herself on her doll, "the china doll with the pink face, the curly blond hair, . . . her blue eyes" (3). The china doll is a model impossible for the child to replicate.

The protagonist recalls her fascination with the black boy next door, "the black boy, son of the cook at the house next door. . . . [S]itting on the wall, dangling his bare legs, he would suck on the mango and smile at me" (10). The black boy represents bravery, freedom, sexuality, and the forbidden ("a white girl shouldn't mix with black boys" [10]). A memorable moment in which he lowers his pants to show the young protagonist "his hard little sex" (111) incites her to reflect both on sexuality and racial origins, as she thinks about how his grandmother was a slave and then wonders about her grandparents and their grandparents and where her own dark skin might have come from.

As an adult, she tries to break free from the racist ideologies of her father and her husband to explore Afro-Brazilian culture. She attends *candomblé* rituals and attempts to recuperate the African traditions of her Afro-Brazilian nanny. Part of the importance of *Woman between Mirrors* is the presentation of a female protagonist "actively embarking in the act of construing a racial identity that goes against the racism she experienced during the years of the military dictatorship" (Sáenz de Tejada 45).

As a life narrative that blurs the boundaries between autobiographical fiction and fictional autobiography, *Woman between Mirrors* makes visible what is often not visible in a more traditional autobiography. Parente Cunha's metafictional text highlights what it means to write "I," or, in this case, *eu*, an *eu* always in dialogue with a *você* and an *ela*.

The Fragmented Self Intensified

Parente Cunha continues her elliptical and ironical play with the master narrative of autobiography in *As doze cores do vermelho* (1988; The Twelve Colors of Red). Eneida Leal Cunha asserts that *As doze cores do vermelho* "redoes *Woman between Mirrors*, intensifying it, expanding it, perhaps I can even say, radicalizing it, in all aspects" (156). The text is constructed of three columns—*eu*: a first person who remembers past events and discoveries; *você*: a second person who dialogues about worries in the present; and *ela*: a third person who narrates future adventures.[12] The columnar format forces the reader visually to confront the multiplicity of the protagonist's identity. We are unable to read the three sections simultaneously. Looking at the open book, it is as though we see the multiple images of the protagonist in the mirror. We look first to the left, then to the middle, then to the right, studying each reflection like a prospective customer trying on clothing in front of a three-way mirror. In a "Las Meninas"–like maneuver, readers of *As doze cores do vermelho* find themselves occupying the physical space of the protagonist of *Woman between Mirrors*. The speaking subject thus reproduces in the reading subject the experience of splitting, the tautness generated by the stretching between identification and otherness, between sameness and difference. Parente Cunha employs a form of deconstructive writing, what Toril Moi explains as "one that engages with and thereby exposes the duplicitous nature of discourse" (9). Thus Parente Cunha's narrative strategies reflect her politics. In order to read the narrative, readers have to accept the fragmented nature of the protagonist's identity. We also have to decide how to read the text: read each of the three columns, turn the page and read the next three; or read through all of the left-hand columns of the text, then all the middle columns, then all the right-hand columns. In this literal way, readers are forced to participate in the construction of the protagonist's identity.

The dialogic relationship of the columns demonstrates the active, relational, heterogeneous, nonidentitarian elements of the dialogism that Bakhtin defines as characteristic of the novel as genre. *As doze cores do vermelho* employs textual effects like the columnar format in order to bridge the gaps in textual meaning. Parente Cunha's narrative bears out Drucilla Cornell and Adam Thurschwell's point that "[u]ltimately, the 'truth' of nonidentity can only be shown, not told" (160). That Parente Cunha does not write solely in the first person singular signals to readers that the generic assumptions of continuous identity are not operating in this self-narration in any conventional way. This self-narration, like the earlier *Woman between Mirrors*, makes clear that the self is not single, unique, or self-identical.

In a prefatory remark entitled "Before Crossing the Rainbow,"[13] Parente Cunha explains her narrative strategy: "At the same time that each column is totally related to the whole, it also possesses an independent life of its own. Fragments and totality, instants and flows of life. To exist is to put together the pieces that remain and coexist in a singular and multiple dimension" (9). Parente Cunha's remarks introducing *As doze cores do vermelho* reaffirm the protagonist's claims in *Woman between Mirrors* that each person has many voices, many sides, many silences.

Just as the three female figures in *Woman between Mirrors* are all writers, in *As doze cores do vermelho* each representation of the self is an artist. Both texts link creativity and the search for some form (albeit provisional) of self-realization. In both texts, the creative space is an alternative space where the woman can create her own reality, one that does not have to conform to "culturally mandated, internally policed and hegemonically poised" norms of what it means to be a woman (DuPlessis 5).

Neither woman feels comfortable in the restricted role of the bourgeois woman in her society. In *Woman between Mirrors*, the protagonist discovers the burden that the female body entails: "I'm weighted down by my own body. When I try to walk I get nowhere" (5). This woman has difficulty walking because her feet have been gnawed away by rats. Similarly, the woman in *As doze cores do vermelho* discovers that being female carries with it many rules about what one can and cannot do:

> Eu devia comportar-me e ter juízo e falar baixo e rir pouco e não gesticular e não mudar a roupa na vista dos outros. Não não ão ã. Sutiã. Já ia começar a usar sutiã para não deixar o peito solto debaixo da combinação. . . . Eu não devia ficar fazendo perguntas. Não devia ficar conversando com os meninos. Aprendia a costurar a bordar a cozinhar eu apreia a ser uma boa dona-de-casa. (14)

> [I should behave myself and be reasonable and talk softly and laugh little and not gesture and not change clothes in the sight of other people. No No No No. Bra. Already I was beginning to wear a bra in order not to let my breasts be free inside my blouse. . . . I shouldn't keep asking questions. I shouldn't talk with boys. I learned to sew, to embroider, to cook and I learned to be a good housewife.]

The same social norms we had seen in *Woman between Mirrors* dominate *As doze cores do vermelho* as well.

In the left-hand columns of *As doze cores do vermelho*, we see the protagonist at school, with her four boxes of colored pencils, wanting to be a painter but with artistic ideas that are too rebellious. When she paints the sky green, the teacher tells her the sky should be blue. She asks indelicate questions related to race, class, and sexuality. She is conscious of the prejudice against the redheaded girl (the daughter of a prostitute) and the black girl and often allies herself with them. The two girls, like the three versions of the self in the split columns, can be read as female alter-ego figures who mirror the subversive desires of the self.

In the central columns, the woman is married to a rigid husband, always identified with his black briefcase. Between her domestic chores and her salaried job, she has little time to paint. Nor does she have liberty to choose her friends because "her husband doesn't like black people" (27). She maintains her friendships with her schoolmates in spite of a husband who won't let her Afro-Brazilian friend enter the house.[14] Like the protagonist of *Woman between Mirrors* and like Alice in front of the looking glass, she always wants to know, "What is on the other side?" (45).

In the right-hand columns is the dream: "She will travel, go, see, and make seen the unformed forms and the red sky and the colors of the colors and the shouted laughter" (37). In this column she goes from being afraid to have an exhibition of her art, to making money on her paintings, buying the bigger apartment that her husband was never able to afford on his salary, and receiving international awards. But success has its price as well.

In *As doze cores do vermelho*, as in *Woman between Mirrors*, Parente Cunha focuses on gender as a social construction, the difficulties confronted when one tries to live outside those social norms imposed on women, and the impossibility of being a unified and univocal subject under such conditions. The linguistic experimentalism already present in *Woman between Mirrors* and more noticeable in *As doze cores do vermelho*—the use of alliteration, the use of words which echo each other, the ludic repetition of the same word or parts of the same word—serves to disrupt any sense of signifying security or univocality.[15] The language of the texts mirrors the themes explored in the narratives.

In *Woman between Mirrors* and *As doze cores do vermelho*, Parente Cunha decenters the autobiographical genre and the female gender. The feminine subject historically has been produced as an object by means of the practices and the discourses of femininity just as the autobiographical subject is constituted by means of the practices and discourses of autobiography. Parente Cunha employs autobiographical fiction as a stage on which she can experiment with the reconstruction of the representative and ideological discourses that constitute the subjectivity of Brazilian women.[16]

Parente Cunha employs her autobiographical metafiction to present a fractured (and nameless) woman whose identity can only be found, perhaps, in the intersections, the silences, the differences, and the variations. She fills the various conflicting and mutually constrictive roles of child, adult, friend, wife, mother, lover, artist. She is all of these things and no one of them alone. Parente Cunha questions the concept of identity when it is used to imprison various different and conflicting angles of a woman/person. Thus she questions the very validity of autobiographical writings if they are dominated by one, all-powerful *eu* (I).

Parente Cunha uses fictional autobiography to show how the "self" is put into question in the self-positioning act of writing, how identities can never be self-identical, and how authority is also contested when the inherited forms of literary discourse are discarded in the creation of new forms. By catching the reader in the play of mirrors, by forcing the reader to participate in the construction of the protagonist's identity, Parente Cunha refracts authority over identity from the author to the reader and reflects in the mirrored surfaces of her textual strategies the very themes she explores in her autobiographical narratives.

As one who both creates and studies literature, Parente Cunha is conscious of forming part of an "explosion" of women's writing in Brazil that started in the 1970s. As she notes, much of that literature, "besides focusing on the question of women's identity, presents characters who are victims of conflicts that trap them between ideological pressures and the desire for freedom" (*Com a palavra o Escritor* 157). She is also conscious of the autobiographical nature of her novelistic production, noting that unlike her poems, "the two novels and various stories are the fictional representation of my life submerged in the asphyxiating oppression of the patriarchal order and of sexist authoritarianism" (157). She affirms that a significant part of her narrative production arises from the mixture of perplexity and revulsion she felt in the face of the absurd roles played by the women she knew as she was growing up in Bahia in the 1930s and 1940s, roles that she still sees today (157). Like the women inscribed in her two autobiographical narratives, Parente Cunha was born and raised in "a typically patriarchal northeast family, upheld by the unbalanced certainty placed in the authority of the head of the household and in a belief in the dependence of the woman, obligated to follow the model of fixed values attributed to the feminine subject" (157). Her early experiences of gender within the family seemingly play a powerful part in her coming to an understanding of feminist thought and theories. Her personal experiences and those of women around her serve as raw material for her writing of metafictional novels that play elliptically and ironically with the master narrative of autobiography. Her heterogeneous and theoretically self-conscious autobiographical acts of narrative resistance stand as powerful rejections of traditional gender restrictions in middle-class Brazilian society. Her autobiographical texts challenge us, as readers, to question conventions of both gender and genre, to ask how those conventions serve to restrict women's freedom of expression, and to question how those conventions might be the very rats gnawing away at the protagonist's (or all women's) feet.

2 / The Self in Exile: Luisa Futoransky's Babelic Metatext

Like Helena Parente Cunha, Luisa Futoransky, in *Son cuentos chinos* (They Are Chinese Tales) and *De Pe a Pa (o de Pekín a París)* (From Pe to Pa [or From Peking to Paris]), plays elliptically and ironically with the master narrative of autobiography. Like Parente Cunha, Futoransky writes novels that can be considered as fictional autobiographies, but are further problematized by their aspects as autobiographical fiction. They are fictional autobiographies in that they tell the life story of the fictional character Laura Kaplansky. They are autobiographical fiction in that they incorporate aspects of Futoransky's life experiences. In his work on the autobiographical pact, Phillipe Lejeune asserts that works are considered autobiographical if and only if the authors declare their autobiographical intention. This obligatory statement can be made in the title, the dedication, the preface (most frequently), or in a concluding note, as Futoransky does in *De Pe a Pa* when she states that "Laura (Falena) Kaplansky was a character I created with part of my melancholy, my vision, my joys, pains and sorrows" (123).[1] According to this criteria, then, *De Pe a Pa* and *Son cuentos chinos*, the other narrative featuring Laura Kaplansky as protagonist, can be considered as falling within that autobiographical pact. Futoransky's texts work the definitional boundaries between autobiography and fiction, between autobiographical fiction and fictional autobiography. By writing at the borders, she bears witness to the constrictions imposed by the conventions of genre and seeks a freedom outside those conventions. Together, *Son cuentos chinos, De Pe a Pa*, and Futoransky's third novel, *Urracas*, can be read as a metatext, an extended series on writing, identity, marginalization, and exile.

Indeed, in a 1993 conversation with Marily Martínez-Richter, Futoransky confirms that she had originally conceived of the three as a trilogy. However, her plan for the second novel was so ambitious that she ended up in the hospital: "There I realized that I should reduce my plans, that it was a question of life or death" (78). She also explains why she changed the protagonist's name from Laura Kaplansky to Julia Bene: "As for the change of name, in order to escape with bitter irony and a pirouette, I will answer you that, since I was tired that in life things were going badly (*male*) for me, in order to exorcise the novel, I called Julia, Laura and Luisa *bene*" (78). That she gives Julia, Laura, and Luisa all the same last name would imply that the flesh-and-blood author and her fictional protagonists all occupy the same level of reality. Futoransky's metatext serves as an excellent example of the problematic authority of the signature.

Throughout this chapter, I explore how Futoransky uses a variety of tropes in her autobiographical fiction to explore issues frequently discussed in criticism and theory on women's autobiographical writings. Her use of proper names highlights issues of identity and language, while her play with language and linguistic multiplicity function as signifiers of a radical Otherness, as a process that relentlessly foregrounds variance and marginality as the norm (Ashcroft, Griffins, and Tiffin 75). Her exilic texts foreground a nomadic subject who continually searches (in her life and in her writings) for a place to represent herself anew.

The Self in Exile

Luisa Futoransky and the protagonists of her autobiographical fiction share much in common, including the experience of exile. Shari Benstock argues that for women, the definition of patriarchy "already assumes the reality of expatriate *in patria*" and that "this expatriation is internalized, experienced as an exclusion imposed from the outside and lived from the inside in such a way that the separation of outside from inside ... cannot be easily distinguished" (20). Futoransky's inscription of exile clearly goes beyond the more common physical or geographical definitions to incorporate the status of women in patriarchal hierarchies.[2]

The exilic experience of Futoransky and her autobiographical protagonists includes that expatriation that is imposed from the outside and lived from the inside. Experiencing displacement and disorientation on various levels, Futoransky uses her autobiographical writings to ponder if there can be greater misfortune than to be female, fortyish, alone, not at all thin, Jewish, South American, and prone to volatile passions? Hers is an abject identity constituted by all that is the negative of society's values in gender, age, race, and physical appearance. It is a nothingness imposed from without, from a patriarchal world of power and wealth.

Futoransky's autobiographical texts showcase a socially abject protagonist, ill at ease with her ethnicity and identity, who seeks to come to terms with and reshape that identity through her writing. The creative process of writing is presented in *Son cuentos chinos* as a possible path toward self-knowledge and self-realization. Admitting that she still does not completely accept her name or her physical appearance, she wants to write until she purges herself of "all my slobbering demons" (55). Her discomfort stems from body politics; for, as Sidonie Smith reminds us, "The body functions as a sorting mechanism whereby the culturally dominant and the culturally marginalized are assigned their 'proper' places in the body politic" (*Subjectivity* 10). Futoransky contests the societal sorting mechanisms that have assigned her to culturally marginalized spaces. She uses her autobiographical writings to contest that oppressive system and to offer other possibilities.

While some women writers chose exile in order to find a place where they can write freely, they frequently find themselves still restricted by the confines of patriarchal language and the often transnationally dominant literary conventions. The exilic texts produced by these writers frequently decenter notions of identity and authority at the same time that they transgress the boundaries of genre and text. Futoransky traces out exile as the path both of her life—"I am a person who works a lot with exile, because there is a lot of exile behind me" (Schwartz, *Writing* 116)—and of her chosen profession—"To be a woman in this area is, in a certain way, to be exiled" (Futoransky, lecture). Futoransky believes that "a woman who can't express herself is an interior exile" (ibid.). In inventing an oral autobiographical account in her interviews and talks, she sees both writing and exile as integral parts of her identity: "I don't really know what exile is, what writing is, what reading is. The only thing I know is that I can't do anything else" (ibid.). For Luisa Futoransky, as for her fictionalized protagonist Laura Kaplansky, to live is to write.

Her autobiographical metafiction shares characteristics with other narratives of exile, which "inscribe a nomadic subject, set in motion for a variety of reasons and now inhabiting cultural borderlands, who may or may not return 'home,' but who necessarily negotiates cultural spaces of the in-between where 'hybrid, unstable identities' are rendered palpable through the negotiation 'between conflicting traditions—linguistic, social, ideological' (Woodhull 100)" (Smith and Watson, *Reading* 194).

Futoransky's first two autobiographical novels inscribe a nomadic subject, Laura Kaplansky, who negotiates cultural spaces of the in-between where her own hybrid, unstable identity is rendered palpable in Futoransky's prose. *Urracas* continues the story of the nomadic subject, now renamed, living in exile in Paris and embarking on a weekend trip to Switzerland.[3] Futoransky's narratives present a protagonist set in motion, away from her place of birth and her family of origin.

Futoransky creates a nomadic autobiographical subject who seeks sanctuary in the interstices of culture and strives to become a protagonist within the various cultures she inhabits. She exemplifies Sylvia Molloy's observation of a certain "disquiet" in texts by Latin American women, which Molloy argues "bespeaks a dislocation of being—more specifically, a dislocation in order to be—that could well be the main impulse behind their writing. One is (and one writes) elsewhere, in a different place, a place where the female subject chooses to relocate in order to represent itself anew" (Castro-Klarén, Molloy, and Sarlo 10).

The creation of exilic subjects, the search for origins, and the dislocation of being can all be linked to elements of Luisa Futoransky's own life and family history. She reminds an interviewer that, "evidently, I can't brag about having various generations of Argentines at my back. My ancestors came between the wars, fleeing from European pogroms." When asked where her family came from, she replies: "My family came from countries that don't exist; they exist, they are formed, they come undone, they kill each other tribally, the Central European countries. They come from that zone that is Moldavia, Romania, Russia, Ukraine" (Pfeiffer 56). The list of identities Marcy Schwartz maps out for Futoransky—"the daughter of Eastern European Jews who immigrated to Argentina, . . . a Latin American resident in Asia, . . . a Latin American living in Paris" (*Writing* 116)—shows that Futoransky has experienced displacement within a variety of geocultural situations, with her identity reconfigured in each location. Futoransky and the narrators she inscribes in her autobiographical metafiction are always outside the imaginary community, always aware of the fundamental fragility of place, skeptical of anything they can call home, yet desirous of finding or establishing a connection to some place that could be a home.

Born in Buenos Aires in 1939, Futoransky knew even as a child that she wanted to be a writer, in particular a poet. She began to travel in the 1970s, "when we wanted to discover our America" (Pfeiffer 54). She traveled in Bolivia and Brazil and then, "as they say in Argentina, I was bitten by the travel bug and I'm still very interested in seeing what is happening just a little bit beyond my nose" (54). With a Fulbright International Writing Program grant, she participated in the University of Iowa's Writers' Workshop. She worked at Radio Peking in China and staged opera in Japan. Her experiences in Asia came "in the years in which my country was suffering under a very bloody dictatorship, and then I grabbed hold of whatever possibilities offered themselves, which were not in literary fields, but in the radio or the opera" (55). She left Asia when she was about forty years old, moving to Paris, where she began to publish prose and continued to write poetry.

The autobiographical narratives Futoransky pens and publishes in Paris highlight her international and intercultural experiences. As travel narratives that also highlight the arena of agency, these texts continually question the dominant ideologies of the societies in which the nomadic protagonist finds herself. Futoransky questions "the domain of socially instituted norms" (Butler, *Bodies* 182), be they instituted in China, Japan, France, or Argentina.

Futoransky's autobiographical narratives of nomadism contribute to the tradition of Jewish Latin American women's writing in which authors inscribe themselves in their own cultures at the same time that "their memory of migrations and often multiple Diasporas has been the essence of their literature and their multiple destinies" (Agosín xx). Futoransky's autobiographical texts exemplify Edna Eizemberg's assertion that "Jewish Latin American fiction is a hybrid mix of the past and the present, the folklore of that place and the presence of 'here,' but it is also a literature that can be tied to the postcolonial discourse of displaced people" (quoted in Agosín xviii). Futoransky's metatext mixes past and present, the folklore of Buenos Aires and the presence of here (whether that here is China, Japan, or Paris) at the same time that it highlights the existence and discourse of displaced people. The dislocations of identity unsettle her understandings of time, space, subjectivity, and community, potentially engendering new patterns of remembering.

Son cuentos chinos is the story of Laura Kaplansky, an Argentine Jew living in Peking, a city that "sometimes makes her nauseous" (21). Kaplansky's narration of displacement shows how the city is "the site for the body's cultural saturation, its takeover and transformation by images, representational systems, the mass media and the arts—the place where the body is representationally reexplored, transformed, contested, reinscribed" (Grosz 249). As an outsider in Peking, Kaplansky experiences the city as an alienating social organization. Much of the text is comprised of commentary on the language, behavior, clothing, and customs she observes in Peking. She records comments from her Chinese colleagues as well as citations from Buddhist, Confucian, and Zen sources, struggling to express in Spanish, and thus understand, these different sentiments and beliefs.

In *Son cuentos chinos*, Kaplansky's inability to speak Chinese forces her into an infantile state where others are always in control. To receive medical care, for instance, she must go to the hospital with an interpreter, "which is a way of returning to kindergarten since one is impotent because of the language and the bureaucratic regulations that make it impossible to do anything without an intermediary" (38). Often consciously, sometimes in a seemingly unconscious manner, Kaplansky connects her unfamiliar experiences in Peking with familiar ones in Buenos Aires in her constant struggle to decode the foreign experiences. Buenos Aires is the familiar territory onto which she attempts to map out the oddly shaped pieces of her Chinese puzzle.[4] Buenos Aires is thus the "absent and enabling signifier" through which her life in Peking "can acquire legitimacy as a subject of literary discourse."[5]

In *After Exile*, Amy Kaminsky similarly notes that for Southern Cone exiles who ended up in Scandinavia, being in a place where the language was unfamiliar meant being "returned to a state of complete dependency" and being "perceived as intellectually incompetent" (68). Kaminsky also picks up Yi-Fu Tuan's distinction between space and place, the latter being a space filled with affect, known and understandable (11). For Kaplansky, Peking is space; only Buenos Aires is place.

In *Son cuentos chinos*, Laura Kaplansky is working in the international section of Radio Peking and living in a small apartment where her pictures are hung on the walls with thumbtacks, "nothing permanent or that indicates staying, at least for now, the insecurity of not having a (real) right to be in the place where one is in passing, marginal or almost outside the law, a constant rejection (one doesn't do that, girl, how shameful!) upon signing contracts and anguish over renewing my passport" (13). The temporariness of her decor and living conditions, her geographic instability, and her linguistic difficulties all reflect her own insecure state of being in the world. The quoted sentence, with its various modifiers, qualifiers, and parenthetical remarks, itself reflects the sense of temporariness and instability. Her marginality takes on criminal

overtones, and she demonstrates reluctance and fear upon perform-
ing legal acts like signing a contract or renewing a passport. Again her
experiences in China are put into a childhood context with the parenthetical admonishment from an unnamed adult, as though her actions
were shameful. Living in exile in a culture so different from one's own
means never really knowing which are the things "que no se hace" (that
one doesn't do). Living in exile also highlights how "the demands placed
on the subject in situations of unfamiliarity and dislocation" make even
more visible the struggle for identity (Bartowski xix).

Laura Kaplansky resigns herself to the thought that in Buenos Aires,
no one remembers her. After so many years living abroad, she remains
linked with her country of birth only by a wrinkled blue passport, a few
world-traveling friends she sees quite rarely, and "the language that I
am living as best I can" (19). She no longer has family in Buenos Aires,
so that "no one conserves the negatives of my photos as a nude baby
in Santos Lugares nor the little rocks that got caught in my first shoes
when I walked proudly holding da-da's hand" (19). Her sense of identity
is threatened both by the fear that she is losing her native Spanish and by
this lack of ties, of material evidence to support the family memories.

Constantly made aware of her status as a foreigner by the strictly enforced divisions in housing, hotels, trains, and shops, she ponders the
fact that "the Orientals harbor a considerable resentment against 'for-
eigners' and under this title they group whites in general, but at the same
time they feel a secret scorn, superiority and intransigence" (21) and
recounts the offensive terms used in Japan and China to refer to foreign-
ers.[6] Not only is Kaplansky marginalized as a foreigner in China, but she
is also devalued within the expatriate community as non-Anglo, non-
European, and poor. She is exiled from power and status even within the
community of exiles in Peking.

Having experienced Peking as a closed system, in *De Pe a Pa*, Laura
Kaplansky moves to Paris—anticipated as a city of greater possibilities—
in order to pursue there her lifelong dream of becoming a published author. All the difficulties she endures during the course of the text, she
endures "due to her desire to try not just to live but above all to write in
Paris" (36). As a child in Buenos Aires, Laura had wanted, variously, to be
a ballerina, a chess champion, a queen, a solitary sailor, or someone with
the ability to become invisible at will. "At age fifteen, she reunited as best
she could these secret ambitions in one that in part contains them" (14)
and became a writer. She published her first poems and articles in the
student newspaper under the name Ruth París: "*Ruth*, obviously in an

attempt to assume the kaplanskiness, . . . and *Paris*, in order to embrace, including herself geographically, the cosmos of the literary myth" (14). She knew, even as a teenager, that for all writers ("except for Borges"), "all breath passed through Paris" (14). Residence in Paris seems so obligatory for Latin American writers that to imagine herself a successful writer she must succeed there.

Whether choosing a new name at age fourteen, or choosing to live in exile, she never escapes her memories of Buenos Aires or her Argentine point of view. For Kaplansky, her country of origin "is like a chronic wound, like smoking since you were 15. At forty-something, it is difficult to conceive of the world without the curtain of your own smoke, without the sonority of your own cough" (11). Her narratives of life in China and Paris are told in a colloquial, *porteño* Spanish that is often hard-pressed to explain the foreign terms and customs she encounters. The frequent inclusion of terms in other languages underscores the impossibility of expressing transnational experiences in any one national language.

Naming the Self

In a metatext that plays close attention to language, to the disparate codes of discourse in international and transnational settings, the use of proper names merits careful scrutiny. Futoransky peppers her prose with proper names both partial and complete, names gleaned from the competing cultures of literature, politics, and commercialism. Together with the multiple citations from other texts, the scattered names serve both to represent the bombardment of cultural codes that constitute late twentieth-century life and to highlight issues of personal, familial, ethnic, cultural, and national identities. In an autobiographical narrative oeuvre that consistently struggles with the question of subjectivity, the protagonist's name itself becomes a contested site of identity.

In *Son cuentos chinos*, Futoransky fills her text with the names of places and objects. She refers to items by their commercial brand names—"la *Gillette*" (67)—and names several international hotels and restaurants as common meeting places for people living in exile. The names of various newspapers, magazines, and radio programs are frequently cited by a protagonist who herself works in journalism; *Time, Newsweek, Paris Match*, the BBC, VOA, NHK, Radio Tirana, Radio Australia, and Radio Moscú are all mentioned on page 96 alone. Futoransky further weaves into her metafictional tapestry names of authors, fictional characters, icons of popular culture, and important figures in world history. Some names stand alone; others form part of long litanies of proper names. Sometimes the complete name is given—Shirley Temple or Domingo Faustino Sarmiento—but more often only a partial name is provided, forcing the reader to decipher the reference. The coarse weave of *De Pe a Pa* includes historical names like "Sadat," "Edison, Thomas Alva," "Mister Bell," and "Mitterand"; international organizations like Doctors Without Borders and UNESCO; and references to various countries. Futoransky's metafictional texts rely on worldly readers familiar with the rich and famous in world literature and aware of events reported in the electronic and print media. By leaving it to the reader of *Son cuentos chinos* to decide that "gabo" refers to Gabriel García Márquez or that "*burda* y *marie claire*" are fashion magazines, Futoransky replicates for the reader the workings her protagonist must undergo to decipher the signs around her. By including references to the worlds of popular culture, politics, science, medicine, literature, and commercialism, she highlights how these diverse discourses all contribute to creating and imposing identities on individual subjects.

By refusing to capitalize the majority of the proper names interspersed throughout her fiction, Futoransky strips them of the power, authority, and uniqueness usually identified with names. Proper names are accorded the same status as common nouns. By not capitalizing "gabo," "evita," "beatles o rolling stones," those nouns are then equated with peach, newspaper, or bicycle. Proper names of the characters within the novel are the least likely to be capitalized: references to her lovers "juanda" and "koumbá" are frequent.

While imposing a definitive name is a gesture of control, employing different versions of a person's name challenges the belief that the self is self-identical. In *Son cuentos chinos*, Futoransky refers to her characters variously. The protagonist's South American lover is evoked a single time as "Juan Daniel Jíbaro Norteño Inca del Perú" (27), other times as "Juan Daniel," "Daniel," "juandaniel," "juanda," or "Juanda." Referring to a friend or lover by a nickname seems natural in an intimate journal; as a narrative technique, however, it serves to disperse the identity of the person.

Futoransky also uses names in her autobiographical fiction to call into question the identity of her own protagonist. Although *Son cuentos chinos* is written in the first person, the protagonist not infrequently refers to herself by name, as "la lauri," "la laura kaplansky," or "laura beatriz kaplansky de morán para el pasaporte" (93). The first two are names by which she is known among friends or coworkers; the last exemplifies an institutional identity. Yet even when specifying her complete name for such an official document as a passport, she undermines the authority by failing to capitalize the name.

Futoransky most radically undercuts the uniqueness of the protagonist's identity not by referring to "lauri" or "laurita," but by slipping into the text two references to "le pequeña lulu" and "su pobre lou" (41; the little lulu, his poor lou), pet names that obviously derive from Luisa, her own name, rather than from Laura, the name of her supposedly fictional protagonist. The traditional boundary between fictional character and flesh-and-blood author is thus partially erased in this metafictional text.

The preoccupation with the protagonist's name, and its relation to her identity, is further developed in *De Pe a Pa*. Being known by one's name implies social recognition, a recognition often missing from Laura Kaplansky's life abroad. Her identity as a foreigner is emphasized by the mistaken versions of her name used by others, as in the note from the concierge that reads, "Mrs. Kapraski, please report to the concierge's desk at once" (53). Such name changes, imposed from without, stress the sense of impermanence and undecidability that accompany the exilic state. In *De Pe a Pa*, the name, as the guarantor of the unity of the person, is problematized, its unity scattered, by exile and mistranslation.

Richard Rand reminds us that proper names refer to singular, absolutely unique beings and as such are "undefinable, semantically ungeneralizable, and hence untranslatable as well. . . . For, as Derrida repeatedly insists, the proper name, unlike the common noun, lies outside the semantic system of a language" (86–87). And in *Prière d'insérer*, Derrida queries:

> The name: What does one call thus? What does one understand under the name of name? And what occurs when one gives a name? What does one give then? One does not offer a thing, one delivers nothing, and still something comes to be. . . . What happens, above all, when it is necessary to sur-name [*surnommer*], renaming where, precisely, the name comes to be found lacking? What makes the proper name into a sort of sur-name, pseudonym, or cryptonym at once singular and singularly untranslatable? (quoted in *On the Name* xiv)

Kaplansky is renamed Kapraski in Paris when her name is found to be lacking, lacking translatability, lacking coherence in a Parisian setting. Her name is seen as at once singular and singularly untranslatable in *De Pe a Pa*.

The unity of her identity, as represented in the name, is further scattered in *De Pe a Pa* by the unwanted nicknames others impose on her, "*La gorda Lauri*, o simplemente *Lagor*" (22; the fat Laura or simply Fatty). In *Son cuentos chinos*, Kaplansky admits, "I still don't totally accept my physical appearance or my name: it's obvious that-I-do-not-know-who-I-am-nor-where-I-am-com-ing-from-nor-where-I-am-go-ing" (55). The careful and deliberate enunciation of each syllable highlights the importance of the sentence. In *De Pe a Pa*, she is still exploring her identity and her "kaplanskidad" (14).[7]

Carefully dispersed throughout *De Pe a Pa* are occurrences of the protagonist's complete name. Much of chapter 2, a chapter full of words beginning with the letter *B*, is addressed (in the second person singular) to a Berenice.[8] The "final and repetitive lament of (Laura Beatriz) Be-re-ni-ce (Kaplansky)" (32) at the end of chapter 2 of *De Pe a Pa* suggests that Kaplansky's "real" middle name is *Beatriz*. Laura and Beatriz are highly charged literary names that cannot but seem obvious allusions, to Dante's Beatrice, his guide through paradise in the *Divina Commedia*, and Petrarch's Laura, the beloved of his sonnets.[9] In Futoransky's fiction, the literary weight of the name Beatriz makes it an appropriate middle name for an aspiring writer at the same time that the original Latin meaning of "voyager through life" seems fitting for an international journalist who has worked in many countries.

While chapter 2 presents Beatriz and Berenice as dual (dueling) middle names for Kaplansky, in the last chapter, Kaplansky is referred to as Laura Falena Kaplansky (114, 117, 123) or as "la Falena" (121). Falena then serves as the last word defined in a novel that features numerous dictionary-style definitions: "FALENA f. (gr. *phalaina*) name of various twilight or nocturnal butterflies also called geometrics" (124). The falena is an elusive creature, just as difficult to capture as identity of the protagonist in this text. The assignation of a proper name should guarantee the uniqueness of a personal identity, but in this narrative the proper name of the main character is decentered. The very center of her name is displaced, dispersed among the various possibilities of Beatriz, Berenice, and Falena. That "la Falena" sounds so similar to "la Fulana" (the Spanish equivalent to "What's-her-name" or "So-and-so") further erodes the uniqueness of the protagonist's personal identity.

The problem of the protagonist's identity is intensified by the repeated transgression of the border that separates character from author. In *De Pe a Pa*, those transgressions are made most obvious in the footnotes, notes that violate the traditionally blank space of the borders or margins of the text. These footnotes highlight how Futoransky always already is an interpreter of her own text. These footnotes, situated both inside and outside of the texts, "represent a reading rather than a writing, primordial sorties into that interpretative territory in which the Other (as reader) stands" (Ashcroft, Griffiths, and Tiffin 61).

In *De Pe a Pa*, footnotes, explanatory prefaces, and dictionary entries can be seen to have similar effects. At the end of a section on Jean Rhys, there is a footnote that blurs the boundaries between Laura Kaplansky and Luisa Futoransky at the same time that it suggests connections between Rhys and Futoransky:

> * *N. de Laura*. Jean Rhys retribuyó el apasionado entusiasmo de la autora, dedicándole en *Vasto Mar de los Sargazos* esta frase, harto significativa: *"Anything might have happened to you, Louise, anything at all, and I wouldn't be surprised"* (Cualquier cosa pudo haberte pasado, Luisa, cualquier cosa y no me hubiera sorprendido.) A mí, tampoco. Merci, Jean. (*N. de la A.*). (23)

> [*Note from Laura. Jean Rhys returned the passionate enthusiasm of the author, dedicating to her in the *Wide Sargasso Sea* this very significant phrase: *"Anything might have happened to you, Louise, anything at all, and I wouldn't be surprised"* (Anything might have happened to you, Louise, anything at all, and I wouldn't be surprised). Me neither. Thank you, Jean. (Note of the Author).]

Here the character Laura Kaplansky, by recognizing the existence of the author, violates the literary conventions dividing fictional and historical reality.[10] The footnote further breaches the chronological order of accepted literary history by indicating that Jean Rhys was referring to Luisa Futoransky when writing the line cited in English in the text.

While the footnote begins as a "nota de Laura," the lines after the citation from Rhys appear to be penned by Luisa Futoransky. The first person appears again, "A mí, tampoco," when Futoransky agrees with the statement from *Wide Sargasso Sea* and thanks Jean Rhys, in French, for the sentiment. The footnote closes with the parenthetical "(*N. de la A.*)"—that is, "nota de la autora," author's note. The footnote, with its three languages and two authors, is a synecdoche of the novel itself.

The dually authored footnote is but one example of how the identity of Laura Kaplansky frequently merges into that of Luisa Futoransky. Laura Kaplansky and Luisa Futoransky share similar names, traits, and experiences as Jewish Argentine women poets living alone in foreign countries.

Laura and Luisa are both five-letter, female names beginning with *L*, and ending with *a*, with two vowels and one consonant in between. Kaplansky and Futoransky share the same Polish/Jewish origin, and the same last five letters. So intertwined are the two problematic identities, in fact, that the back cover of the Anagrama edition of *De Pe a Pa* mistakenly refers to Laura Kaplansky as Luisa Kaplansky, an error that apparently escaped the attention of copy editors (or, perhaps, was left to catch the attention of readers).[11]

The final footnote of the novel attempts to explain the relationship between the author and character: "Laura (Falena) Kaplansky was a character I created with part of my melancholy, my gaze, my joys, pains, and sorrows. Through Laura, a kind of candid and sometimes lucid admirer, I tried to explain what it is to be a poet out in the world, with certain aggravating circumstances: an older woman, poor, Jewish, Argentine, and alone" (123–24). In the footnote, the first-person speaker is presumed to be Futoransky, addressing the readers and admitting the autobiographical nature of her protagonist. She goes on to explain that she could have continued with the story of Kaplansky, but decided one day, "Laura, that's enough."

In traditional narratives, the author of the novel and the characters in that novel are considered to exist in different planes of reality, one historical and one fictional. In the last sentence of the footnote—"and I realized, Laura, that's enough"—is that Laura talking to herself, or Luisa Futoransky addressing her fictional character? Because of the earlier "Pude haber seguido con ella" (I could have continued with her) in which the first person singular of "pude" would be Luisa speaking and the "ella" would refer to Laura, we have to assume it is still Futoransky speaking. But the terms of the enunciation have changed. The footnote begins with Futoransky addressing the readers and referring to her protagonist in the third person. By the end of the footnote, she addresses the protagonist directly, effacing the lines between fiction and reality. In the footnotes, as in the use of proper names, Futoransky denies singularity of self to both protagonist and author, dispersing and intermixing their identities.

The abundance of forms of naming and representing the self in Futoransky's texts shows "a need to fix the boundaries of an elusive textual persona" (Castro-Klarén, Molloy, and Sarlo 111) but also highlights the impossibility of fixing those boundaries. Futoransky's use of names and her mimicry of forms of naming problematize representation and the referential throughout her autobiographical metatext, making her an excellent example of how Latin American women writers engage autobiographical genres and conventions.

The Babelic Self/The Babelic Text

The autobiographical fictions Futoransky creates from her exilic experiences are paratactic texts, patched together with pieces of free-verse poetry, dictionary definitions, ads from newspapers, diagrams for a house, footnotes, and other marginalia. Words and sentences from other languages interrupt her *porteño* Spanish. Competing cultural codes and discourses abound. The protagonist struggles to establish agency while living in a textual Tower of Babel.

Futoransky calls on the powers of magic, opening *De Pe a Pa* with an explanation of the word *Abraxas* (a name of God, a magic formula, a word derived from the Hebrew *berajá*, blessing, or *abrac*, bolt of lightning or thunder).[12] A copy of an inscription of the word is followed by the statement that the word has degenerated into our current "abracadabra." "Abracadabra" is then presented along with its dictionary definition and a version of its letters in the form of a triangle (see figure 1).

From the very first page of *De Pe a Pa*, then, Futoransky presents her readers with the varied texture of her narrative weave. The opening page offers a dictionary definition, a copy of an old drawing, Hebrew words, and a triangle of letters that looks like a word-search puzzle. The remainder of the autobiographical novel is similarly eclectic, highlighting "the iconic and constitutive function of language" (Ashcroft, Griffiths, and Tiffin 55). *De Pe a Pa* is a patchwork narrative, pieced together out of "Laura's unconfessable reflections," "Laura's early morning notes," sample personal ads ["GOODLOOKING YOUNG DOMINATRIX urgently seeks domestic (eventually sexual) slaves" (19)], the labeled architectural diagram of a house (34), various dictionary definitions, the cast of characters for an opera, some poetry, and one page that is a collage of ads from a Paris newspaper (71; see figure 2). As with the inclusion of photographs or maps in the autobiographical narratives of Ana María Shua or Shirley Sterling, Futoransky incorporates different media that "juxtapose other geographies to that of the verbal narrative" (Smith and Watson, *Reading* 72). The heterogeneous modes and media highlight the fragmented and multiple characteristics of her narrated "I"s. The "I" in Futoransky's autobiographical metatext is neither unified nor coherent.

The fragmentation and multiplicity are also reflected in the terms in

FIGURE 1. This page comes before the first page of chapter 1 of *De Pa a Pa (o de Pekín a París)*, setting up the reader for the paratactic text to follow. Reprinted courtesy of Luisa Futoransky.

English and French that mix in with the Spanish sentences of *De Pe a Pa* just as occasional words in Japanese or Chinese appear in the text of *Son cuentos chinos*. This "technique of selective lexical fidelity which leaves some words untranslated in the text" is often used to convey a sense of cultural distinctiveness, which not only "acts to signify the difference between cultures, but also illustrates the importance of discourse in interpreting cultural concepts" (Ashcroft, Griffiths, and Tiffin 64). Doris Sommer might refer to these terms as "artful maneuvers for marking cultural distance" (*Proceed* x). Linguistic multiplicity in Futoransky's novels then functions as "a signifier of a radical Otherness, not just as a construct which continually reinserts the gap of silence, but as a process which relentlessly foregrounds variance and marginality as the norm" (Ashcroft, Griffiths, and Tiffin 75). Futoransky's exilic autobiographical

FIGURE 2. This collage of French-language ads appears in the middle of the novel. Reprinted courtesy of Luisa Futoransky.

novels develop specific ways both to constitute cultural distance and to bridge it. By drawing attention to themselves, the competing codes and disparate discourses encourage the reader to be suspicious of the inherited literary discourse and codes that sustain the dominant ideological structures that serve to marginalize Laura Kaplansky.

The chapters of *De Pe a Pa* are arranged in a not quite consistent alphabetical series. An alphabetical arrangement of an autobiographical work, while unusual, is not entirely unique: *Roland Barthes par Roland Barthes* also employs an alphabetical arrangement of scenes and reflections to present the self. His alphabet, like Futoransky's, is incomplete: his entries run from *A* to *T*, while Futoransky's go only from *A* to *H*. In Barthes's text, the "I" and the "he" intermingle, like the "I" and the "she" in Futoransky's texts.

In Futoransky's fictional autobiography, almost every chapter names, and provides a dictionary definition of, an object. The first chapter is introduced by the definition of the term "abracadabra"; the second chapter, entitled "¿Be de bagre o bella?" [*B* of gawdy or beautiful?] is burdened by words beginning with the letter *B*, strung together into babbling sentences: "El Baal Shem Tov bebe té con buñuelitos y reflexiona ante las brasas en el homónimo Bodegón de la Buena Familia, y diligentes, Borges y Bioy recogen el reto y el boceto" (30; Baal Shem Tov drinks tea with little rolls and thinks in front of the coals in the homonymous Good Family Diner, and, diligently, Borges and Bioy gather up the challenge and the sketch). Reading more like a playfully random list of *B* words than like a narrative conveying a coherent story line, the chapter stands as a Tower of Babel.

The biblical story of the Tower of Babel is indeed significant here, both as a foundational myth linking names with the establishment of identities and as an example of language losing its capacity to hold meaning. The Genesis story takes place at a mythical time when "the whole earth was of one language, and of one speech" (Gen. 11:1). Having brick and mortar, the people said, "Go to, let us build us a city and a tower, whose top may reach unto heaven; and let us make us a name, lest we be scattered abroad upon the face of the whole earth" (Gen. 11:4). Like the aspiring author Kaplansky, the people in the biblical story want to make their name famous. Their massive tower will be a visible mark to announce the presence of their identity and ensure their continuity in time.

Yet, in the biblical story, the tower is never finished, and the people do not achieve their goal of making their name famous; rather, they have a name imposed on them by others only after failing in their project.

They are renamed in the multiplicity of meanings Derrida gives "*re-nom-mant*," both the renaming of *renommer* and the renown of *renommée*. The biblical story of the Tower of Babel reflects Derrida's discussion in *Prière d'insérer* of the name of God, "there where the Sur-Name names the unnameable, that is, at the same time what one neither *can* nor *should* name, define, or know, because, to begin with, what one sur-names then slips away *beyond being*, without staying there" (xv). The unnameable is given the name Babel.

The name Babel comes from the Hebrew verb *balbel*, to confuse. The biblical story of Babel is a story of the struggle for power and authority over identity. By trying to confirm and celebrate their own identity, the people in the story of Babel reject God as the creator of all identities. God reacts not by killing the people who tried to usurp his control over naming and identity, but rather by confusing their language, that they may not understand one another's speech. Unable to communicate with one another, they are unable to create and maintain meaning, unity, and identity.[13]

Similarly, Laura Kaplansky finds herself often unable to create and maintain meaning, unity, and identity. Not only does she speak a differ-ent language than the people around her in China and France, but their cultural codes are different. In *Son cuentos chinos*, she recounts that for the Chinese, "peach = longevity; for us, sweet skin, adolescent skin that I no longer have" (18). The second chapter of *De Pe a Pa*, with its seemingly unrelated sentences emphasizing the letter *B*, replicates for the reader the sense of confusion the protagonist feels in Paris, her sense of living in a French Tower of Babel.[14]

In Jorge Luis Borges's "The Library of Babel," the narrator lives in a universe that consists of one vast library presumed to contain all pos-sible verbal representations of reality. The librarians can find meaning neither in the majority of the books themselves nor in their order in the library. China is as indecipherable to Kaplansky as this Borgesian library. For both Borges and Futoransky, the narrative of Babel tells of the inadequateness of one language to another, of the deficiency of lan-guage to itself and to meaning. Futoransky's narratives similarly tell of the inadequateness of one tongue to another—of her *porteño* Spanish to these Chinese and French experiences and customs—and serve as an ex-ploration of the impossibility of translation. Futoransky's autobiographi-cal narratives highlight the gap between the experience of place and the language available to describe it. The unease with this gap can lead to "a radical questioning of the relationship between language and the world, an investigation into the means of knowing rather than into what is, or can be, known" (Ashcroft, Griffiths, and Tiffin 137). In trying to bridge the gap, Futoransky experiments with figuration, tropes, twists, and turns in her attempts to represent and explicate her experiences in lands not her own.

The Tower of Babel not only shows the multiplicity of tongues, but also exhibits the impossibility of finishing. The story of Babel does not write beyond the ending; rather it posits the impossibility of an ending. Futoransky encounters the impossibility of finishing her own Babelic texts: *Son cuentos chinos* and *De Pe a Pa* both stop at seemingly arbitrary points.

As a common noun, "Babel/babble" means confusion, in the myth referring both to the confusion of tongues and to the confusion of the architects in finding the structure of their tower interrupted. But Voltaire, in his *Dictionnaire philosophique*, protests: "I do not know why it is said in *Genesis* that Babel signifies confusion, for *Ba* signifies father in the Oriental tongues, and *Bel* signifies god; Babel signifies the city of God, the holy city. The Ancients gave this name to all their capitals" (quoted in Derrida, "Des Tours de Babel" 168). Babel would thus be the name of God the father, with God using his name to mark the city of confusion, the city where understanding was no longer possible.

De Pe a Pa, a text that begins with another word that is a name of God, continually shows that understanding is not always possible for Laura Kaplansky in Paris. After the figurative Tower of Babel that is the second chapter, the letter *C* carries the third chapter, commencing with a dictionary entry for the word *casa* (house) that includes different set phrases employing the word and various "related ideas" (33) in that semantic field. A detailed architectural diagram of a house follows the dictionary definition. The chapter completes the theme by describing Laura Kaplansky's difficulties in finding an apartment to rent in Paris. Her search for an apartment, a room of her own, is a synecdoche for her experience of exile. Here we also find a mise-en-abyme section discussing a proposed journal, the first issue of which would be dedicated to the letter *T* (41–42). Subsequent chapters follow alphabetically, with definitions of *divan, espejo, fiambre, gallo* and *gallina* (sofa, mirror, cold meat, rooster, and hen).[15] Chapter 10, marked as "(Optional)," returns to the beginning of the novel with its title, "ABRACADABRA," and mirrors the style of the second chapter, this time filled with words beginning with the letter *A* (98–103), including the very important (and thus completely capitalized)

"ARGENTINA" (102). Chapter 11 does not feature a letter, while the final chapter defines "hospital" as an "establishment where poor people and pilgrims are taken in for short periods of time" (115). Laura Kaplansky/ Luisa Futoransky, as nomadic subject, is both poor and a pilgrim.

Francine Masiello has argued that Futoransky's art emerges in part from a desire "to move within the landscape of language, to celebrate its liquidity and its aleatory force, to move beyond representation in order to focus on voice and sound" (43). Just as Parente Cunha disrupts the storyline in her autobiographical fiction with her language play, so too in the work of Futoransky "anecdote gives way to sound itself and allitera-tion becomes the connection between cultures" (Masiello 43). That the chapter of *B* words ends with "Curtain!" suggests the staging of speech, the performance of language.

It is significant for an English-speaking reader that the text ends be-fore reaching *I*. The self can neither be found nor enunciated. It is also significant for this autobiographical work that the text ends with *H* and "Hospital," as Futoransky has stated that the work that went into writing the second novel put her into the hospital (Martínez-Richter 78).[16]

This emphasis on the alphabet plays off the novel's title. This title, like *Son cuentos chinos*, comes from a colloquial expression that is in-corporated multiple times in the novel. "Cuentos chinos" is a colloquial expression roughly equivalent to the English "tall tale," a long, compli-cated story that is full of lies. That Futoransky titles a work of auto-biographical fiction "*Son cuentos chinos*" complicates any discussion of "autobiographical truth." *De Pe a Pa* evokes an elementary school lesson in syllable formation, pa-pe-pi-po-pu, used to teach children to read. If Futoransky is writing beyond the ending, severing the narrative from conventional structures of fiction and consciousness about women, then her texts can be seen as helping to teach readers to read, to read beyond the ending, to read for alternatives not made available to women in the traditional romance plots.

The Self as Struggling Writer

Futoransky's life narratives showcase a struggling author always want-ing to be somewhere else. The beginning of *Son cuentos chinos* displays a desire for displacement: "I can think of various places to think about in order not to be where I am now" (9). She thinks, in this specific moment, of the house where she lived for four years in Japan and the Lion's Door in Jerusalem, but in each autobiographical text she continually reenacts this "paradox of diasporic rootlessness" (Spitzer 8).

Futoransky's first-person narrator struggles to find order and coherency in her world and in her work, getting dizzy because "I don't know what isn't worth saying and what I have to continue saying" (10). She begins her text by rejecting dominant, male-authored literary models as inadequate for her stories. Like the narrative voice of Julieta Campos's *Tiene los cabellos rojizos y se llama Sabina*, who claims that if that were a real novel, it would have had to begin with the first sentence of Marcel Proust's *A la recherche du temps perdu*, Luisa Futoransky's narrator is self-conscious about her narrative beginning. As she explains, "I can't begin this saying: 'I was born in 1632, in the city of York' like Robinson, because I was born in Buenos Aires the fifth of January of 1939" (10). Futoransky's protagonist acknowledges that the canonical male-authored text, with its narrative conventions, will not serve to tell her story. That the protagonist shares the same place and date of birth as Luisa Futoransky highlights the autobiographical nature of the text and exemplifies how, in autobiographical texts, there is a reality that checks fantasy and narrative desire.

Although Kaplansky (like Futoransky herself) must support herself with other jobs, "do what I never wanted to do, stick my ass in an office all day, day after day" (16), her sense of identity is always tied to being a writer, her frame of reference is always literary. *Son cuentos chinos* teems with references to other texts and other writers, mostly male. Kaplansky alludes to *Tres tristes tigres* with her chapter title "TRISTES TES . . . de té/de trabajo/de tigre/de tesoro de la juventud" (87; SAD T's of tea / of work / of tiger / of the treasure of youth). Her text nods to *The Tales of the Arabian Nights* (113) and includes quotations from Ray Bradbury, Gabriel García Márquez, T. S. Eliot, William Faulkner, D. H. Lawrence, and Roberto Arlt. *De Pe a Pa* also plays on a strong intertextuality, mixing in authors, literary texts, popular songs, and fairy tale characters. The frequent inclusion of other texts emphasizes her self-identification as a writer, her dream of the day when her name will be as famous as these and her words will be cited. Julia Watson's observation that autobiography "is located at an uneasy nexus of past—the retrospective record of one's life—and future—the wishes, dreams, and aspirations of the subject-in-process" seems an apt description of the autobiographical novels of Futoransky (317). Futoransky's texts also bear out Watson's claim for autobiography's multidirectionality, as the eruptions of the present moment of writing continually disrupt the story of the past events.

While very aware of her alienation as an exile and of her low-class status within the community of exiles, Kaplansky seems unable to escape from the internalized precepts of the commodification practices that victimize women and women's bodies, seeing them as exchange objects between men. Always the author, she seeks solace in other authors whose life experiences and writings mirror her own.

Kaplansky, identifying with Rhys as another exiled woman writer who lived for a period in Paris, wishes that they might have met or that she could have at least had the opportunity to send Rhys "a devout little card: Thank you so much for how well you write, Ma'am, and very happy New Year!'" (*De Pe a Pa* 21). Kaplansky decided to read something by Rhys upon reading that Rhys was born in Martinique, "and without another thought, she decided that she must be black, so that reading her would mean knowing a little bit more about blackness and thus she would get a little closer, even if it was in such a way, to her never very well understood Djagó, Zairean and Mongolese" (21). Like so many of Kaplansky's actions, her reading of Rhys's fiction is motivated by a desire for a better relationship with a man.

The first Rhys story Kaplansky chooses to read is also selected by virtue of a personal identification: "Fifí la grosse" (in *Left Bank*), because Kaplansky is often called "*La gorda Lauri,* o simplemente *Lagor*" (22). Exposing her pain at the supposedly affectionate nickname results in a change in voice from the third person singular to the more intimate first person singular: "something that hurts *me* quite a bit, but *I* have to act as if it were nothing, because they say it is affectionate" (22, emphasis added). Underscoring her emotional anguish, the first person continues in her oft-repeated fantasy of being born thin, with blue eyes and lots of money, before being replaced by the third person singular to refer to Laura.

Kaplansky recounts how Jean Rhys was forgotten for more than twenty years until, rediscovered, "they began to shower her with national and other prizes. Just out of guilt. Jean, when she went to receive one of the prizes, said to them, simply and without even any anger or sadness, 'A little late, don't you think?'" (22). *De Pe a Pa* contains several references to Futoransky's own dream of receiving literary prizes, especially the Nobel (61).

Enough similarities can be traced between the lives and fictions of Jean Rhys and Luisa Futoransky to make the self-identification with Rhys understandable. Both writers employ paratactic narrative styles, drawing "the reader's attention to the fact that all narrative originates around a gap, a sense of incompletion and loss" (Druxes 60). Both authors draw heavily from their own experiences as women and exiles to write their fictions, inventing female characters who are versions of earlier selves, thus both sharing a "telling of self," and preserving "an alterity for her present self, a distance from the scenarios of victimization she evokes" (Druxes 63). By entering into dialogue with their earlier fictionalized selves, each writer can "repeat commodification scenarios in which she is no longer the passive sufferer but the active narrator, wielding a compensatory control over her female characters" (Druxes 64). Futoransky notes in an interview that she can't reread her own work because she is no longer the same: "I can't reread my work, it would be absurd. . . . We are one way in a determined period, with the eyes of a determined period: we will never be the same even if we go to bathe in the same river. There is always fiction" (Pfeiffer 58). Futoransky admits to the autobiographical nature of her works, but insists on their fictionality as well, stressing the claim that all autobiography is fiction in that the self inscribed on the pages of the text is one that does not exist outside the text.

Rhys's narratives feature female protagonists whose situations are similar enough that critics often write of a "Rhys woman";[17] Futoransky's first two novels share the same protagonist while her third novel, Urracas, focuses on a woman who shares many characteristics with the earlier protagonist. Both authors place at the center of their narratives women who would not qualify as heroines of conventional novels, thereby de-centering that inherited narrative structure and the values that underlie it. The female characters of both authors struggle to be heard, to be recognized as possessing subjectivity, within a social structure and a literary discourse that does not easily grant them subjectivity.

The protagonists of Rhys and Futoransky's fiction are displaced middle-class women who seem to gravitate toward major cities as sites where they may gain (an often precarious) economic independence and some sense of subjecthood. In these narratives, the city is "the condition and milieu in which corporality is socially, sexually, and discursively produced" (Grosz 242). Futoransky's exilic fiction serves to demonstrate the corporeal relationship between the protagonist and the various foreign cities in which she lives.

In a metatext written in the margins between autobiographical fiction and fictional autobiography, the protagonist's self-identity as writer is crucial. Laura's sense of herself as a writer is reflected in the frequency with which she compares life and literature in her narrative: "life is much messier, less clear than novels. in books people begin and end things in a few hundred pages. no one gets left hanging nor retraces his/her steps, . . . in novels things are presented as less mixed-up and confused and the protagonists tend to do less unmotivated damage than in life, in novels people don't get erased nor disappear so easily as in life. . . . but life doesn't have semantic or semiotic problems nor does it lack words or style and novels do" (163–64). In this ironic passage, much longer than the section included here, Laura thinks she prefers life in novels over real life; but at the end, speaking as a writer, she recognizes that novels also present difficulties not present in real life. That her own novel, written as an intimate journal, presents a slice of life is thus reaffirmed by virtue of its being "mezclada y confusa" (mixed-up and confused) like her characterization of the events in real life. Blurring the distinction between fiction and reality, constantly undermining the illusion that literary discourse constitutes a process of mimetic representation, Futoransky's text unites the confusion and incoherence of real life with the semantic, semiotic, and stylistic problems of fiction.

In *De Pe a Pa*, Kaplansky's self-identification as writer and reader continues. Her construction of *De Pe a Pa* is paratactic: pieces of the narrative are placed side by side without subordination or any ranking of literary styles, reflecting the random, associative connections of the protagonist's consciousness in response to her environment. She marks off one chapter as "optional" (98), for, as Laura has earlier stated: "(As a reader, I like it when authors, when they get into the type of troubles that I do, let me know, put up an announcement of warning and complicity in said pages: *optional*)" (84). Not only is Laura Kaplansky writing the type of narrative she would like to read, but she is also coaching the readers on how to appreciate her text.

That she is writing the kind of narrative she would like to read seems apparent in her ending of the book with a section of notes "for those who are interested in the fate of the story's protagonists after the limited situation of the literary plot" (123). A note that informs readers that Laura continues to write poetry carries with it the footnote discussed above: "Laura (Falena) Kaplansky was a character that I created with part of my melancholy, my gaze, my joys, pains and sorrows. Through Laura, a kind of candid and sometimes lucid admirer, I tried to explain what it is to be a poet out in the world, with certain aggravating circumstances: an older woman, poor, Jewish, Argentine and alone" (123–24). In this footnote, the boundary between protagonist and author is blurred as the author admits to having created the character with pieces of herself. The patchwork metaphor functions, then, not only for the text, but also for the protagonist.

The footnote continues: "I could have followed her through interior and exterior scenes as coarse and as cutting as the Malvinas War . . . but all of a sudden, since that is how big decisions are made, those that mature slowly, today I got up and I realized, Laura, that's enough" (124). Here there is no conventional nineteenth-century narrative ending of marriage or suicide, no textual tying up of loose ends. Futoransky rejects both the traditional endings made available for women characters in the literary canon and the ideological structures those endings serve to sustain. In her alternate fictional space, the story just stops.

Yet the story continues in Futoransky's third novel, *Urracas*, a first- and third-person narrative that relates the amorous difficulties and international travels of Julia Bene, an Argentine woman living in Paris. It is another metafictional text that confronts issues of language, writing, and identity, another text on and by a woman writing (in) exile.

Together, *Son cuentos chinos*, *De Pe a Pa*, and *Urracas* form an autobiographical metatext on writing (in) exile, one in which the main character's spatial mobility enables her to foster a critical sense of herself as a female subject. In creating this metatext, Luisa Futoransky rejects many of the elements of the dominant fictional structure in order to write beyond the ending, to write another script for another type of female protagonist, one who does not fit into the role of heroine in the traditional romance plot. At the same time, she invokes certain conventions and expectations of autobiography only to create dissonance and disquiet with those expectations. She questions the uniqueness and authority over identity traditionally accorded proper names, draws attention to how language serves to construct experience, and blurs the boundaries between art and life as well as between fiction and autobiography. Borrowing heavily from Borges and others, she constructs autobiographical intertextual narratives about a Latin America woman's life outside Latin America. She writes to contest the societal sorting mechanisms that have assigned her to culturally marginalized spaces and struggles to create autobiographical fictions in which she might author other possibilities for herself and her thinly fictionalized protagonists. In Luisa Futoransky's autobiographical metatext, we have an autobiographical manifesto that stakes a claim for other perspectives on identity, experience, and ways of knowledge. While society places value only on certain female bodies and identities, Futoransky uses her autobiographical writings to claim a space where there is value in the knowledge, experience, and identity that comes from being female, fortyish, alone, not at all thin, Jewish, South American, and prone to volatile passions.

PART TWO

FROM SELF TO FAMILY TO NATION: THE FAMILY SAGA AS AN AUTOBIOGRAPHICAL GENRE

A country is soon impoverished when it is robbed of its stories. Or when its children neglect to tell or invent others in their place.
—NÉLIDA PIÑON, *CAETANA'S SWEET SONG*

In *Nation and Narration*, Homi Bhabha refers to "a particular ambivalence that haunts the idea of the nation, the language of those who write of it and the lives of those who live it" (1). In this section, I focus on the autobiographical genre of the family saga used to tell the story of a nation. The sagas studied here are narratives that signify a sense of "nationness" (Bhabha 2) at the same time that they demonstrate that ambivalence about the idea and the realities of the nation. If we take Hannah Arendt's idea that the society of the nation is "'that curiously hybrid realm where private interests assume public significance' and the two realms flow unceasingly and uncertainly into each other 'like waves in the never-ending stream of the life-process itself'" (quoted in Bhabha 2), then we can read Nélida Piñon's *The Republic of Dreams* and Ana María Shua's *The Book of Memories* as curiously hybrid texts where private interests (the realm of autobiography) assume public significance (the realm of narratives on the nation, or, to use Doris Sommer's term, "foundational fictions"), with the two realms flowing unceasingly and uncertainly into each other in the never-ending streams of life and literature.

With the narrations of the nations discussed here, we can see how the marginal or the minority is a "substantial intervention into those justifications of modernity—progress, homogeneity, cultural organicism, the deep nation, the long past—that rationalize the authoritarian, 'normalizing' tendencies within cultures in the name of the national interest or the ethnic prerogative" (Bhabha 4). The South American dictatorships of the 1970s and 1980s (like the Indian residential school systems in the United States and Canada discussed in chapter 6) put into stark relief what happens when authoritarian regimes rationalize the justifications for their aberrant actions in the name of the national interest. Shua's and Piñon's narratives are substantial interventions into those justifications. The two authors employ their family sagas to present new narratives of the nation, narratives that participate in the "turning of boundaries and limits into the *in-between* spaces through which the meanings of cultural and political authority are negotiated" (Bhabha 4). Resisting the meanings of cultural and political authority that dictatorial and patriarchal regimes would seek to impose, Piñon and Shua use their narratives to negotiate other possibilities, to create in-between spaces. Their texts remind us to question "[w]ho and what determines which stories ultimately become woven into the national narrative?" (Andrews 4). I read their narratives as political attempts to tell counterstories that contest the dominant narratives, dominant narratives that would claim the exclusive rights to telling the story of "the nation." In claiming those exclusive rights, dominant narratives claim the story of "the nation" as a particular form of property, one that they own. While the dominant narratives of the nation exclude the voices, concerns, and experiences of many members of the national community, Shua and Piñon write to give voice to other members of their national communities. *The Book of Memories* and *The Republic of Dreams* provide examples of how, through acts of remembering, individuals and communities narrate counterhistories coming from the margins, voiced by other kinds of subjects than those who hold power in the nation. In this way, individuals and groups may also "engage in narrative acts of critical self-locating through which they assert their cultural difference and right to self-determination," or they may employ their personal narrating to bear witness to different forms of trauma (Schaffer and Smith 4). Their stories thus enable new forms of subjectivities and different futures for themselves and others.

Doris Sommer has shown the connections between the establishment of modern Latin American nations and the projection of their ideal histories through the novel. Authors of early Latin American novels were also "fathers of their countries, preparing national projects through prose fiction, and implementing foundational fictions through legislative or military campaigns. At the turn of the nineteenth century, there was already a page-long list of Hispano-American writers who were also presidents of their countries" ("Irresistible" 73).[1] As these are "the very foundational romances that helped prepare the familial and often hierarchical rhetoric that recurs in Latin American politics" ("Irresistible" 89), the novels Sommer discusses can be seen as part of the tradition Shua and Piñon both engage and resist.

Nélida Piñon and Ana María Shua are prolific authors who have produced narratives that reflect the richness and diversity of their nations. Like Gabriel García Márquez, who told the story of his nation via the story of a family in the monumental novel *Cien años de soledad* (1967; *One Hundred Years of Solitude*, 1970), both Nélida Piñon, in *A república dos sonhos* (1984; *The Republic of Dreams*, 1989), and Ana María Shua, in *El libro de los recuerdos* (1994; *The Book of Memories*, 1998), employ family sagas to explore questions of national identity. In an autobiographical novel that has been called "both a family and a national chronicle, a record of individual lives that take on meaning in the historical process of nation-building" (Espadas 52), Piñon tells the heroic saga of a Brazilian family with its origins in Galicia. Breta, the granddaughter in the novel, is to write the story of the family. Piñon, like her character Breta, is the granddaughter of Galician immigrants and has inherited from her own grandfather Daniel this desire to "hacer las Américas" (to make it in America; literally, to make the Americas). Piñon lives out that dream through her writing, with each book a new journey, a new conquest, the foundation of a new imagined community.

Like the narrators of her autobiographical novel, Shua is from a family of Jewish immigrants in Argentina. She has remarked in an interview with Fernando Reati that "[t]o tell the life of a family is also to tell the life of a country" (quoted in Buchanan, "Narrating Argentina" 84, translation mine). The telling of stories—the stories of people's lives, the stories of a family, the stories of a country—structures both *The Republic of Dreams* and *The Book of Memories*. Sylvia Molloy has argued that "the Spanish American autobiographer forays into the past through familial . . . reminiscence" (*At Face Value* 9); in this section I chart out the forays of Nélida Piñon and Ana María Shua as they fictionalize their own family stories in order to create novelistic accounts of their nations.

In remembering their own family stories as a base from which to create their fictions, both authors reflect on the problematic nature of memories. Memory is foundational to both their books and their countries. Indeed, a nation has been called "a soul, a spiritual principle" with "the possession in common of a rich legacy of memories" as the first of two elements considered constitutional to that spiritual principle (Renan

19). Shua's novel, *The Book of Memories*, highlights memories in its very title and has been seen by many as part of a Jewish literary tradition that underscores the importance of memory. While Piñon's title refers to dreams rather than memory, memories, dreams, and storytelling are always already intricately interwoven in her text. The importance Piñon places on memory is further underscored in her interviews and talks. In her inaugural speech as the first female president of the Brazilian National Academy of Letters, she explains: "I told stories because my memory is the collective memory of my feminine gender. A remote memory that was present throughout the painful pilgrimage of humanity on earth. A memory that was the caretaker of history, the protector of the myths that brought warmth to the living rooms and irrigated the imagination, the legends, the poetry of all, in short, that helped to soften the loneliness of mankind" (quoted in Teixeira 26). That Piñon is conscious of herself as a memory is also made obvious in an interview with Claudia Posadas, where she reflects, "I am conscious that I am a memory and therefore what I do is accumulate events of my personal geography" (2). *The Republic of Dreams* is a chart of her personal geography and genealogy.

Piñon's and Shua's family sagas serve, in part, as their family's collective biographies, and assure the authors that their lives have transpersonal significance and are embedded in historical chains that link Galicia to Brazil and Eastern Europe to Argentina. Writing a fictionalized version of the family history allows the authors (both granddaughters of immigrants) the opportunity "to make narrative sense of the radical discontinuity of their American experience and impose on it a frame of narrative coherence" (Watson 298).

Just as we have seen how the autobiographical texts of Helena Parente Cunha and Luisa Futoransky are constructed at an uneasy nexus of past and present, in my discussions of the autobiographical novels of Nélida Piñon and Ana María Shua, we shall see how their texts inhabit that uneasy nexus, as they present the wishes, dreams, and aspirations of the subjects (and nations)-in-process.

Piñon's and Shua's narratives both relate multigenerational stories beginning with a patriarch who immigrated to South America as a teenager and went on both to build a family and to amass a fortune. The description from the back cover of *The Book of Memories*—"the history of a family so distinctive, so unique and special, that perhaps it resembles your own" (my translation)—fits Pinon's family saga as well. Both autobiographical texts present the story of a family that is both unique and representative of other South American families. In both autobiographical novels, the history of the family represents the history of the nation at the same time that it questions the whole notion of the "History" with a capital *H* of a nation that itself ignores the histories of the individuals who make up that nation. These Argentine and Brazilian narratives incorporate a variety of voices and discourses to challenge any monolithic presentation of their respective nations.

In telling the histories of their countries, both texts address issues raised by living during a dictatorship. That context of violence and repression is not just a background for the story but a crucial, internal dimension of the text. As Shoshana Felman and Dori Laub note in *Testimony: Crises of Witnessing in Literature, Psychoanalysis, and History*, reading for both the *contextualization of the text* and the *textualization of the context* allows readers better insight into "the political, historical, and biographical realities with which the texts are dynamically involved and within which their particular creative possibilities are themselves inscribed" (xv). We shall see in the chapters to follow how *The Republic of Dreams* and *The Book of Memories* are both dynamically involved in the political, historical, and biographical realities of their nations. The authors' critique of gender subordination "takes on its specific urgency, and its historical specificity" in relation to the political context of the dictatorships of Brazil and Argentina (Kantaris 3). Elia Geoffrey Kantaris argues that for Southern Cone women writers, "this unleashing of despotic violence is perceived to be bound up with a complex of masculine power and identity within which 'woman' becomes the central yet excluded or disavowed term" and that the authors' awareness of gender as a crucial social and political aspect marks what she calls "an epistemological shift in both the practice and the theory of culture in Latin America" (3). The attention to gender politics in the works of Shua and Piñon contributes to their importance as major contemporary Latin American writers.

The Republic of Dreams and *The Book of Memories* are both "vehicles of criticism or social action against events that exceed the writers' control" (Fuchs 197). The Brazilian and Argentine dictatorships are obviously events that exceed the control of Piñon and Shua; however, by writing those events into their texts, they demonstrate a narrative control over events they could not control in their own lives.[2] Often, when autobiographical works are written in response to catastrophe, women writers look past their own time and place to represent themselves in broader historical contexts. *The Republic of Dreams* explores the long range of both Brazilian and Galician history, while *The Book of Memories* moves from Jews escaping repression in Nazi Europe to Argentina's Dirty War. In this way, these autobiographical family sagas confuse, conflate, and manipulate time, highlighting how memory commingles past and present times.

In both texts, we see a preoccupation with women's roles in society and in the family, with the curtailment of personal freedoms in patriarchy and dictatorship, and with the importance of artistic freedom and imagination. Both family sagas trace families who have emigrated from Europe to the Americas and in which the members of the younger generations are expected to carry the memories of the older generations. We see how, in Shua's *The Book of Memories*, photographs are "ghostly revenants, are very particular instruments of remembrance, since they are perched at the edge between memory and postmemory, and also, though differently, between memory and forgetting" (Hirsch 22). The concept of postmemory is another element that serves to tie together the two autobiographical family sagas.

Postmemory "is distinguished from memory by generational distance and from history by deep personal connection" (Hirsch 22); it is "a very powerful and very particular form of memory," a memory carried by the younger generations. Those who have grown up dominated by the stories of events that happened before they were born, "whose own belated stories are evacuated by the stories of the previous generation shaped by traumatic events that can be neither understood nor recreated" (Hirsch 22) live with this experience of postmemory. In *The Book of Memories* and in *The Republic of Dreams*, we see one family in which the ancestors are Jews who leave Europe to escape from the horrors of the Holocaust and start a new life in America, and one family in which the patriarch leaves poverty in Galicia to make his fortune in the Americas. Both are families in which the younger generations grow up dominated by narratives that preceded their births. Both families also live through, and are marked by, the traumatic events of dictatorship in Latin America, events that can be neither understood nor re-created. Both literary texts are made up of multiple voices, exemplifying how the formation of a person's identity is tied, in part, to the life stories and fictions of others.

In writing the autobiographical novels, both authors draw from their own family histories, but also from their fertile artistic imaginations. When Shua is asked in an interview whether *The Book of Memories* is autobiographical, she responds: "Everything is autobiographical and nothing is. I can follow the line of each one of these characters and tell where I got each of their characteristics. . . . The house is that of my Arab grandparents who lived there with their ten kids. I took that house, took out that family and put in a Polish family" (Collette, *Conversación al sur* 141). She further explains that the grandfather in the text is a mixture of the worst traits of her own two grandfathers. Her mixture of autobiography and fiction has confused even her own family members; one of her aunts called her and asked, "Why did you make me fat in the novel?" (142).

What is of interest here is the ways in which both authors employ the family saga to write the story of the nation. Both authors stress the role of stories and memories in personal, familial, and national identity formation. Their texts reveal a performative memory that involves the repetition of the stories by which one's identity is constituted, whether that one is an individual person, a family, or a nation. Both texts invoke and contest the ways in which dictatorial regimes impose "truths" on their citizens via the compulsory repetition of prior and subjectivating norms. Shua and Piñon present alternate stories of their nations as a way of resisting, subverting, and displacing those norms. By presenting the (fictionalized) histories of their families as the histories of their nations, they expand the auto-bio-graphical genre from the self/the life/the writing to the family/the life/the writing to the nation/the life/the writing, writing themselves into their nation's literary history and into a literary tradition I call *natiobiography*.

3 / Re-membering the Nation by Remembering the Family: Ana María Shua's *The Book of Memories*

Ana María Shua was born in Buenos Aires, in 1951, to a Jewish Argentine family. She published her first book, *El sol y yo* (1967), when she was sixteen years old and has gone on to publish prolifically in a variety of genres, including the novel, short story, poetry, and children's literature. Shua's interest in Jewish culture, tradition, and humor is evidenced by such books as *Risas y emociones de la cocina judía* (1993), *Cuentos judíos con fantasmas y demonios* (1994), and *El pueblo de los tontos* (1995). Shua has received numerous literary awards, including two for her first book of poems, and she was awarded a Guggenheim for her work on *El libro de los recuerdos* (1994; *The Book of Memories*, 1998).

The Book of Memories tells the story of several generations of the Jewish Argentine Rimetka family. Like the narrators in her text, Shua is from a family of Jewish immigrants. *The Book of Memories* can be read as a text based on family genealogy and history that is an attempt to preserve Shua's cultural memory and to come to terms with the history and stories of her family and her country, characteristics often cited as common to third- and fourth-generation Jewish Latin American writers (Lockhart xxii).

Memory is a central theme of Shua's narrative, as it is of many autobiographical texts. Indeed, Steven Sadow, in his introduction to *King David's Harp: Autobiographical Essays by Jewish Latin American Writers*, points out that "in writing that is both Jewish and autobiographical, memory is of the utmost importance. Memory of the old country, parents and grandparents, arrival and culture shock, growing up, places lived in, 'making it in America,' artistic, business, or political achievement, anti-Semitism and the Nazis" (xvi). He goes on to note that there is "ambivalence about personal and collective memory, a constant evaluation of Jewish identity as a personal issue and in a Latin American context" (xvi)—all issues that we can trace in Shua's text (and in the autobiographical narratives of Luisa Futoransky discussed in chapter 2).

Other critics writing on Jewish Latin American literature have also underscored the issue of memory. Nora Glickman writes of the primacy of memory in the works of Latin American Jewish writers explicitly pre-occupied with Jewish issues. Many of these authors have written of their own memories and of their ancestors' memories, blending together the personal and the collective histories. Glickman writes of authors who "share a history of exile that consists of memories of uprooting, perse-cutions, pogroms, and irrational hatreds" (300) and who persistently incorporate their families into their fictions in ways that attest, "both positively and negatively, to their enduring attachment to the richness and pain of the Jewish experience" (321)—descriptions that fit Shua's work here as well. Marjorie Agosín, in her introduction to *Passion, Memory, and Identity*, discusses how the "gestures of writing become the retrieval acts of memory" so that "all literary acts are also acts of re-membering" (xii–xiii). She traces a number of fundamental themes and concerns in the Jewish literature of Latin America, including the three that mark out the title of her collection. Agosín asserts that the unify-ing tradition for Jewish women writers in Latin America is the memoir, arguing that it is in memoir that "Jewish women writers assume their own identities, remember through the voice of the father or the mother, but at the same time feel the world from their position as outsiders. The act of writing memoirs that document exiles and arrivals and that in-corporate, through personal experiences, what it means to be Jewish in Latin America is probably the most powerful contribution these writers can make" (xiv). Agosín argues that being Jewish means living always in two worlds, the past (which is recuperated through memories) and the present (xviii). Shua recuperates the past world through memories at the same time that she inscribes her self and her family into Argentine (and Jewish Argentine) culture. The memories of migration and multiple diasporas are crucial, but so too are the memories of family vacations and financial ventures.

In *The Book of Memories*, Shua presents the life of the family, like the life of the South American country, full of everyday events like childhood soccer games, impetuous love affairs, successful and failed businesses, family disputes, political and economic problems. It is a life full of contradictions, surprising and sometimes incredible events. As noted on the back cover of the original Spanish edition, "it is the story of a family so unique and special that perhaps it resembles your own" (translation mine).

Argentina has been home to one of the largest Jewish communities in the world, and, in certain ways, the Rimetka family is representative of many Jewish Argentine families: they are of Eastern European descent; they live in Buenos Aires, specifically in el barrio Once (a neighborhood that has been particularly associated with Jewish immigrants in the twentieth century); and they show changes in social, economic, and educational levels from one generation to another. The grandfather started out as a traveling salesperson on a bicycle; he has grandchildren who are psychologists and journalists.

Shua's narrative begins with the history of this grandfather, who escaped Poland because "he wanted to build America, but not this America, the other one, you know, the real one, the one up north" (1–2). Because the grandfather was an army deserter, he had to wait for the death of some young man who was not a deserter in order to buy his documents and be able to emigrate. That was how he came to be Gedalia Rimetka and, since the false documents were not sufficient to immigrate to the United States, how he ended up in Argentina, "that's America too, but not quite" (3). Thus the first story of the novel is one of immigration, of the loss of personal identity and the beginning of a new identity, with a new name, in a new country with a new language and new customs.

And the name Rimetka is not even the name of the man who died in Poland, but "a combination of auditory expertise and orthographic arbitrariness" of the civil registry employee who took the grandfather's information in order to make his Argentine documents (7). The history of the last name provides an opportunity to reflect on national identity: "Like so many other immigrants, the Rimetka family had acquired an intensely national name, a truly indigenous product, much more authentically Argentine than a correctly spelled Spanish surname, because Rimetka never existed in Grandfather's homeland, or in the original language or, for that matter, in any other country or time in history" (8). This quotation puts into question what is authentic, what is Argentine, and who has the right to declare themselves authentically Argentine.

Shua's challenge to the definition of "Argentine" is particularly significant in light of the sometimes still existing belief that the Jews are not "real" Argentines, at least not if they practice their religion or if they identify, in a religious or secular manner, as Jews.[1]

The grandfather's story also shows how it is that the name, as the guarantor of the unity of the person, is problematized by exile and mistranslation, as we have previously seen in the discussion of Luisa Futoransky's autobiographical metafiction. Again, we remember Richard Rand's assertion that proper names refer to singular, unique beings and thus are "undefinable, semantically ungeneralizable, and hence untranslatable as well" (86). The grandfather receives the name Rimetka in Argentina when his last name (which is not even his) is found lacking, when it lacks the ability to be translated, when it lacks coherence in an Argentine context. The name is seen as singular and as singularly untranslatable in the new country and in the new language. The family name, as that which guarantees the unity of the person and the family, is problematized, its unity dispersed with exile and mistranslation. In an autobiographical narrative that struggles with the question of subjectivity, the family name thus becomes a negated site of identity. (Shua's own last name is a simplification of her Lebanese paternal grandfather's name: Schoua.)

The story of Gedalia Rimetka and his family is told by the multiple narrators, narrators who are themselves unnamed members of the family. If "a large part of Jewish identity is found in the recurring habit of telling stories" (Siskind 96), it is appropriate to highlight the intergenerational storytelling pleasure at play in the construction of *The Book of Memories*, a text constructed of conversations, testimonies, questions, and responses from various members of the Rimetka family. Ilan Stavans notes that this narrative construction "pays tribute to a recognizable device in Jewish letters. More specifically, in Yiddish literature: to the unfolding of the story while two guys talk" (80), a tradition Stavans asserts presents Jewish life as a debate, an encounter, a "clash of opinions" (81). With the various narrative voices contradicting each other about what happened to different people in the family, *The Book of Memories* might easily be read as a continuous clash of opinions.

For, indeed, the narrative voices that make up the text seem never to agree on any event or on the characterization of various family members. They disagree on the profession of their grandfather:

Grandfather Gedalia was always a moneylender, even in Poland.

Grandfather Gedalia couldn't have been a moneylender in Poland because when he came over he was still very young.

There are people who charge interest while they are still in their mothers' wombs. There are people who, as they're being born, make mortgage loans to the midwives.

Moneylender is just an elegant way of saying loan shark.

There is nothing elegant about being a moneylender. (14)

They have a "clash of opinions" on his character and observance of Jewish traditions as well:

Grandfather Gedalia never ate pig's meat because it was against his religion.

Grandfather Gedalia never ate pig's meat in public.

Grandfather Gedalia was a pig. (15)

With their repetition, biting humor, and wordplay (often more successful in Shua's original Spanish than in the English translation), these two exchanges regarding the profession, character, and traditions of Grandfather Gedalia are typical of those found throughout the novel. They serve as examples of how subjectivity is constructed relationally—for each member of the family has his/her own opinions on the subjectivity of the others.

Although some of the characters in *The Book of Memories* consider their Jewishness an important part of their personal and cultural identity, the traditions seem more important than the faith itself. The stories have many references to the cultural traditions of the Rimetka family, usually references that appear as small details inside other stories. Most frequently they are related to members of the first generation, to the grandfather, the grandmother, or her brother, Uncle Sansón, who came on Saturday afternoons after having walked "block after block in order to celebrate Saturdays at his sister's house, because it is forbidden to travel by car on the Sabbath. He had to knock on the wrought-iron door with his umbrella handle because it was forbidden to ring the bell on Saturday" (124). In the description of the family house, we have a reference to the "bedroom where Gedalia, who believed in nothing, had slept in one bed and Granny, who didn't believe in anything either, slept in the other, all due to that curious, faithless religion that at times they prayed to but that prohibited them, for instance, from sleeping together in the same bed" (133). According to one of the narrators, Grandfather Gedalia did not follow the religion, "[b]ut he followed tradition. Mainly to keep up appearances" (12), using religion as an excuse to do what he wanted to do anyway, like kick Aunt Judith out of the house. A narrator recalls how the grandfather always said that there was a certain citation in the Talmud and, after saying it in Spanish, would repeat the phrase in Hebrew. And without commentary on the part of the narrator, the next paragraph continues: "Aunt Clara's grandchildren went to a school that taught Hebrew. After that, whenever he would quote the Talmud, he wouldn't repeat it in Hebrew anymore" (12). This example highlights how Grandfather Gedalia used the authority of the Talmud and the authority of the Hebrew that he supposedly spoke to impose his patriarchal will over his wife, his children, and his grandchildren.

The use of certain terms in Polish and Yiddish in the novel serves to display a sense of cultural distinction, something that not only "acts to signify the difference between cultures, but also illustrates the importance of discourse in interpreting cultural concepts" (Ashcroft, Griffiths, and Tiffin 64). The multiplicity of codes in the novel functions as a signifier of Otherness, with Shua's work developing specific ways both to constitute cultural distance and to bridge it. By drawing attention to different uses of language and to different languages, Shua encourages her readers to be aware of the ways in which the various discourses and codes can sustain the dominant ideological structures of a society. Her multivoiced text resists the imposition of any one "truth" or settled meaning.

Another chapter that emphasizes religion and Jewish identity is the one entitled "La babuela" ("Granny").[2] In this chapter, the grandmother speaks, as a first-person narrator, from the cemetery, and addresses the question of language: "But can you really say something important in this language? Can you really say things you believe, say what comes from deep inside you, from your gut? Are there words for those things in Spanish? Spanish, bah. What kind of language is this?" (139). As part of the generation that was born and raised in Poland and only learned Spanish as an adult, *la babuela* has never felt comfortable in Spanish. For the grandmother, there is a gap between lived experience and the language available to describe it. Several members of the other generations remark that sometimes the grandmother said things not very clearly, because "she wanted to express it with a proverb but she always got it backwards in Spanish" 79.[3]

When she says, "Eso es lo bueno de estar aquí, que con todo el mundo se puede hablar. Casi todos hablan idioma" (166; "That's the good part about being in this place, you can talk to the whole wide world. Almost everyone here speaks something" [140]), readers have the impression that the grandmother is buried in a Jewish cemetery.[4] She finds the cemetery to be a less alienating place than the city itself; in the cemetery she can talk with everyone, and everyone celebrates the same holidays. When interviewed from beyond the grave by her grandson, *la babuela* asks him to tell her children to change the photo on her monument for one taken when she was much younger: "[S]o for Hanukkah and Purim, which are happy celebrations, they would let us make up our faces like in the photos. During the rest of the year we have to go around with faces looking like we were on our death beds, and I don't even want to talk about mine" (141). The emphasis on Jewish culture, traditions, and language reminds readers of the strong Jewish community in Argentina and of the role Jews have played in constructing the Argentine nation. The emphasis on the photograph and its role in constructing the identity of the grandmother—even after her death—is an example of the role of the photograph in the family story and the ways in which "power is deployed and contested within the family's visual dynamics" (Hirsch 9).

In the younger generations, the traditions are not as strong. Aunt Judith converted and had a church wedding, saying that "she couldn't care less where she got married—she didn't believe in religion anyway—and the only thing she wanted to do was live with Uncle Ramón" (43). Although Silvestre respected his father's traditions more than Judith did, "he didn't believe in God or the Devil, or religion or anything, he even disliked the Hebrew Club because, he said, it would get young people together with the excuse to play sports or to meet socially and then, afterward, on Fridays, they would be subjected to occult rabbinical interpretations of the Scriptures. For him, religion was the opiate of the masses" (82–83). With this quotation, readers can not be sure if the reference to the Devil is religious or political as there are also references to Juan Perón as the "Diablo Coludo" (43).

A Subject Constituted in Gender, Multiple, and Contradicted

In addition to religion and language, gender is vital in the construction of personal identity. Shua's text provides examples of the subject "constituted in gender, to be sure, though not by sexual difference alone, but rather across languages and cultural representations; a subject engendered in the experience of race and class, as well as sexual, relations; a subject, therefore, not unified but rather multiple, and not so much divided as contradicted" (de Lauretis 2). The subjects of *The Book of Memories* are constituted by way of language and representation; the stories by which we come to know the subjects serve, with their own contradictions, to present them as multiple and contradictory subjects.

Shua presents the grandfather as a very traditional man who liked to humiliate his wife. When she spoke, he said, "she has a big mouth and so she talks" (12); when he did not like the food, "he would throw it on the floor, say, for instance, when there wasn't enough salt or it wasn't hot enough" (13). If the grandmother interrupted him when he was speaking, "his eyes would well up with tears and he'd look at her as if to say 'now that I'm finally old and decrepit doesn't anyone show respect anymore?'" (13), yet he always interrupted her. And when Silvestre, as a little boy, told his parents that the teacher wanted them to speak only Spanish at home, Grandfather Gedalia "liked the idea. . . . because it gave him the opportunity to humiliate his wife in front of his children (which gave him much pleasure)" (18–19).

In contrast to the more traditional gender roles of the grandparents, we see in Aunt Judith a girl, and later a woman, who resists and rejects the traditional roles reserved for her gender. She preferred soccer to sewing and was worth two players in the neighborhood soccer games. She was considered "an independent woman who was ahead of her time" (35). Later, when Silvestre remembers his sister Judith, it is as a woman "who had suffered so much, but who was so strong, quick to respond, foul-mouthed, quarrelsome, and always defiant, capable of scandalizing her own children" (165). Shua presents a woman who, rejecting the norms of the patriarchal society in which she lives, is punished by life, but does not repent. Her friend Martita also rejects the roles reserved for women: "Martita wasn't afraid of anybody or anything. . . . Martita studied law at a time when most women didn't study at all" (47).

Although the audacious women who go against patriarchal norms have to pay a price, the woman who tries always to live within those norms is not happy either. In a section focalized by Clarita, Judith's sister, we see her as the one who "wants to do everything right. She wants to be a good daughter and a good wife and a good mother. Until now, Clara has always done things right. That's why it's not fair that she isn't happy" (65). She married an older man to please her father. She represents the woman who has no opinion of her own: "Clara would see things through her father's eyes, through her husband's eyes and, finally, to speak through her son" (165). She is the woman who serves, as Luce Irigaray notes, as the mirror for the man. In *This Sex Which Is Not One*, Irigaray asserts: "The rejection, the exclusion of a female imaginary undoubtedly places woman in a position where she can experience herself only fragmentarily as waste or as excess in the little structured margins of a dominant ideology, this mirror entrusted by the (masculine) 'subject' with the task of reflecting and redoubling himself. The role of 'femininity' is prescribed moreover by this masculine specula(riza)tion and corresponds only slightly to woman's desire" (30). Clarita serves as the mirror to reflect the male, playing a feminine role that does not correspond to her own desire—indeed, one that leaves no space for her to have any desires of her own.

Masculine desires also come under scrutiny. A section on prostitution scorns men who could not choose a woman from photos or videos, because to prefer one woman would "reveal something more personal or intimate or less masculine (as if it's not real macho to decide on one woman over a bunch of others because, when all is said and done, a pussy is a pussy and, if he's a real man, one is as good as another)" (130). Photographs (and the visual gaze) are again crucial here for the ways in which they reveal and contest subjectivity, intimacy, and gender. Another example of the social construction of masculinity comes in the section in which *la babuela* asserts that "a man has to have ambition, he has to fight to make it in life" (148). The commentaries that the various members of the family make about the appropriate roles for each gender serve to show the ways in which both gender and identity are constructed in and through language, and how discourse serves to produce knowledge and power.

The Imbrication of Photography and Narration

In making evident how discourse serves to produce knowledge and power and how gender and identity are constructed in and by language, *The Book of Memories* makes narration itself a key issue of the text. The stories narrated have as their source the "Book of Memories," the supposed family album with photos, documents, and stories. The Book of Memories is the authoritative text of the family; when a question comes up about which is the correct version of what happened to a particular uncle or a certain cousin, one of the narrators will ask: "And The Book of Memories? What does it say?" (49). The Book of Memories is the collective memory of the family, the authority to be consulted and cited. It exemplifies what Marianne Hirsch affirms in *Family Frames: Photography, Narrative, and Postmemory*, that "[f]amily pictures depend on such a narrative act of adoption that transforms rectangular pieces of cardboard into telling details connecting lives and stories across continents and generations" (xii). In Shua's text, we never see those rectangular pieces of cardboard—indeed, we cannot be sure of their existence—yet the family stories told in the autobiographical text form that narrative act of adoption that makes us want to believe.

Hirsch's work on family photographs helps to illuminate the use of the family album in this Argentine novel. Hirsch affirms that "photographs, as the only material traces of an irrecoverable past, derive their power and their important cultural role from their embeddedness in the fundamental rites of family life" (5). While the past is always irrecoverable, family histories invoking both the Holocaust and Argentina's Dirty War emphasize even more painfully the irrecoverability of the past at the same time as they emphasize that to move from the past into the future, "memory must be spoken. It is not through amnesia that deep pain becomes almost bearable, but rather through an acknowledgement of it" (Andrews 151).

Hirsch's discussion of how contemporary artists and writers have incorporated family pictures in their work, interrogating the family and its traditions of representation, is pertinent here, for "this work of contestation appears not so much in actual family photographs as in meta-photographic texts which place family photographs into narrative contexts, either by reproducing them or by describing them" (8)—as Shua does in *The Book of Memories*. It is in the context of metaphotographic textuality and in self-conscious contextuality that photographs disrupt a familiar narrative about family life and its representations, "breaking the hold of a conventional and monolithic familial gaze" (8).

Her series of issues and questions brought out by the family album as a mode of representation of the family, while somewhat lengthy, is worth citing here for its relevance to Shua's text:

How is the familial subject constructed through looking, and what do photographs tell us about this process? How does photography mediate family memory and family ideology? Can the technologies and cultural forms that interpellate us also be used to contest that interpellation: can the camera and the image, in the words of Jo Spence, be used for its "unfixing" rather than its "fixing" qualities? What are the relationships of looking and power, and how do the camera and the album intervene and mediate these relationships? How does photography insert itself into a heterogeneous tradition of familial representation, and how does it inflict and shape this tradition? How are these relationships marked by national

tradition, gender, class, race, ethnic community? Are there distinctive representational traditions, divergent "familial gazes," particular memorial traditions? (12)

Shua's narrative, organized around the trope of the family album, the
Book of Memories, speaks to how photography mediates family memory
and family ideology, how the camera intervenes in relationships of looking and power, and how photography works in the familial relationship
of a Jewish Argentine family with roots in Eastern Europe. The use of the
family photograph on the grave of *la babuela*, discussed above, is an example of a particular memorial tradition. That the grandmother asks to
change the photograph on her grave for one taken when she was younger
highlights how photographs serve to create subjectivity. That the request
is made to a family member underscores how family members serve to
construct and contest subjectivity through their relationships and their
gazes.

Of course, the family album within Shua's narrative is problematic as
an album that does and does not exist. Shua's use of the family album
urges us to reflect on the uses, the limitations, and the power of history and memory. Shua's Book of Memories is like the "memory box"
employed by Steve J. Stern in *Remembering Pinochet's Chile*. In his work
on the history of Chile during and after the Pinochet years, Stern is interested in understanding what social truths or processes allow people
to tell stories in particular ways, how great atrocities can make conventional narrative strategies seem inadequate, and how we can conceive
of memory under devastating circumstances. Stern chooses a metaphor
that enables him "to picture memory as competing selective remem-
brances to give meaning to, and find legitimacy within, a devastating
community experience" (xxviii). His metaphor, one whose description
seems apt also for Shua's Book of Memories, is that of "a giant collectively
built memory box. The memory chest is foundational to the community,
not marginal; it sits in the living room, not in the attic. It contains several
competing scripted albums, each of them works in progress that seek to
define and give shape to a crucial turning point in life, much as a family
album may script a wedding or a birth, an illness or a death, a crisis or a
success" (xxviii). Stern goes on to describe his "memory box" as one that
also contains the loose photographs and items that seem important but
that do not fit into the main scripts, asserting that it is "a precious box
to which people are drawn, to which they add or rearrange pictures and
scripts, and about which they quarrel and even scuffle" (xxviii).

Shua's Book of Memories is collectively built by the members of the Rimetka family, is foundational to the family, appears to sit in the living room (although there are times when the various members of the family claim not to be able to find the book), contains several competing versions of the events in the family's (and the nation's) history, and is a precious album to which the members of the family are drawn, adding and rearranging materials, quarrelling and scuffling over both the items held therein and their interpretations of those items.

Shua's Book of Memories is, in many ways, like Stern's description of the memory box, serving as a narrative tool that functions like a repository of the collective memory of the Rimetka family and, by extension, of Argentine society. In an interview with Nora Domínquez, Ana María Shua explains: "The voices of the characters are not credible; each one has his/her own version. So I realized that I needed that book of memories that is clearly a ploy because it doesn't have a physical form, it doesn't appear as an object and no one goes to a box to look for it. Rather I decided that it was the condensation zone where the memories of everyone come together, the small, partial and arbitrary memories they all agree on" (6; quoted in Buchanan 86). The fact that the mere existence of what appears to be the authoritative text for the Rimetka family is pure fiction makes the reader reflect on how other authoritative texts can be fictive as well.

Although the narrators of the family say the Book of Memories is their only absolutely reliable source, as a metanarrator, it is frequently not a reliable narrator. There are blank pages, and others that have been torn out of the book. There are key elements of the family histories that are not explained in the Book of Memories, bearing out Hirsch's assertion that the conventions of family photography "are designed to keep the family's secrets and to protect it from public scrutiny. Family albums include those images on which family members can agree and which tell a shared story" (107). Pictures that contest or diverge from the agreed-upon story get discarded rather than included. In Shua's text, there are interesting passages in which one member of the family wants to tell about a certain event in the family history and another member does not want that story told, so that one of the main issues underlying the novel is which stories can be told, and which cannot. Like Toni Morrison's *Beloved*, Shua's *The Book of Memories* asks which are the stories *not* to be passed on.

The question of which stories can and cannot be told within a family history or within an autobiography again raises the problematic nature of autobiography, always teetering between the classifications of fiction and nonfiction. Shua's text—teetering on the borders of autobiography, fiction, and family saga, constructed around photographs it doesn't include but including other photographs—reminds us also that "photography and autobiography operate in a parallel fashion, both deliberately blurring the boundaries between fact and fiction, between representation and creation" (Adams, *Light Writing* 20). Every autobiography, like every photograph, is both representation and creation, so that the inclusion of photographs within autobiographical texts seems particularly appropriate, as Timothy Dow Adams argues in *Light Writing and Life Writing*.

In taking a photograph, we take a picture, in the present moment, of that which is about to become a memory, capturing that which is about to become the past, that which is about to be remembered as past. In writing an autobiography, we write, in the present moment, of that which is now the past, that which is now remembered as past. Photography and autobiography both operate at the interstices of memory and imagination.

While Shua's *The Book of Memories* does not include the pages and photographs of the family album it makes central to its text, it does contain two photographs, ones that carry greater importance because of the very centrality of photographs in the narrative. The cover photo of the original text is a black-and-white photograph of a child dressed as an adult, in a black top hat, a white shirt with a collar, a dark vest and jacket, and striped trousers, with the right hand tucked into the trouser pocket and the left hand hanging down at the child's side (see figure 3). The child is standing on a tiled floor in front of a wall, looking directly at the camera, with just the hint of a smile on a serious face. Ana María Shua's name is in capital letters, in black at the top of the page, just above the top hat. The title of the book is also in capital letters, in white (with a grey back shadow) across the waist and stomach area of the posed figure. The name of the publisher, Editorial Sudamericana, is in the same font as the title, but in a smaller size. The only spot of color on the front cover is a red bow tie, superimposed onto the black-and-white photo. The red tie draws attention to itself in its contrast to the black and white of the rest of the photograph and draws the viewer's eyes to the face. With the black-and-white photograph, readers are tempted to suppose the photograph to be an old family photograph, perhaps of one of the characters as a child. Although the clothing seems masculine and the hair is cropped short, a viewer may also be tempted to "read" the photograph as one of a younger Ana María Shua, playing dress-up. (That cross-dressing might then remind readers of the family photograph of Frida Kahlo in which Frida is dressed in men's clothes.) The presentation of Shua's name directly over

FIGURE 3. The cover photo of the original Sudamericana edition of *El libro de los recuerdos* may suggest a young Ana María Shua dressed in male clothing, but it is a photo of her husband as a young boy. Reprinted courtesy of Ana María Shua.

the photo on the cover seems to serve as an identificatory marker, to turn the photograph into a self-portrait. Certainly the cover must be read as a protonarrative that comments, in some way, on the contents of the book. We are asked to interpret the cover photograph to be and not to be a self-portrait for a book that is and is not an autobiography.

Indeed, Hirsch likens the photograph and the autobiographical act, arguing that the "illusion of the self's wholeness and plenitude is perpetuated by the photographic medium as well as by the autobiographical act: both forms of representation rest on a profound misprision of the processes of representation" (84). Both photography and autobiography have "a fragmentary structure and an incompleteness that can be only partially concealed by narrative and conventional connections" (84). Hirsch asserts that the family portrait can be read as a self-portrait just as "the self-portrait always includes the other, not only because the self, never coincident, is necessarily other to itself, but also because it is constituted by multiple and heteronomous relations" (83). So how then can the cover photograph—which is, in fact, a photograph of Shua's husband when he was a young boy dressed up for a wedding[5]—be read as both self-portrait (of Shua) and family portrait (of her family/of the family portrayed in the book)?

The reader who opens the book finds, on the inside front cover, another black-and-white photograph, a head shot, this time of the adult Ana María Shua (see figure 4). The photo of the smiling author is set over the biographical information given about her, in the third person. Readers who read Shua's text in the English translation or the 2007 Emecé Spanish edition find another photograph on the front cover, one of three women bearing a strong family resemblance (see figure 5). The older woman is in the center, with the younger women's faces leaning in on either side of her head. That familial relationship is stressed in this photograph—from 1942, of the author's grandmother, mother, and aunt[6]—makes it an appropriate choice for the cover of an autobiographical work that stresses family photographs, that emphasizes multiple voices, and that presents different viewpoints expressed by members of different generations of the same family. In discussing Shua's work, I deliberately conflate the self-portrait, autobiography, and family portrait, as Hirsch does in her work, in order "to explore the continuum on which these genres uneasily define themselves. This continuum between self-portrait/allo-portrait and family picture traces the subject's constitution in the familial and the family's visual reflection of the individual subject. It defines the process of subject-formation in the field of vision and it makes the taking

FIGURE 4. Photo of Ana María Shua from the original Sudamericana edition of *El libro de los recuerdos*. Photo by Silvio Fabrykant. Reprinted courtesy of Ana María Shua.

and reading of photographs central to its contemporary manifestations" (85). Shua's text rests on a continuum between the genres of novel, auto-biography, self-portrait, family photograph album, and national history; it traces both the subject's constitution in the family and in the nation as well as the family and the nation's visual reflection in the individual subject; and it makes the reading of photographs central to its project.

For Shua's text is an intimate history, giving the readers the impression that they know these characters and are listening to their stories. The narrative is created out of many voices; the singular, authoritarian, unifying voice of the traditional omniscient narrator has been replaced by the dialogic discourse, the heteroglossia described by Bakhtin. The events in *The Book of Memories* are presented with commentaries by the various members of the family, commentaries that frequently represent different points of view. The narration of the chapters is often interrupted by short dialogues, in the form of questions and answers, sometimes in italics. The narrative structure mimics the common ritual, in family gatherings, of relatives participating in the shared remembering and telling of family stories. The retelling of family stories reinforces the family history and the sense of family in the various members, even if they do

FIGURE 5. The cover photo used on the English language edition of *The Book of Memories* (University of New Mexico Press) is another family photo, of Ana María Shua's mother, aunt, and grandmother. Reprinted courtesy of Ana María Shua.

not all agree on the versions told by other members of the group. The unnamed narrative voices that represent members of the Rimetka family often disagree on their versions of family events and at times deliberately deceive each other but not the Book of Memories: "But she couldn't deceive The Book of Memories because it's much more difficult to deceive. If at times The Book of Memories doesn't say the full truth, it's because it doesn't want to, not because it doesn't know the truth" (108). The Book of Memories is personified here, as something that can want or not want, in some ways becoming yet another member of the boisterous family. The contradictions and the different versions of events presented by the family members reflect how we all remember differently not only our family histories, but also our national histories.

A Story of Dictatorship

As a story of the Rimetka family and the Argentine nation during the twentieth century, *The Book of Memories* is, in part, a story of dictatorship and oppressive regimes. In the chapter entitled "Time of Fear," Shua writes of the collective fear felt by the Argentine people during the military dictatorship of the 1970s and 1980s.[7] It is a chapter that disputes one of the authoritarian discourses whose power Shua challenges, that discourse that purports to tell what happened in Argentina during the so-called "Proceso de Reorganización Nacional" (Process of National Reorganization), more frequently called simply "el proceso," "la guerra sucia," or the Dirty War. Shua displaces that hegemonic discourse with the unofficial knowledge of the members of the Rimetka family, putting into question history's claim to represent the past objectively. *The Book of Memories* continually reminds us that there is no version of the past that is not always already mediated.

It is significant that this chapter begins with a commentary on the Book of Memories, a commentary that merits quoting here because of its relevance to the question of interpretation:

> The Book of Memories is our only legitimate source. That's why it can make you so mad: even though what it tells you is true, it never tells you everything, it simply doesn't provide all the information.
>
> At times, people lie, distort, or exaggerate things and give their own version: that is, they interpret. But The Book of Memories limits itself to providing only the facts as they happened; it's as if they were happening that way at the moment we consult it. It also contains original documents whose authenticity is verifiable. (91)

This ironic passage insists that the Book of Memories limits itself to presenting the events as they happened. It does not interpret the events, as people are wont to do. Of course, it is one of the narrators who says that the Book of Memories is an absolutely reliable source and that the narrators are persons and therefore not reliable because they sometimes lie, distort, or exaggerate. So, as readers, we cannot rely on this narrator who tells us that the Book of Memories is absolutely reliable. And we cannot trust in his (her?) words when we are told that the Book of Memories contains original documents of verifiable authenticity. Shua employs a very Borgesian tactic here, granting power and authority to documents that are purportedly historical and verifiable.

The chapter contains an intercalated text, in italics, about the "time of fear," a literary text written by a member of the third generation of the Rimetka family. The insertion of the text not only serves as political commentary on Argentina's Dirty War, but also offers another opportunity to reflect on the distinction between fiction and history or fiction and journalism:

> In reality, when all is said and done, this document is just fictional literature and not an example of investigative reporting or a testimony about the times when the events take place. Its relationship to the facts is indirect; you could almost say the author uses them ad hoc, mixing them with invention and certain conventional literary tricks. It's not anything like a historical text. (Even though at times a short story or a novel can help to understand or to imagine more easily a period in time than a list of names and dates that ends up forgotten or confused with the truth of what happened to the people involved.) (92)

That the version of the events ultimately deemed the most satisfying is a fictionalized one shows that the need to address the issues of the past in a fruitful way may take precedence over the need to establish an empirically verifiable version of history, if, indeed, the latter were even possible.

The parenthetical remark also reminds us that the need to engage people with an ethical issue often requires creating a situation in which they can enter imaginatively into the lives of distant others and have emotions related to their imaginative participation in those lives (Nussbaum xvi). Shua makes this argument for fictional literature here, but we can also extend it—throughout these chapters—to life writing.

Playing with "the truth of what happened" is also an occasion for resistance, a way of resisting politically or culturally provided versions and identities and creating alternative ones. The problem of how to represent violence in literature is one that many Argentine authors confronted during the period of repression and one with which they continue to struggle (Buchanan 88).[8] While this chapter concentrates on life during the Dirty War, the memory of that particular period of Argentina's past becomes a prism through which we see and interpret other parts of the family saga, just as the horrors of the Dirty War are, for many Argentine Jews, a haunting repetition of their parents' or grandparents' experiences during the Nazi regime. Because the Book of Memories is presented as a physical entity, a body of knowledge, a body that at some points cannot

be consulted because it has disappeared, the disappearance of the often personified Book of Memories then evokes the disappearances of
Argentine citizens during the Dirty War.

The use of the intercalated text on the Dirty War also highlights the
way in which meaning is constructed and produced. When the censorship of authoritarian regimes prohibits the public narration of certain
stories and certain truths, other stories are narrated in order to articulate
the marginalized and the silenced. We can read the struggles against the
authoritarian fathers in Shua's *The Book of Memories* and Nélida Piñon's
The Republic of Dreams as obliquely figuring a struggle against the oppressive, dictatorial states of Argentina and Brazil.[9]

The feminist texts of Shua and Piñon challenge the sociopolitical
forms of authority wielded by the military governments. As Beatriz Sarlo
explains, "If the regime's discourse was characterized by the closing off
of the flow of meanings and, as a result, it indicated obligatory lines for
the construction of meaning, offering a poor and one-directional com-
municational model, in which a very reduced number of figures wore
out the representations of the social and the individual, of the public and
the private, of the present and of history, the literary discourses could
propose a practice of open meanings, of a chain that doesn't close, of
abundant figurations" (40). Shua's narrative proposes this practice of
open meanings and abundant figurations that resist the authoritarian
discourses of dictatorship and patriarchy. Shua consciously plays with
the genres of fiction, history, testimony, journalism, photography, and
autobiography, genres that are ingested, digested, and rearticulated by
the novel. In this way, Shua puts into question the "truths" that each of
these genres purports to tell. By defying the authority of these genres,
Shua challenges the dominant discourses that dictate the value systems,
the institutions, and the structures of power in Argentine society.

The reflections of the Argentine poet Manuela Fingueret on the importance of writing under dictatorship returns us to the topic of Jewish
women's writing with which I opened this chapter: "For me, it [writing]
was a way of opposing authoritarianism and the death of an era in which
diversity was a dangerous and clandestine activity under the dictatorship. Since the return to democracy, the understanding is that the in-
soluble nexus between the nature of being Jewish and being Argentine, is
essential in a country that is still struggling to grow as a nation" (quoted
in Agosín xvi). Certain scholars of Jewish Latin American writing have
noted that the presence of the Jewish Diaspora itself serves as a challenge
to the supposed homogeneity or coherence of nation states, a concept or

ideology vital in the elite dominant discourses of many South American countries, particularly under dictatorship (Vieira 2). Undoubtedly, Shua uses her autobiographical writing to oppose authoritarianism, both within the family and within the nation.

Shua's challenge to dominant discourses is successful enough that her text's generic identity is itself questioned by some critics. David William Foster asserts that it is neither novel, bildungsroman, nor family saga but rather a work that "focuses on what one might call metonymic aspects of Jewish life in Argentina that, in a somewhat fuguelike way, are elaborated around often grotesque individuals and outrageous incidents that are strikingly singular in delineating aspects of Jewish life and identity" ("Recent" 42–43). Similarly, Piñon's *The Republic of Dreams* has frequently eluded the characterization into literary genres by critics, "due precisely to the fact that the novel moves between various literary currents without necessarily attaching itself to any single one, and for being, above all, a negation of absolute forms of seeing and representing the world" (Sobral 69). Both authors resist dominant discourses of genre, identity, gender, history, and nation.

The story of the Rimetka family presented in Shua's semi-autobiographical narrative serves as a vision, or a version, of Argentine history in the twentieth century. The members of the Rimetka family reflect (and reflect on) various aspects of the national story. Shua's text presents an alternate history, one that often resists and rejects the official story presented by the military government of the time. Both autobiography in its broadest sense and the particular autobiographical genre I explore here (the semi-autobiographical family saga used to tell the story of the nation) are appropriate genres with which to challenge the authoritarian discourse of dictatorship, which would impose one truth, one history, one story. Each autobiography and each family saga unsettles that one imposed truth with a multiplicity of stories, memories, and versions of events.

In the end, *The Book of Memories* is about how to tell a story, about what can and cannot be told, and about the ways in which the stories we tell serve to construct personal, family, and national identity. In constructing her text, Shua uses her own family stories, memories, and photographs to pen the story of a fictionalized family, blithely blurring the boundaries between autobiography and fiction, between family history and national history, between light writing and life writing, adding a new text to this genre I call natiobiography.

4 /   The Autobiographical Text as Memory Box: Nélida Piñon's *The Republic of Dreams*

Nélida Piñon's autobiographical *A república dos sonhos* (1984; *The Republic of Dreams*, 1989), like Ana María Shua's *The Book of Memories*, is about storytelling and the ways in which the stories we tell construct personal, family, and national identity. Like Shua, Piñon draws from her own family history in writing an epic narrative that represents the history of a nation. *The Republic of Dreams* tells the heroic saga of a Brazilian family with its origins in Galicia. Breta, the granddaughter in the novel who is to write the family story, proclaims, "If I hadn't become a writer, grandfather, I was going to become a tramp" (612). Piñon, like her character Breta, is the granddaughter of Galician immigrants and has inherited from her own grandfather Daniel this desire to "hacer las Américas." *The Republic of Dreams* charts her own voyage, her own geography, as a response, perhaps, to Piñon's lament, in an interview with Catherine Tinker, that "woman has always been a remote soul, distanced from herself, as if she were a continent without land, a geography, waiting to be named" (quoted in Castro-Klarén, Molloy, and Sarlo 79). In *The Republic of Dreams*, Piñon names her continent(s) and her geography at the same time that she bears out her claim that "[w]e were the books of our ancestors; we're their copyright" (79).

Piñon holds a solid place in Brazilian, Latin American, and world literatures. Her honors, awards, and honorary doctorates are too numerous to mention here, but it might be recognized that she was the first woman to be elected president of the Academia Brasileira de Letras (Brazilian Academy of Letters) in 1996, serving during the one hundredth year of the Academy's existence; the first woman and the first Brazilian to be awarded the prestigious Juan Rulfo Prize for Latin American and Caribbean Literature, in 1995; the first Brazilian selected for the Prince of Asturias Award of Letters (2005); and the first woman selected for the University of Guadalajara's Julio Cortázar Chair, a distinguished professorship established by Carlos Fuentes and Gabriel García Márquez. Her work has been translated into many languages, and her short stories have been widely anthologized.

Nélida Piñon was born in Rio de Janeiro in 1937. Her maternal grandparents, Amada and Daniel, immigrated to Brazil from Galicia. (Piñon's first name, Nélida, is an anagram of Daniel.) She grew up listening to the stories of her grandparents, stories of their lives as well as the tales of Galician legends and myths they passed on to the younger generations. Those stories became "the starting point of a complex web of fact and fiction that nurtures Piñon's fertile mind. The author collected their tales, captured their memories, and embarked with them on a laborious task of spinning the fine threads of her own creativity into a compelling body of work" (Teixeira 22). That many adult autobiographers and writers come from storytelling families is hardly surprising, for, as John Paul Eakin notes, "the child's immersion in a rich narrative culture of family storytelling doubtless informs the adult's autobiographical impulse" (*How* 118). Nélida Piñon dedicates *The Republic of Dreams* to those family members whose stories she heard, those who came to Brazil:

> In memory: Amada Morgade Lois
>
> Daniel Cuiñas Cuiñas
>
> Lino Piñon Muños
>
> to: Maíta Cuiñas Peres
>
> Avelina Cuiñas Brito
>
> Celina Cuiñas de Almeida
>
> Antônio Cuiñas Morgade
>
> and to my mother: Carmen Cuiñas Piñon (5)

Piñon relates her passion for myths to her Celtic roots: "I believe strongly in myths, in ancient stories. Yes, perhaps my interest in literature has to do with cultural genetics. The Celts were great storytellers, stories outside of time that others followed" (Riera 46). This connection between storytelling and Celtic heritage is echoed by the grandfather in *The Republic of Dreams* when he reminds his granddaughter, "This gift we have for telling stories is owed to the fact that we're Celts, Breta. It's our greatest heritage" (72).

In *The Republic of Dreams*, telling stories—the stories of people's lives as well as the stories of the history and the building of a nation—is a central theme intricately interwoven with other themes of dreams, memories, eroticism, politics, the relationship between reality and illusion, and the roles of the artist and the writer. While these topics can be discussed separately with some success, they are always already interwoven in the text, impossible to separate out completely.

The Republic of Dreams begins with the impending death of the family matriarch, Eulália. During the week that she is dying, the family members gather in the household, remembering past events and conflicts, sharing stories. Gathered together are her husband, Madruga, her faithful servant and companion Odete, the living children of Madruga and Eulália (Miguel, Bento, Antônia, and Tobias), and the grandchildren. The most important representative of this third generation is Breta (daughter of Madruga and Eulália's deceased daughter Esperança), the granddaughter who is to record the family story. Throughout the text, with trips back and forth in time, readers learn of Madruga's childhood and his decision to travel to Brazil to make a new life. We learn of the founding of his fortune and of his family. We meet his lifelong friend, Venâncio, whom he met on the ship from Spain to Brazil. The history of the family is interwoven with the histories of Brazil and Galicia, with Breta designated as the one to write the family saga.

The Sensual Art of Storytelling

Throughout *The Republic of Dreams*, Piñon sets up stories as something that enriches life, nourishing both the people and the nation. Just as *A doce canção de Caetana* (1987, *Caetana's Sweet Song*, 1992) intermingles the pleasures of sex and the pleasures of food,[1] *The Republic of Dreams* mixes food and stories. Sensual pleasures, they are to be taken in together, each enriching the taste of the other: "In Xan's hands, the stories were like a porridge thickened with milk. It had to be eaten hot, by the spoonful" (317). Xan's grandson Madruga likens the stories his granddaughter Breta tells him to rich cream, comforting, sustaining: "And to charm me even more, she went on telling me stories. And as she poured the warm milk into the mouth, the rich cream that trickled through her lips enticed me to live" (229). Madruga explains to a Brazilian acquaintance that it is a Galician tradition to mix stories with food and drink:

"Where I come from, we have the habit of drinking and telling stories at the same time" (519). In both places, we see people telling stories in bars and taverns or over drinks at home.

Madruga's grandfather Xan creates his stories like a great chef, mixing "the ingredients" (317) while Eulália's father, Dom Miguel, also liked to tell stories during and after meals:

> After the pudding, into whose preparation there had gone more than twenty-four egg yolks, of a vivid yellow, Dom Miguel invited Eulália to keep him company as he drank his coffee and smoked his cigar. Only then, his heart uplifted by nature, ash-grey and barely visible through the windowpanes clouded with mist, did Dom Miguel tell Eulália the stories to which, in her old age now, she had begun little by little to contribute ingredients of her own to strengthen them, as the one last effort that life still demanded of her. (416)

Again, the telling of stories is associated with food, particularly as it comes after a passage delineating the parts of meat that come from butchering a pig. Eulália's contributions to the stories are ingredients; stories are doled out like bits of culture and dreams.

That cooking and storytelling are linked arts is obvious not only in Piñon's narratives but also in her interviews. In an interview with Paul Sneed, she asserts: "The imagination frees itself to the degree to which you yourself set it free. The more you free your imagination, giving it subsidiaries and ingredients, the more the imagination grows. You must give it yeast, like the yeast you put in a cake for it to grow, in bread, to ferment the imagination. Life is yeast for the imagination" (21). The nourishing aspect of storytelling recalls the concept of postmemory, as we can see how the younger generations in these texts (like the authors themselves) are raised on stories, fed stories by the older generations.

Some of the descriptions of storytelling in the novel are also apt descriptions of Piñon's narrative style in *The Republic of Dreams*. Madruga's grandfather Xan was recognized in Galicia as "a master of the insuperable art of telling popular stories, Xan had only to open his mouth, with a straw-paper cigarette invariably dangling from it, for a solemn silence to ensue" (97). He could tell long, complicated stories, with many digressions. He added details and never yielded to pressure to shorten a story: "If a story takes a year before it's told, it would be a crime to lop off its beauty and imagination. If a person has no ear for them, he can go live in hell. Or begin living without them" (98). Such a statement, coming about 100 pages into a more than 650-page novel (748 in my Portuguese edition, 663 in my English edition), warns readers that if they have no ear for a long novel, they can go live in hell as well. Piñon is not lopping off the beauty and imagination of her grand saga either.

Another description of Xan's storytelling aptly describes Piñon's narrative style in *The Republic of Dreams*: "Xan interwove facts and legends in colorful, lively language. And whenever he needed to graft new elements onto the story, he opened parentheses, though without losing the thread of the plot by so doing" (97). Piñon's narrative interweaves facts—dates and names of historical figures from Brazilian, Galician, and world history—and legends, employs a colorful, lively language, and frequently enters into long diversions to recount earlier episodes in the family's history before returning to the present-moment conversation between two or more of the family members. Her complex combination of narrators, focalizers, time periods, and locations is captivating enough to keep readers engaged throughout the long narrative.

Although the narrators, focalizers, time periods, and geographical locations change in this family saga, storytelling remains a constant. Madruga wonders aloud to Breta whether he might not have left Galicia, "conquer[ed] the waters of the Atlantic, endure[d] humiliation, just so you, my granddaughter, would tell our story someday? Xan's story, Dom Miguel's, Eulália's, Odete's, the story of all of us anonymous dramatists who don't know how to write?" (631). Madruga's words bear out the idea that the family's history is made up of the histories of the individual people therein, just as a nation's history should reflect the histories of all those anonymous dramatists who don't know how to write. Piñon's presentation of history resists the imposition of a national history written by the elite of the country.

Breta's fate as the one who is to tell the stories of her ancestors is alluded to repeatedly. While Madruga and Venâncio struggle over which of the two men is to tell the stories of their lives and their fractious friendship, Madruga acknowledges that they "shall be free of each other only when Breta, in the future, frees us of this mutual responsibility and begins to speak for us" (404). They can only be free when she tells their story for them.

Breta is prepared for this role as the family chronicler from her youth. Madruga trained Breta, starting when she was still a little girl, to be a good listener to his stories:

Sitting beside me, self-absorbed, he reeled off strange names, and

events I had never had any part in. Teaching me to respect the
flow of his storytelling. . . . Some of the episodes, fragmented and
disjointed, undoubtedly did not reflect his own story. Though
Madruga didn't seem to be bothered by that fact. Since he had
learned from Grandfather Xan that only a teller of tales able to fer-
tilize and broadcast collective stories had merit.

His aim was to instill in me the cult of invention, long present in
his family. Even before Xan. This being a Galician custom. (66–67)

Breta, even as a young girl, is interested in hearing Madruga's stories. He
repays her interest "by recounting scattered episodes. As though anonymous voices were speaking through me. In particular those oldsters who
came to Sobreira before me" (17). Madruga shares stories, or parts of
stories, he heard from Xan and the other old men of Galicia with his
Brazilian granddaughter.

Piñon's family saga exemplifies how the nation and the family are
forged through the act of storytelling. Madruga takes Breta traveling
around Brazil, just as his grandfather Xan occasionally took him on trips
in Galicia. She is to learn about Brazil through these storytelling travels
with her grandfather, but Madruga realizes that he learns about Brazil
through her eyes as well, "as Breta described the landscape in minute
detail. Without sacrificing, at the same time, the pleasure of telling a
story. Through such a practice forcing me to learn by heart a country
that risked becoming abstract and inaccessible to her as well. And whenever I asked her to clarify an ambiguous episode, Breta rewarded me by
inventing another story. Doing so in a questioning tone of voice, like
Grandfather Xan's. Thereby forging herself and the country in which she
had been born" (223). Here Breta begins to take on the role of Xan, telling stories, inventing new stories that serve as digressions in the original
narrative, even taking on his tone of voice. As it is through storytelling
that one forges oneself into one's country of birth, Piñon's text exemplifies the power of narration in the process of nation building. Breta, as the
fictionalized version of the author, shows how Piñon herself forges a story of Brazil through her autobiographical writings. Breta grows up as the
grandchild expected to be a writer, to take the wealth of material passed
on to her by Madruga, Eulália, Venâncio, and the others and write out
their grand story. In her life and in her writings, the Galician ancestors
will live on, just as they live on in the narratives of Nélida Piñon.

Although the principal line of storytelling is traced out from Xan to
Madruga to Breta, other lines exist as well. Eulália's father, Dom Miguel,

is a devoted storyteller, one prone to lose himself "in the labyrinths of a thousand tirelessly contrived stories" (448). Eulália grew up listening to his stories and, after his death, occasionally tells stories to her own children "in her eagerness to preserve the memory of her father, Dom Miguel" (3). She most frequently tells stories to Miguel, the child she named after her father. The stories they share bind Eulália more closely to Miguel than to any of her other children. Piñon's novel shows how shared stories bind people together into real and imagined communities. Throughout this study, I argue that women writers of the Americas, feeling that the official stories of their nations do not include them, write themselves into the national imagination through their own autobiographical writings.

While Eulália most frequently shares stories with Miguel, she does sometimes share stories with the other children. When Esperança was upset after a dressing-down from Madruga, Eulália would tell her stories in the kitchen, "in a voice that grew softer and softer, with the risk that Esperança might understand exactly the contrary of what her mother was telling her. Till Esperança realized that Eulália was really talking to herself and not to other people" (423). Storytelling is, as always, a way for Eulália to return to Sobreira, to return to her father's house and to the world of dreams the two shared.

Listening to her mother's stories leads Esperança to believe "that this was far from being a family trait. It was much more like a fate. As though she and her brothers and sisters were destined to follow the same paths. All of them equally inclined to develop, to a high degree, a talent for telling themselves the story of their own lives, as a means of believing in human existence" (423). They seem destined to be a family of autobiographers. But the stories of their own lives are difficult to tell for, just as in the family saga of Ana María Shua, the family members here have trouble agreeing on what really happened, whose version of the story is authoritative, who has the right to author the stories of their individual and collective lives. When Miguel and Breta argue over their differing interpretations of Miguel's life choices, Breta grows tired of the arguments, realizing "we were both consuming a narrative from which we were withholding basic elements. Duped by lies and hollow mockeries. We were mere incompetents when it came to total confessions. Just because we sensed that there was a collective story ruling our lives" (240). Questions of autobiographical truth trouble the siblings before they even begin to author their life narratives.

Madruga also realizes that the collective story, the family saga, is the only story worth telling. When he watches his children and grandchildren fighting over the division of belongings and resentments on the eve of Eulália's death, he knows that "the only way of uniting them is to prove to them that their stories, taken individually, aren't worth a thing. And that they'll make sense, or will one day be told, only if this saga is enriched through the presence of all of them" (613). Of course, in *The Republic of Dreams*, Piñon tells their stories not individually, but as a grand family saga, a monumental narrative enriched by the presence of each of the characters.

The Memory Box

Pertinent to the family saga Piñon pens is the idea of the memory box, employed by Steve Stern in his work on Pinochet's Chile and discussed in chapter 3 in connection with *The Book of Memories*. *The Republic of Dreams* includes actual memory boxes—the meticulously polished and carefully guarded wooden boxes in which Eulália collects memories for each of her children—as well as more metaphorical ones, including Eulália's jewel box, the strongboxes various characters have in their banks, Venâncio's secret diary, the corners of Madruga and Eulália's house, even the old men of Galicia.

With memories, dreams, and the careful construction of reality all constant themes in this novel, the memory boxes created by the matriarch of the family are an important recurrent motif. The beautiful wooden boxes were gifts from Madruga to Eulália, one for each child, all different, boxes to which only she had access. While the memory box discussed by Stern is a "giant collectively built memory box" (Stern xxviii), the boxes Eulália creates are of her own sole creation out of "material that in the future would enable the children to tell their stories thanks to the facts stored in them" *(Republic of Dreams* 155). Again, the ability to tell one's own story is stressed here. But to what extent will the stories told be their own if it is their mother who is choosing the "facts" that will form the basis of these stories? And just what are the "facts" Eulália is contributing? Eulália is supposedly storing "facts" in the boxes, but as her contributions often were leaves she had carefully collected, dried between the pages of her missal, and then distributed between the boxes, these memory boxes underscore problematic issues in the construction and interpretation of autobiographical narratives.

Readers do not know what the boxes contain, other than the leaves and pretty bits of nature that catch Eulália's eye and are then deposited in the boxes. Not even Madruga knows what may be guarded therein: "I once asked her whether it was odds and ends of her children, or her own life that was distributed among the six boxes, thus making it difficult to trace the precise development of the story, the exact sequence of events. She did not answer" (446). Even Madruga is denied entrance to the "universe where she had woven together the precarious story of her family" (446).

In these citations, as throughout the semi-autobiographical novel, the ideas of memory and stories are inseparable. The memory boxes, collectively, constitute the place where Eulália weaves together the story of her family and, individually, serve to contain a story for each child. Madruga wonders about Eulália's eagerness to testify in this way to existence of the children, "As though they lacked direction and were more than a little uncertain. And as though their coming into possession of their own stories depended solely on their mother. Could this have been Eulália's intention?" (447). If their coming into possession of their own stories depends solely on their mother's efforts in creating these memory boxes, the children prove themselves not at all anxious to take on possession of those stories, as we shall see below.

The partial exception to the mystery involving the contents of the boxes is the box of Tobias, the youngest son of Madruga and Eulália. A major element in his memory box is the handwritten notes Venâncio left for his infant godson each Sunday during the Spanish Civil War. Venâncio's notes tended to be full of bitterness and disillusionment, but always ended "But we'll win even so" (155). Madruga worried that his son's cradle was being overburdened by such a cruel reality as the baby's bed became "the weekly repository of Venâncio's anxiety" (155). Tobias grows up closer to Venâncio than to Madruga, more linked to Venâncio's dreams, disillusionment, and despair than to Madruga's desires, drive, and decisive deal making.

On her deathbed, Eulália dispenses the boxes to children not eager to receive them. The oldest son, Miguel, hides behind one of his brothers, hoping not to receive his box first: "He was afraid his mother would unveil his life from an intimate, unbearable perspective. Or that cruel, depressing messages would leap out of one of the open boxes" (531). Each child is so anxious to flee from unpleasant discoveries that none of Eulália's children examines the contents of the boxes now in their possession. Bento takes his to his office, where he closes himself in to confront "his inheritance. A legacy that Bento would willingly have renounced, had it been up to him" (551). Opening the box at last, he breathes in the scent his mother had worn during the years of the Spanish Civil War. Slamming the box shut, he finds the scent has impregnated him: "He ran to the bathroom, turned on the faucet, allowing the water to splash out onto the marble bench. He soaped his hands, scrubbing them with the nail brush" (551). Unable to face what is in his box, he pours out the contents onto his desk and, without looking at them, divides the contents and dumps them into three manila envelopes which he seals and on which he writes "TO BE OPENED AFTER MY DEATH" (551). He immediately deposits the envelopes in his safe deposit box in the bank. Thus the contents in the polished wooden memory box lovingly guarded by Eulália until the eve of her death are placed in a new, more institutional/industrial memory box to await Bento's death.

Miguel takes his box, unopened, in the car, stopping on the Rio-Niterói bridge, where he stops "just long enough to dump the contents of the box into the sea. Free in space, they looked like a flock of fat birds. His eyes did not follow them till they fell into the water" (557). Like Bento, Miguel is afraid to look at the memories saved for him by his mother, unable to face her version of his life. While Bento locks his mother's memories of him into the safe deposit bank for a future generation to confront, Miguel places his beyond the reach of any generation.

Antônia puts her unopened box into her closet, and Tobias, the youngest, leaves his box, also unopened, on the floor of his childhood bedroom in the family home, telling his godfather he will come back to claim it someday. The only box that is coveted by the family members is that of Esperança. Eulália gives the box to Breta, telling her: "Your mother was beautiful and wild. Esperança was like a Galician gorse bush. With flowers and thorns at the same time. Affectionate and prickly" (533). Breta receives the box and wonders: "What could there be inside that could possibly explain her mother's life? She ran her fingers carefully over the surface of the smooth-textured wood. She felt that she was caressing Esperança herself" (533). The memory box brings her mother back to her, becomes the physical presence to replace her mother's absence. Miguel covets the box that embodies his beloved sister but is denied her body once again. Breta is the only one to know what is in Esperança's box, recognizing that "Esperança's sole remains were myself and the box" (648).

In addition to these boxes created for each child, boxes that become such tormented legacies, is the box that Eulália creates for herself. A year after the Spanish Civil War, Madruga presents Eulália with a box in which she can preserve her own memory. Madruga spends a week in the downtown antique shops searching for the perfect piece, finally giving her a bright-red box, painted with a vegetable dye extracted from bra-zilwood. As he explains to her: "When I was a boy, I dreamed of having a box to hide chips of wood, papers, round river pebbles in. No matter what, but far from Urcesina's watchful eye. I wanted to keep my secrets safe. But nobody ever thought of giving me a box. Not even Grandfather Xan. And now it's too late to realize that dream. What good would it do me? It seemed to me, though, that this would please you, Eulália. It's yours, and I'll never open it" (594). For Madruga, such a box is a dream, a dream to contain secrets and memories. Eulália is delighted and im-mediately places her first memory in the box.

It is not until much later in the novel that readers learn what is in Eulália's box. Like the boxes she creates for her children, it mostly con-tains objects "that, by chance, she had little by little collected on her way back from church" (591). As she nears the end of her life, she asks Odete to clear out all those superfluous items, for she seems "eager to rob her own life of all the hard evidence. As though she recognized that she had gone too far in those years. Tempted, surely, by vanity, she had stuffed the box too full of useless memories" (591). What is collected in her memory box is, contradictorily, both "hard evidence" and "useless memories."

What Eulália chooses to keep from her box are three notes, yellowed with age. The first note bears the date of 27 October 1927, the date on which the body of her infant son, the first Bento, was tossed into the Atlantic Ocean after his death at sea, on the return journey to Brazil from Galicia. This note is the first item Eulália ever placed in her box. The second note bears the date 19 June 1956, the date of Esperança's death in a car accident. The third note is a blank sheet of paper, folded like the other two, and put into the box at the same time as the slip of paper with the date of her daughter's death. The blank sheet is so that "I won't forget my destiny. As soon as I close my eyes, have them write the date of my death on it. It's a task I can't take care of myself" (597). For Eulália, the note symbolizes her gravestone in Sobreira, the Galician gravestone she gave up by moving to Brazil.

Eulália's other memory box is her jewelry box, with each item con-tained therein having its own story, as precious memories are encrusted alongside the precious stones. When Eulália is on her deathbed, she asks Odete to bring her the jewel box. Odete is, outside of Eulália, "the only one to tell the story of each jewel" (47). Eulália entrusts the stories, just as she entrusts the care of the jewels and the jewelry box, to Odete. When Odete occasionally asks to hear again the story behind a piece of jewelry, Eulália finds herself wondering: "How to be scrupulous about details concerning an episode dating back, for example, to February 1940 and still respect its spirit unconditionally? How to be faithful to a memory that constantly failed her? Or preserve stories that time, of its own accord, undertook to sacrifice or to leave behind for good?" (52). All of Piñon's characters struggle with the interrelated questions of memory and storytelling, as they constantly tell each other stories in a struggle to author their own stories rather than live the stories others want to impose upon them. The constant emphasis on memory and storytelling is apt in a semi-autobiographical novel that uses the family saga to tell the story of a nation. Each character in the novel tells a story of the family and the nation, just as each jewel in Eulália's box tells a story from her life.

Not lost on Eulália is Odete's interest in the stories and the loving attention Odete lavishes on both Eulália and the jewelry. Indeed, Breta remarks once that watching Odete polish Eulália's jewelry is like seeing her "burnishing with emery the body of an imaginary lover" (52). Because of the fascination Odete displayed for Eulália's gold bracelet, a wedding present from Madruga, Eulália is determined that the bracelet will be Odete's upon Eulália's death. Although Odete protests her employer's intention, Eulália knows that "nobody deserves the bracelet as much as Odete. Always trailing along after her to pick up the fearful, blood-red pieces of the story that she kept letting fall to the floor" (64). Since Eulália's memory box is described as blood-red, the reference to the "blood-red pieces of the story" Odete picks up when Eulália lets them fall ties Odete to Eulália's memory box. Odete is, in some ways, the memory box of Eulália, the one who guards the bits and pieces of Eulália's life that seem important to her but that might pass unnoticed by those writing the major scripts.

Other people are likened to memory boxes as well. The old men of Galicia are "veritable echo chambers of memory" (182).[2] Madruga's grandfather Xan was "able to count on a memory with a file of names in perfect order. In fact, Xan prided himself on being the registry office of the village" (318). Madruga, then, inherits "from his grandfather a spirit given to examining reality as though it took the form of a box, inside which we were imprisoned" (335). The memories held in the various memory boxes in *The Republic of Dreams* are contested ones, multiple memories that compete against each other, memories that are elusive and ever changing.

In a way, we can see how not just *The Republic of Dreams*, but all the autobiographical texts explored in this study are memory boxes. They are all works in progress, inscriptions of a subjectivity that is itself always in progress, always changing. They are in different ways collectively built. Some reflect the voices of various members of a family. Others reflect various (competing) versions of the self. All seek to define and give shape to crucial moments in the lives of the authors at the same time that they open up new possibilities for future generations.

The Elusive Boundaries between Reality and Dreams

Caught up in that memory box, living between the past and the present, Eulália is just one of Piñon's characters struggling with the boundaries between reality and illusion, between reality and dreams, between reality and memories, often not knowing where those boundaries lie. She admits that "she herself had difficulty pinning down the exact localities of a marriage lost in some hidden compartment of her memory" (64). Furthermore, since childhood, she would wake with a start, finding herself "unable, at the end of each day, to add her various pictures of the world to her heart, as though there were a family album in it" (254). Her heart is a family album, like the "Book of Memories" discussed in the previous chapter. And like the multiple narrators of Shua's text, Eulália often finds herself unable to reconcile the disparate pictures from her life and her world.

In the previous chapter, I cited Timothy Dow Adam's comparison of the workings of photography and autobiography, "both deliberately blurring the boundaries between fact and fiction, between representation and creation" (20). Eulália embodies that blurring of boundaries in her own difficulties distinguishing between fact and fiction. Eulália decided early in life that "reality was only an immense portrait that would little by little turn yellow as it passed through the memory of each person" (254). Reality is an artistic creation that affects, and is affected by, the memories of each person. *The Republic of Dreams*, as an artistic creation of Nélida Pinón, is affected by the memories Pinón has of her family, her own life, and her travels in Brazil and Galicia.

Believing, as Eulália does, in the necessity of solitude for the creation and maintenance of dreams and memories, she not only creates the memory boxes for her children, but also divides "the house into zones, named after the mountains of Sobreira" (417). Each child is given a region, "with the right to take refuge in it without the danger of foreign invasions. Save for one by Madruga, whose invader's instinct did not respect private territories" (417). She designates areas of the house for each child in order to provide them safe spaces to dream, naming them after the mountains in Sobreira to encourage the children to remember their connections to Galicia and their Celtic roots. That they are given the right to take refuge in their spaces without the danger of foreign invasion indicates the degree to which this family is not one of dreamers, but of warriors, pirates, conquistadores. The children battle each other and their dictatorial father for the individual freedom and identity they find hard to achieve in a large family headed by a tyrannical father.

Just as Madruga's children struggle to be independent from their father, so too does Venâncio, Madruga's best friend, have to fight to be himself and not the replica of Madruga that Madruga would have him be. In his struggle to distinguish reality from illusion and to understand his own place in Brazil, Venâncio keeps a secret diary for three years. As his mental condition deteriorates and he finally concedes to enter an asylum, he brings the secret diary to Madruga's house one Sunday, "to be handed over to a faithful guardian" (171). Venâncio entrusts the diary to Eulália, asking that no one read it but her. The diary is also seen as a repository of memories, with Eulália clasping the diary to her breast "moved by an object filled with memories" (172). Venâncio's secret diary is a memory box of another sort. It is, in part, the story of Madruga, Venâncio, and Eulália, but it is also a feverish imagining of Brazil in an earlier century, Venâncio's attempt to discover Brazil by rewriting its history. Contradictory and chaotic, the diary contains multiple, competing versions of personal and national history that serve to cancel out any single, definitive version of history or truth. Dictatorships, whether Franco's in Spain or the various Brazilian dictatorships discussed in Piñon's saga, seek to impose a single, definitive version of history. Venâncio refuses to accept those versions and struggles to create alternate versions in his life and in his diary. His own autobiographical narratives are acts of resistance to authoritarian regimes. By focusing on the violence of dictatorships that seek to impose unitary systems and truths, Venâncio reminds us that any political formation has, at its origin, deeds of violence, as unity is so often achieved by means of brutality.[3]

Breta, Madruga and Eulália's granddaughter, becomes a memory box of another sort as she listens to the stories told by Madruga, Venâncio, and others. She is designated by Eulália as the sole heiress of Venâncio's secret diary and told by Miguel, "You are the only one who will give us continuity" (660). Breta is ambitious and eager "to gather together and tie in a neat bundle the stories sprung from a popular source, personified by Grandfather Xan" (70). Furthermore, she is the grandchild chosen by Madruga to inherit all his documents, papers, mementos: "It calmed him to think that Breta would zealously guard his belongings. The one who would inherit the papers, letters, books, portraits. He categorically forbade his family access to all his personal mementos. No one was to touch or lightly finger his memories. Breta was responsible for separating the material, burning what she thought best" (46). The wear and tear she sees in her grandfather's body and face remind her that "collecting his memory is a task that should not be put off" (175).

For Breta is to write the story of the family. She realizes that Madruga and Venâncio are both "eager for me to get around someday to writing the book about those immigrants who crossed the Atlantic in different eras, intending to cast anchor in Brazil forever" (661). But she also knows that her role as storyteller, as chronicler of the family history, is not an easy one. For she will tell "[a] story that has its risks, however. Certain precious pieces will be missing. After all, and I repeat once again, to whom do I owe fidelity? Nobody owes fidelity to life. It confuses us and encumbers us from one end to the other" (661). The book she will write will be yet another memory box, one that contains several, competing scripts, each one trying to give shape to a crucial memory or turning point in a life. The memory box that is her book, along with the other memory boxes discussed above, are then all nestled into the larger memory box that is *The Republic of Dreams*.

Just as we have seen how Helena Parente Cunha and Luisa Futoransky use their autobiographical fiction, in part, to make visible the normally hidden decisions made by the autobiographer in writing her text, Piñon uses Breta (and the other storytellers intercalated in her text) to make visible the struggles undergone by storytellers, novelists, and autobiographers. The question "to whom do I owe fidelity?" is one that echoes throughout her text and throughout my study of women's autobiographical writings in the Americas.

Not only does Piñon structure *The Republic of Dreams* around the interrelated issues of memory and stories, but she often focuses on those topics in her interviews and in her speeches, including the inaugural speech at the Brazilian Academy of Letters cited above. In an interview in *World Literature Today*, she explains both that "the role of a writer is this, to collect and legitimate emotions: to narrate them, if possible, or outline and sketch them and capture moments of history, capture an epoch" and that "[l]iterature . . . is an art of intelligence, an art of memory, an art of narrating. When you narrate, you tell the lost stories" (19). In her autobiographical novel, she collects and legitimates the emotions expressed by her ancestors and evoked in her being as she listened to their tales of Galicia, the stories of their own lives and adventures. Like the grandmother Eulália who tells stories "in her eagerness to preserve the memory of her father, Dom Miguel" (3), Piñon tells a wealth of stories in *The Republic of Dreams* to preserve the memories of her ancestors, so that her family's stories and history will not be lost. She writes her family into and out of the histories of Galicia and Brazil. The lives of the family members are always interwoven with the history of Brazil.

As a narration of the history of Brazil in the twentieth century, *The Republic of Dreams*, like *The Book of Memories*, is also a story of dictatorships and their impact on the family. Tobias, the youngest son, is a lawyer who has worked to defend political prisoners since 1968. For the most part, these are clients he has never met, as "most of them [are] not even allowed visitors. Shut up in filthy cells, in a lamentable state. It was even suspected that many of them had died without their families being able to claim the body" (30). Descriptions of the fates of these prisoners, and of the torture they endure, are stories not to be passed on—Tobias spares his mother the rendition of graphic details—but ones that must be shared to render a more complete version of the nation's history. Thus, Piñon includes in her text the stories Tobias could have shared with his mother: "Purposely not telling her that, not far from Leblon, on the other side of the Rebouças tunnel, on the Rua Barão de Mesquita, certain men, in every way resembling her son, were at that moment shoving a bottle up the anus of a woman they'd just caught. A penetration that from the first cruelly tore the edges of the narrow circular opening, meant to expand only enough to expel human feces. . . . Till they ended up shoving the bottle all the way inside the woman's body, rending the bowels and veins essential to her existence and her dignity" (539). The inclusion of actual place names in Rio de Janeiro locates the secret actions of the military regime into the daily history and common space of the city.

Indeed, dictatorship is seen by many in the text as part of Brazil's very character. Miguel claims that "the poor Brazilian Constitution is a patchwork quilt that's had rape committed on it a thousand times" (273). Madruga is experienced enough with dictatorship that he can feel a new one approaching: "We'll soon have a dictatorship. Either of the left or of the right. You can tell by the stench. It's the same stench as always. It hasn't changed" (108). Tobias laments to Venâncio that the Brazilian system turns all men into tyrants: "Our institutional freedoms have always been a farce. . . . Beginning with the judicial system, a cripple that can't stand up to strong regimes. And so we all turn into tyrants. Of the same breed as Getúlio Vargas, Médici, and others. . . . We've done nothing but waste a patrimony that some people call a nation, others a country or a fatherland. Brazil lies to itself at every turn. And there is no elite worse than ours. It condemns the weak and the poor to extermination or to exile. The exile of silence and social nonparticipation. Of debarment from their human rights" (31). Tobias suffers under the horrors inflicted on his fellow citizens during the military dictatorship and puts himself at risk by defending those the government has marked out as subversive, but Madruga seems more resigned and pragmatic.

Breta's life is also marked by her experience with the dictatorship. Having been involved in leftist politics, she finds herself at a point in which it is no longer considered safe for her to remain in the country. She is one of many Brazilians who left the country, roaming from one embassy to another, one country to another, looking for refuge: "All of them having left Brazil with marks of violence on their bodies and minds" (281). Breta wonders what would have happened to her had she been caught trying to leave the country. Having been spared the worst, she wonders if she has the right to be upset or if she should not feel grateful to the military regime since it gave her a nice chance to live in Paris: "The unwished-for loneliness, the impossibility of returning being scarcely worth noting then? Would there be an amnesty capable of making those who had been exiled, those who had been tortured, forget the offense they had endured? And merely because the dictatorship had offered exiles the comfortable, well-trodden path to Europe, and to some the title of professor in some foreign university, ought it to decide that it had neatly settled its account with History?" (413). Piñon uses the thoughts and emotions of Breta and the other members of the family to question the role of dictatorship in the history of Brazil, to question how history is to judge those dictatorships and the people involved in and affected by them.

By including different perspectives within the family on the various dictatorships in Brazil and Spain (including those whose businesses prosper), Piñon represents the plurality of opinions in Brazil at the time. Just as Shua employs the unofficial knowledge of the Rimetka family to displace the official and authoritarian discourse of the Proceso, thus putting into question history's claim to represent the past objectively, so too does Piñon employ the unofficial knowledge of Madruga's clan to displace the official stories written by the various dictatorial regimes in twentieth-century Brazil. Both *The Republic of Dreams* and *The Book of Memories* continually remind us that there is no version of the past that is not always already mediated as these texts actively resist the imposition of authoritarian truths.

Dictatorships strive to impose, through whatever means necessary, a univocal, authoritarian discourse, a single interpretation of reality. Literature often seeks to resist that authoritarian, single voice. As Beatriz Sarlo reminds us, in the passage previously cited, while the authoritative discourse of the military regime in Argentina was characterized by a closing off of any play of differences, "los discursos de la literatura podían proponer una práctica justamente de sentidos abiertos, de cadena que no cierra, de figuraciones abundantes" (40). *The Republic of Dreams* and *The Book of Memories* propose that practice of open meanings, of a chain that is not closed, of abundant imaginings that resist the authoritarian discourses of dictatorship and of patriarchy.

Artists like Nélida Piñon and Ana María Shua help preserve and contest the histories of Brazil and Argentina, respectively, by preserving the fictionalized stories of their own families. In both family sagas, we are presented with the retelling of a family and a nation's past not as independent entities but rather as interdependent ones. As in many autobiographical texts, the retelling of the past is central to the authors' task of defining themselves in their own terms. Deborah Cohn argues that Spanish America's "dialogue with the historical record plays a key role in wresting the past from the colonial and neocolonial powers whose needs have dictated—*pre*-scribed beforehand and *de*-scribed, as it were, afterwards—their own" (41). Feminist scholars also argue that women writers of autobiographical texts enter into dialogue with the historical record in order to wrest it from the patriarchal values and norms that would seek to define them. In the works of Ana María Shua and Nélida Piñon, we see vivid examples of these struggles against patriarchal, colonial, and neocolonial powers.

These struggles are presented in the stories of the families and of the nation. Shua and Piñon stress the role of stories and memories in the construction of personal, familial, and national identities. Their autobiographical family sagas reveal a performative memory that involves the repetition of the stories by which identity (personal, familial, or national) is constituted. Their autobiographical texts are acts of narrative resistance: they resist the ways in which dictatorships seek to impose truth and insist on presenting alternative stories of their nations. By writing autobiographical fiction in which the (fictionalized) stories of their own families are presented as the histories of their nations, they open out the auto-bio-graphical genre from the self/the life/the writing to the family/the life/the writing to the nation/the life/the writing, creating literary texts that can be located in a literary tradition I call *natiobiography*.

BEARING WITNESS TO THE SELF AND THE COMMUNITY: TESTIMONIAL WORKS BY INDIGENOUS WOMEN

Indeed, being Indian in the United States is inherently political, and as both Joy Harjo and Audre Lorde have written, "We were never meant to survive." In light of this, I see my personal story as bearing witness to colonization and my writing as a testimony aimed at undoing those processes that attempt to keep us in the grips of the colonizer's mental bondage.

—GLORIA BIRD

In this section and the paired chapters to follow, I take up a literary term, *testimonio*, which is most often used in relation to works created in Latin America, and seek to broaden our understanding of that term and genre by using it to analyze life narratives by two First Nations women of British Columbia.[1] While the term *testimonio* is sometimes unfamiliar to literary scholars working outside Latin American studies, bringing the term to a discussion of Indigenous Canadian texts can deepen our understanding of the genre and of the texts discussed in the following chapters, Lee Maracle's *Bobbi Lee: Indian Rebel* and Shirley Sterling's *My Name Is Seepeetza*.

Testimonio, like autobiography, raises questions about the subject's terms of self-representation, who has the power to change those terms and under what circumstances, and how different circumstances can change the rhetorical strategies employed (Bartow 230). The dynamics of a life narrative genre that "lays bare the struggles with authority, agency and self-legitimation existing in all forms of narrative" (Bartow 25–26) also make that genre an act of narrative resistance, one that can uncover mechanisms of oppression and lay out paths toward political and social change. *Testimonios*, written out of the life experiences and struggles of peoples from different nations in the Americas, offer alternatives to the national identities prescribed by the dominant cultures.

Since 1970, the Casa de las Américas has awarded a prize in the category of *testimonio*, serving in some ways as the mark of recognition of the testimonial work as a separate genre.[2] The genre received increasing critical attention throughout the 1980s and 1990s. The numbers of articles published in scholarly journals, including special issues dedicated to testimonial literature, and the number of university courses that included (most commonly) *Me llamo Rigoberta Menchú y así me nació la conciencia* (1983; *I, Rigoberta Menchú, An Indian Woman in Guatemala*, 1984) all attest to the genre's popularity.[3]

The controversy marked by David Stoll's 1999 study of Rigoberta Menchú's book and her work in Guatemala caused further discussion and debate about the legitimacy and authenticity of the testimonial genre. Stoll challenges the veracity of many elements in Menchú's story and asks readers to "face the limitations of *I, Rigoberta Menchú*" (282), setting off a firestorm of controversy and debate that reached national media outlets in the United States. Asserting that "even if it is not the eyewitness account it claims to be, that does not detract from its significance" (282–83), Stoll does seem able to recognize that her story "has helped shift perceptions of indigenous people from hapless victims to men and women fighting for their rights" (283). At the end, he affirms that, "[b]y pointing toward a more equitable relation between the two great ethnic groups in Guatemalan history, her book is a national epic. The key passage in *I, Rigoberta Menchú* is the first one: that 'my story is the story of all poor Guatemalans.' Even if the life told is not particularly her own, even if it is a heavily fictionalized heroic life, she achieved what she intended in a way that one person's actual life never could" (283). Here he seems to evince some understanding of one of the characteristics of *testimonio*, that the story told is not an individual story alone but one that tells the story of an oppressed group.

Indeed, a large portion of the debate can be discussed in terms of the genre of *testimonio* and how that genre should be read or understood. Stoll, not trained as a literary critic, lacks the generic understanding of *testimonio* held by many of those who have contested his reading of Menchú's text. As Elzbieta Sklodowska states so nicely: "[W]here Stoll spots lies and fabrications, I see allegories and metaphors. In short, I see a text" (256).

The Stoll/Menchú controversy and its reception in varied political and academic circumstances bears out Leigh Gilmore's assertion in *Autobiographics* that "whether and when autobiography emerges as an authoritative discourse of reality and identity, and any particular text appears to tell the truth, have less to do with that text's presumed accuracy about what really happened than with its apprehended fit into culturally prevalent discourses of truth and identity" (ix). Clearly, the culturally prevalent discourses of truth and identity vary in different political camps, in different academic discourses, and in different worldviews (Indigenous and non-Indigenous). For example, Cherokee author Marilou Awiakta, in discussing a traditional story of Selu, notes that "revealing spiritual truth, not facts, is the purpose of Selu's story" (16), so that different versions may make use of different places or change arrows to more contemporary weapons like guns, but "what cannot be changed are the spiritual base and the spine of the story" (16). Awiakta's worldview is clearly different than Stoll's but may, perhaps, be more evocative of Menchú's.

In *Reading Autobiography: A Guide for Interpreting Life Narratives*, Sidonie Smith and Julia Watson suggest that autobiographical truth should be seen as something different from what is normally considered factual truth, asserting that self-referential writing is an intersubjective process, so that "the emphasis of reading shifts from assessing and verifying knowledge to observing processes of communicative exchange and understanding" (13). In their description of autobiography, it is "an intersubjective mode [that] lies outside a logical or juridical model of truth and falsehood" (13). Smith, Watson, and Gilmore, as theoreticians of autobiography, all approach the concept of truth from a different perspective than that employed by Stoll.[4] Smith and Watson's stress on "processes of communicative exchange and understanding" seems closer to values expressed by many tribally affiliated authors and scholars. A lengthy rehearsal of the circulation and reception of Menchú's text (and Stoll's book) would show again that issues of ethics, truth, judgment, and authenticity are both culturally specific and highly contested.

Even apart from the specifics of the politically charged Menchú/Stoll debate, there have always been questions about the definition of the testimonial genre. The genre inevitably raises issues about disciplinary boundaries between literature and anthropology or between oral histories and literary works, as well as matters of distinctions between testimonial literature and autobiography, questions about identity and authority, and concerns about the construction of personal, cultural, ethnic, and national identity. The widespread nature of the debate is exemplified by the 1991 publication of a special issue of *Latin American Perspectives* dedicated to testimonial literature in Latin America.[5] In their introduction, "Voices for the Voiceless," coeditors Georg Gugelberger and Michael Kearney contrast testimonial literature—produced by subaltern people on the periphery of the colonial situation—to the conventional writing about the colonial situation produced at the centers of colonial power.

In spite of critical attention paid to testimonial literature, there is neither a set definition of the genre nor a set canon. Testimonial texts have been called "hybrids, partaking of various qualities but possessing no single unifying identity" (Maier 4). However, I offer the definition of George Yúdice as a useful one for our discussion of this particular autobiographical genre. Yúdice describes *testimonio* as "an *authentic* narrative, told by a *witness* who is *moved* to *narrate* by the *urgency* of a situation (e.g., war, oppression, revolution, etc.). Emphasizing *popular oral discourse*, the witness portrays his or her own *experience* as *representative* of a *collective memory* and *identity*. *Truth* is summoned in the cause of *denouncing* a present situation of exploitation and oppression or *exorcising* and *setting aright* official history" (quoted in Gugelberger and Kearney, 4, emphasis in the original). Many of the same elements are emphasized in the oft-cited definition provided by John Beverley: "By *testimonio* I mean a novel or novella-length narrative in book or pamphlet (that is, printed as opposed to acoustic) form, told in the first-person by a narrator who is also the real protagonist or witness of the events he or she recounts, and whose unit of narration is usually a 'life' or a significant life experience." Beverley goes on to note that "because testimonio is by nature a protean and demotic form not yet subject to legislation by a normative literary establishment, any attempt to specify a generic definition for it, as I do here, should be considered at best provisional, at worst repressive" (24–25).

One topic of debate involves the generic distinctions between testimonial literature and the various genres with which testimonials share some characteristics, like autobiography, ethnographic life histories, slave narratives, and holocaust literature. Like testimonial works, slave narratives and holocaust literature have both documentary aspects and the intention of forcing the reader to reexamine the official histories of oppressed peoples. Slave narratives and holocaust literature often focus on the story of a single individual as representative of a collective memory and identity, to use Yúdice's terms. Such narratives also seek to exorcise and set aright official history, another part of Yúdice's definition of *testimonio*.

But slave narratives and holocaust literature differ significantly from testimonial literature in that the situation of exploitation and oppression they denounce is most often a past one. Testimonial literature addresses present situations and looks to future solutions, to revolutionary solutions, to a transformed society as envisioned by the witness telling her story. (Such future-oriented perspectives do not deny the traumas of the past, but work to transform them into possibilities for the present and future.) Gugelberger confirms this distinction when he defines Holocaust testimonies as basically documentary, with the *testimonio* described as something "that wants to effect change and is quite different from documentary writing" (4). In making his own generic distinctions, Beverley insists that "[t]estimonio may include, but is not subsumed under, any of the following textual categories, some of which are conventionally considered literature, others not: autobiography, autobiographical novel, oral history, memoir, confession, diary, interview, eyewitness report, life history, *novela-testimonio*, non-fiction novel, or 'factographic literature'" (24–25).

Testimonials differ from the traditional autobiography in which the person writing his or her autobiography sees that particular life as exemplary, unique, individually significant. In contrast, Rigoberta Menchú reminds us: "I'd like to stress that it's not only my life, it's also the testimony of my people. . . . My story is the story of all poor Guatemalans. My personal experience is the reality of a whole people" (1). Domitila Barrios de Chungara of Bolivia similarly stresses that hers is not just a personal story, beginning her text: "I don't want anyone at any moment to interpret the story I am about to tell as something that is only personal. Because I think that my life is related to my people. What happened to me could have happened to hundreds of people in my country" (15). In *Mankiller: A Chief and Her People*, Wilma Mankiller (principal chief of the Cherokee Nation of Oklahoma from 1985 to 1995) acknowledges that "[e]specially in the context of a tribal people, no individual's life stands apart and alone from the rest. My own story has meaning only as long as it is a part of the overall story of my people" (14). In these life narratives by Native women of the Americas, the self is defined not in individual terms but in collective terms, as part of a collective struggle, as part of a communal identity. As Yúdice asserts, "[T]he speaker does not speak for or represent a community but rather forms an act of identity-formation which is simultaneously personal and collective" (15). Many tribal scholars present a similar concept of identity, one built on a weblike or spiraling structure with connections to all one's relations, past, present, and future. In *God Is Red*, Vine Deloria Jr. explains: "The possibility of conceiving of an individual alone in a tribal religious sense is ridiculous. The very complexity of tribal life and the interdependence of people on one another makes this conception improbable at best, a terrifying loss of identity at worst" (201). Deloria goes on to quote Harvey Cox's remarks, from *The Secular City*: "Tribal man is hardly a personal 'self' in our modern sense of the word. He does not so much live in a tribe; the tribe lives in him. He is the tribe's subjective expression" (201). So too does Doris Sommer, in "Not Just a Personal Story," affirm that in testimonial literature, the "singular represents the plural not because it replaces or subsumes the group but because the speaker is a distinguishable part of the whole" (108). Readers often attribute part of the power of testimonial works to the sense that the story told represents an infinite number of people. Sommer also points out the resistance strategies of *testimonio*, suggesting that the genre may be "a medium of resistance and counter-discourse, the legitimate space for producing that excess which throws doubt on the coherence and power of an exclusive historiography" (111).

Testimonial literature at times seems an inherently contradictory term, as it presents a challenge to the very concept of the literary and confuses the issue of the authorial signature. Who has the right to speak or to write? What forms are considered appropriate for their utterances to take? (Godard 185). *Testimonio* challenges the concept of authorship, as political power and publishing space is ceded to the "authentic" voices of marginalized persons and groups rather than to elite authors (Bartow 13). While authors of autobiographies are considered just that, authors, with all the authority granted thereby, no one is quite sure what to call those involved in the production of a *testimonio*. Rigoberta Menchú spoke her story out loud to someone else (Elizabeth Burgos-Debray)—someone of a different country, a different race, a different ethnicity, a different social and economic class, a different educational level—who wrote the text. In such a multilingual and transcultural process, it can be hard to say who the author is and where the authority lies. The first edition of the text, published by Editorial Argos Vergara in September 1983, lists the author as Elisabeth Burgos.[6] The English-language version, published by Verso in 1984, is edited and introduced by Elisabeth Burgos-Debray. The Spanish-language edition of *Me llamo Rigoberta Menchú y así me nació la conciencia* published in 1985 by Siglo Veintiuno Editores lists Elizabeth Burgos as the author. These differences in attribution or definition of roles highlight the crucial questions of authority and authorship.

The differences in the name of the woman who produced the text with Menchú are also striking—Elizabeth (with a *z*) Burgos, or Elisabeth (with an *s*) Burgos, or Elisabeth (with an *s*) Burgos-Debray—in light of the fact that the "errors" or "inaccuracies" challenged by David Stoll in his book were sometimes as small as a personal name.

In part, the authority of testimonial works lies in the lived experience of the people telling their stories. As readers, we grant authority to Rigoberta Menchú or Domitila Barrios de Chungara, neither a professional writer at the time they told their stories, because of the profound nature of their struggles, struggles to live, to feed themselves and their families, to exist as human beings of worth and value in societies that do not recognize their value, societies that sometimes do not recognize their very existence.

Just as *testimonio* is a complicated and contradictory term, so too is the term "Native American autobiography," spawning its own critical discussion that revolves in part around debates and disagreements over definitions. In *For Those Who Come After: A Study of Native American Autobiography*, Arnold Krupat argues that Native American autobiography is itself a contradiction in terms, as he considers autobiography a European invention of comparatively recent date and asserts that "[t]here simply were no Native American texts until whites decided to collaborate with Indians and make them" (5). While many of Krupat's claims are strongly disputed by other scholars in the field,[7] his list of questions about the mode of production of Native American autobiography are similar to those raised by testimonial works in Latin America. To cite just some of his queries:

> How well did the various workers (Indian informant-speaker, white editor-transcriber, and also apparently in all cases at least one translator, usually part-Indian and part-white) know one another's language? Under what auspices was the text produced, and what claims were made for it? Was its inscription sponsored by anthropological science and, if so, through a museum or university? . . . Was it sponsored poetically, religiously, morally, or in the interest of revitalizing some aspect of American practice? What were the apparent intentions of the producers and what benefits did they derive from their collaborative project? (7–8)

Just as the *testimonio* in Latin America came to be in a certain historical period, Krupat argues that it is only with the westward movement of the whites, with the Indian Removal Act and the Trail of Tears, that Indians are seen as historical subjects with stories to tell.

Indian autobiographies were often envisioned by the whites involved in their production as textual spaces for the Indian to admit defeat. Yet, "the production of an Indian's own statement of his inevitable disappearance required that the Indian be represented as speaking in his own voice. . . . And it is in its presentation of an Indian *voice not as vanished and silent*, but as still living and able to be heard that the oppositional potential of Indian autobiography resides" (Krupat 35, emphasis added). As in the Latin American *testimonios*, the concept of giving voice to a repressed segment of society is stressed.[8]

Anthologies and critical works on Native women in North America often echo the notion of giving voice to the voiceless. As readers of the published criticism on *testimonio* and autobiography, we must listen carefully for the ideologies invoked in each use of the term "voice" by the various critics writing on Native texts. For, as Lois Parkinson Zamora reminds us, "as a critical concept, 'voice' responds to specific ideological and psychological imperatives" (*Contemporary* 6). Paula Gunn Allen argues that only recently have American Indian women chosen to define themselves politically as Indian *women* as their status has declined seriously over the centuries of white dominance, "as they have been all but *voiceless* in tribal decision-making bodies since reconstitution of the tribes through colonial fiat and U.S. law" (*Sacred Hoop* 30, emphasis added). Julia Emberley affirms that "[g]iving 'voice' in print culture is one way Native writers empower themselves and claim themselves as agents of their own cultural traditions" (73). Kimberly M. Blaeser's "Native Literature: Seeking a Critical Center" grew out of her recognition that "the literatures of Native Americans have a unique voice and that voice has not always been adequately or accurately explored in the criticism that has been written about the literature" (53). Coeditors Laura Klein and Lillian Ackerman begin their introduction to *Women and Power in Native North America* by noting that "[s]ilence surrounds the lives of Native North American women" (3) and asserting that the chapters in their book "give voice to the silences" (4).

Similarly, in *Writing the Circle: Native Women of Western Canada*, editors Jeanne Perreault and Sylvia Vance present their anthology as a collection of voices that had not been widely heard and that have been missing from all Canadians' understanding of their society and literature (xi). Noting that the systemic racism and sexism in Canadian society make every stage of writing and publishing less accessible to Native women,[9] the two non-Native women organized the anthology. In the preface, "Here Are Our Voices—Who Will Hear?" Emma LaRocque (Métis) reminds us that "[t]o discuss Native literature is to tangle with a myriad of issues: voicelessness, accessibility, stereotypes, appropriation, ghettoization, linguistic, cultural, sexual, and colonial roots of experience, and, therefore, of self-expression—all issues that bang at the door of conventional notions about Canada and about literature" (xv). While the idea of voicelessness (first on LaRocque's list) echoes the title of Gugelberger and Kearney's introduction to their special issue on the Latin American testimonial "Voices for the Voiceless," LaRocque takes issue with that term, questioning whether the Indian and the Métis were voiceless. LaRocque acknowledges that many Natives were illiterate in Canada into the 1970s, even into the 1990s, because of the failure of the Canadian educational system to impart basic writing and reading skills to Native youth. And while being illiterate can make one voiceless in a country that revolves around the printed word, LaRocque concedes, it certainly did not mean that the Native peoples had no words, no literature, no wealth of knowledge.[10] As LaRocque asserts, "The issue is not that Native peoples were ever wordless but that, in Canada, their words were literally and politically negated" (xi). In the chapters to follow, we look at two Indigenous Canadian women who have used their words and their voices to tell their stories and the stories of their peoples, reading their personal narratives within the context of testimonial and autobiographical theories. I discuss *Bobbi Lee: Indian Rebel* by Lee Maracle as an example of *testimonio* and highlight the testimonial aspects of what I classify as an autobiographical first novel, *My Name Is Seepeetza*, by Shirley Sterling. My discussion of these two works within the framework of *testimonio* examines vital issues of authority, agency, and self-legitimation in Native literatures.

Maracle and Sterling use their life narratives both to uncover the mechanisms of oppression in Canadian society and to discover the means of resistance and survival. Their texts reveal how they have been subject to an education that would make them subjects in the colonizers' language, beliefs, and values, while repressing their own Indigenous languages, beliefs, and values. Their autobiographical acts give witness to their resistance to the colonial repression and to the continuing strength they draw from their Native cultures. In another context, Simon Ortiz (Pueblo) has written of a culture of "resistance against forces that would destroy life. It is by the affirmation of knowledge of source and place and spiritual return that resistance is realized" (11). My readings show how Sterling and Maracle resist the forces that would destroy life. I read their affirmations of knowledge of source and place and spiritual return as their realization of resistance. Unwilling to be defined by the norms of white Canadian society, Sterling and Maracle insist on their own self-definitions (in part) through their autobiographical writings.

5 /   "The Life of Bobbi Lee Is about Why We Must Talk": Testimonial Literature as a Call to Action

Lee Maracle, a member of the Stó:lô Nation, of Salish and Cree ancestry, was born in 1950 and raised in Vancouver, British Columbia. *Bobbi Lee: Indian Rebel* marked the beginning of a writing project that has continued in both autobiographical and other genres. The original version of *Bobbi Lee* was published in 1975, the year of the first general assembly of the World Council of Indigenous Peoples (WCIP), held in Port Alberni, Vancouver. At the general assembly, WCIP developed a definition of the "Fourth World," as formed by Indigenous minority peoples. Chadwick Allen has argued that the WCIP's development of a narrative definition of Indigenous peoples, rather than a set of criteria, is part of "a project of post-colonial literature and autoethnography that both engages and attempts to counter the First World's dominant discourses of master narrative and ethnic taxonomy" (237). The WCIP and Lee Maracle might be seen as colonized subjects undertaking "to represent themselves in ways that *engage with* the colonizer's own terms" (Pratt 7).

Maracle's *Bobbi Lee* is a work that attempts to counter the First World's dominant discourses of master narrative and ethnic taxonomy. *Bobbi Lee* is referred to on the back cover of the 1990 edition as an autobiography, yet Maracle discusses in an interview with Jennifer Kelly the difficulties she encountered in getting the book published, being told by many that "*Bobbi Lee* was too political to be autobiography" (82). Comments on the political nature of *Bobbi Lee* continued after publication as well. In *American Indian Women, Telling Their Lives*, Gretchen M. Bataille and Kathleen Mullen Sands make a distinction between Maria Campbell's

Halfbreed and Maracle's *Bobbi Lee*, claiming that *Halfbreed* "lacks the strident voice of *Bobbi Lee: Indian Rebel*" (116). Bataille and Sands assert that narratives such as Maracle's play a minor role in the genre of Native women's autobiography because "autobiography is not a particularly effective mode of writing for the promulgation of political theory or action, and hence usually not adopted by writers with pragmatic goals" (136). Such an assertion is clearly based on an understanding of autobiography as something other than political.

Yet for many autobiographers, critics, and activists, autobiography is always political. Gloria Bird (Spokane) proclaims: "To me as a writer, everything is motivated by a political agenda. Indeed, being Indian in the United States [and Canada] is inherently political, and as both Joy Harjo and Audre Lorde have written, 'We were never meant to survive.' In light of this, I see my personal story as bearing witness to colonization and my writing as a testimony aimed at undoing those processes that attempt to keep us in the grips of the colonizer's mental bondage" (28). Not only does Bird link writing and political goals here, but in doing so she employs many of the same terms used in descriptions of *testimonio*, with references to her personal story, bearing witness, writing as a testimony. Like the Native women in Latin America whose *testimonios* are discussed above, Bird understands "that our position within a system that is designed to deny us is tenuous and continually threatened and that there is truly strength in the numbers of witnesses who can carry our stories forward" (29). Bird asserts that witnessing and testimony become "viable tools" in the struggle for decolonization "by providing details of individual processing of the complexities of inheritance that living in the aftermath of colonization provides" (29).

Bird understands the political leverage that can be provided by witnessing and *testimonio*. To make a claim that Native women's autobiography is not (or should not be) political is another attempt to silence the (political and activist) voices of Native peoples. Joanne R. DiNova (Ojibwe) claims that too much of the critical work on Native autobiographies has been based on "a fundamental failure to acknowledge the sovereign status of the First Nations, which inevitably permits the objectification of, and proprietary orientation towards, the people and their stories" (54). DiNova proposes an Indigenous criticism that grows out of the texts themselves, and questions definitions of Native autobiography that work to silence Native claims to sovereignty.

Bataille and Sands' claim that autobiography is not an effective mode of writing for the promulgation of political theory or action also goes against an understanding of *testimonio*, as used in the field of Latin American literatures, as clearly understood by Bird, and as I extend it here to a discussion of *Bobbi Lee*. Recall Yúdice's definition of *testimonio*, which refers to the truth being "summoned in the cause of denouncing a present situation of exploitation and oppression or exorcising and setting aright official history" (Gugelberger and Kearney 4), or Bartow's assertion that "testimonial discourse posits an alternative national identity from the bottom up" (231). As a testimonial work, *Bobbi Lee* denounces the oppression of Aboriginal peoples in Canada (and the world) and proposes an alternative national identity. References to Maracle's work as "too political," "strident," or "Canadian Marxist" strive to define the politics of her discourse into silence.

Since all discourse is political in some way, many authors and critics criticize any false division between politics and literature. Roberto González Echevarría asserts that literature is the equivalent of critical thought in Latin America, and "critical thought most certainly includes politics" (3). So too does contemporary literature by Indigenous peoples in the Americas serve as both critical thought and political thought. Jace Weaver (Cherokee) coins the word "communitism"—a combination of community and activism—noting that "[l]iterature is communitist to the extent that it has a proactive commitment to Native community, including what I term the 'wider community' of Creation itself. In communities that have too often been fractured and rendered dysfunctional by the effects of more than 500 years of colonialism, to promote communitist values means to participate in the healing of the grief and sense of exile felt by Native communities and the pained individuals in them" (xiii). Craig Womack (Muskogee Creek–Cherokee) asserts that "Native literary aesthetics must be politicized and that autonomy, self-determination, and sovereignty serve as useful literary concepts. Further, I wish to suggest that literature has something to add to the arena of Native political struggle. The attempt, then, will be to break down oppositions between the world of literature and the very real struggles of American Indian communities, arguing for both an intrinsic and an extrinsic relationship between the two" (11). Womack urges a literary criticism "that emphasizes Native resistance movements against colonialism, confronts racism, discusses sovereignty and Native nationalism, seeks connections between literature and liberation struggles, and, finally, roots literature in land and culture" (11). DiNova calls for an Indigenist criticism that, in the simplest terms, "examines literature in terms of what it is doing for (or against) the people" (53). Paul Chaat Smith (Comanche) echoes

Gloria Bird's assertion that being Indian is inherently political, reaffirming that for Native people, "It was a political act simply to be human in the contemporary world" (32).

While Weaver, Womack, DiNova, and many others make strong arguments for Indigenist criticism, the desire of others to separate politics and literature can, and often still does, serve as an excuse to exclude Native authors. On September 16–17, 2006, the Guthrie Center hosted a gathering entitled "The Resilience of the Human Spirit: An International Gathering of Poets." According to their Web site: "This conference is an extraordinary gathering of poets who have experienced war, genocide, prison, execution of loved ones, oppression, racism, exile, and despair— and who use the power of their voices to bear witness to the resilience of the human spirit. During the weekend, there will be panels, intimate conversations, writing workshops, and readings by acclaimed poets." The list of participants did not include a single Native poet from the United States or Canada, even though Native poets can and do speak to "war, genocide, prison, execution of loved ones, oppression, racism, exile, and despair." When the Ohlone-Costanoan Esselen Nation poet Deborah Miranda sent an e-mail to one of the conference organizers to ask about the incredible omission of any Native American speakers, Miranda was told that the conference "is not activist in nature. It is not a place for political debate or to air grievances. . . . It is about using poetry and language to build bridges of understanding and create change." Such a response seems to imply not only that Native authors cannot use poetry and language to build bridges of understanding and create change, but also that their works are only political, not literary.[1]

Just as *Bobbi Lee* was deemed too political to be autobiography, Maracle recounts that her 1990 collection *Sojourner's Truth and Other Stories* "was not published at first because the stories were too controversial" (82). Maracle's works have not been easy to publish, as they do not always fit neatly into traditional (Western) literary genres or conform to the expectations often held by mainstream publishers as to what Native literature should be. In *The Sacred Hoop*, Paula Gunn Allen argues that the worldview often held by Native writers does not allow for the strict separation of literary genres: "It is reasonable, from an Indian point of view, that all literary forms should be interrelated, given the basic idea of the unity and relatedness of all the phenomena of life" (62). Maracle would seem to support Paula Gunn Allen's words. In a July 2000 interview with Margery Fee and Sneja Gunew published in 2004, Maracle talks about her efforts "to find a way to alter the language to suit my own Salish sensibility" (211), something that "has created somewhat of a controversy literarily for me, not of big difficulty because people like reading me. It doesn't really matter what English professors say about me, as long as people continue to like reading what I have to say" (211). Maracle believes she has been successful in bringing changes to genres and disciplines: "I've brought emotionality to writing, I've brought emotionality to politics. I've brought emotionality to sociology, I've brought spirituality to all of those things that literary critics say is not literary, and I managed to do it in a literary manner. I brought change to the language; I brought change to perception" (213). Regardless of how her works are classified by publishers, booksellers, and librarians—as fiction, autobiography, biography, bildungsroman, poetry—Maracle strives always to write with a Salishan sensibility, to transform language and genres to suit that sensibility. A comprehensive study of her collected works (beyond the scope of this study) would reveal their communitist nature.

That her works do not always fit so neatly into the traditional canonical forms of the dominant society can make publication difficult, but so too can the fact that, as Agnes Grant notes, the written tradition of Canada "often overlooks Natives because Natives are not generally considered a living, contributing factor in all facets of Canadian society" (125). As Anna Marie Sewell, in "Natives on Native Literature: What Do We Rightly Write?" notes, "It has taken a long time for Native writers to gain access to mainstream publication, so that we could talk about our reality; and those who led the way brought with them uncomfortable truths" (20). Maracle is a writer who has brought uncomfortable truths to the pages of her texts.

In her interviews, Maracle often weighs in on issues being debated in literary fields. She argues that white writers are much less capable of writing Native characters than Native writers are of portraying white characters, claiming that it "has to do with hierarchy and the way it works. The people at the bottom see more clearly what's happening than the people at the top seeing down" (Kelly 83). Maracle notes that whites are hugely unaware of the racism and oppression intrinsic in Canadian society because whites can afford to be unaware and apathetic while Natives cannot (Kelly 81). Their very lives and identities are at stake.

The racist ideology Maracle critiques in all her writings is not just an idea or a value system. Ideology is a material practice, and Natives, most particularly Native women, live under the brunt of that brutal material practice. Maracle not infrequently makes the connection between racism and sexism: "It's like the woman question. Men aren't very good in the realm of anti-sexism. Their intentions might be there, but they haven't done much anti-sexist work" (Kelly 83). Maracle continually stresses how racism operates as sexism within the Native communities and how sexism operates as internalized racism.

While Maracle's work, like that of other Indigenous authors in the Americas, is often referred to as postcolonial, Maracle rejects the label of postcolonial frequently being used to discuss Indigenous literature because "[f]or us . . . there has been no revolution in this country. We're still colonized. So postcolonialism has no meaning for us whatsoever, which is why it never comes up in discourse between us. We're still fighting classical colonialism" (Kelly 83). In *Bobbi Lee: Indian Rebel*, the very subtitle of the work underlines Lee Maracle's self-positionality as a fighter.

Bobbi Lee, like some of the Latin American *testimonios* discussed earlier, was created out of the collaboration of a Native woman and a white academic/activist. In 1972, Lee Maracle told her life story to Donald Barnett, chairman of the Liberation Support Movement. Maracle dictated her life story into a tape recorder, as part of a project on life writing undertaken by members of a Marxist political group to which she belonged. Those hours of tape were distilled and edited into the original edition of the work, which went out of print fairly quickly. In 1990, the Women's Press in Toronto republished the text as *Bobbi Lee: Indian Rebel*. The 1990 edition includes the original 1975 text as well as a foreword by Jeannette Armstrong, and introductory material and an epilogue, both by Maracle. My references are to the 1990 edition.

In the prologue to the 1990 edition, Maracle explains: "There are two voices in the pages of this book, mine and Donald Barnett's. . . . We had disagreements over what to include and what to exclude, disagreements over wording, voice. In the end, the voice that reached the paper was Don's, the information alone was mine" (19). Maracle's prologue makes explicit what is often not expressed in the collaborative testimonial work between two people of different races, different classes, different ethnicities. Like Rigoberta Menchú, who claims that there are many things Indigenous people in Guatemala will not share with whites, Maracle explains that she "didn't, couldn't tell him everything" (19). There were truths too painful to share with a white man. That Maracle claims that the voice that reached the paper was Barnett's also questions to what extent testimonial literature does "give voice to the voiceless" and would seem to support Krupat's assertion that "the structure of Indian autobiography is ultimately the responsibility of the Euramerican editor" (111).[2]

In her foreword to *Bobbi Lee,* Jeannette Armstrong asserts both that "the telling of the Native sojourn through the quagmire of Canada's colonialist past is an extremely important human document to Canadian literature" and that in "the movement of the life of Bobbi Lee, what unfolds is the story of many natives" (15). Like the Latin American testimonial works, Bobbi Lee's story is presented as not just a personal story. Her story presents the harsh realities of her life and allows the readers to see those realities, as Armstrong notes, "through the mix of native and non-native values and customs jammed together for survival purposes" (15). Armstrong asserts the importance of autobiographical and testimonial projects for Native communities, suggesting that "the telling of our lives, the back-tracking, the map-making through the treacherous terrain of our individual experiences is perhaps a more important exercise than we Native people readily appreciate" (15).

Mapmaking through the Treacherous Terrain of Bobbi Lee's Life

Bobbi Lee: Indian Rebel is a narrative of childhood and adolescence. The first chapter of Maracle's text, entitled "Turbulent Childhood" (21), tells the story of a girl born in Vancouver in 1950 and raised in poverty on the mudflats of the North Shore. Her mother was born in a large Métis community in Lac Labiche, Alberta, the daughter of a French man and an Indian woman. Her father was born in Goodsoil, Saskatchewan, on a small farm. The family house had originally been a boatshed and was without heating, hot water, or electricity. Even when they later got electricity, she reports, "the place was always cold and damp" (22). Her father sometimes worked on boats but other times left the family to go north to fish; "he rarely came home and never sent mom any money" (24). Bobbi's older brother and grandfather went crabbing, and Bobbi's mother earned money selling the crabs. Her brothers also got paper routes or worked as caddies at the golf course. Bobbi started taking in washing and ironing for white families when she was just seven years old. They all worked in the family vegetable plot. Bobbi Lee's story helps exemplify how "poverty is one of the most effective tools that has been and continues to be used by Canadian society as a means of subjugating, dominating, exploiting and even destroying the human targets of its racism" (Damm, "Dispelling" 104).

The tale of Bobbi's youth is one of systemic violence and racism. Her parents fought frequently, with the father away for extended periods of time. When he was home, he often was both violent and drunk, calling Bobbi's mother a "dirty old squaw" (34). The father's drinking impacted the kids in a variety of ways: "When they had parties—which was almost every week—dad got drunk and made us kids drink beer too. He would then make us dance and do other stupid things—which I really hated" (23).

As a young girl, Bobbi "was often left with a woman named Eileen Dunster—whom I called 'Aunt Eileen'—because dad kept beating me up and mom didn't like it" (23). Her father routinely beats her brother Ed and throws him against the wall (24), her mother threatens various men with an axe (25), Bobbi and her brother Roger drag their three-year-old sister Joan through brambles. Bobbi's family is ostracized by many of the other families on the mudflats, due in part to their race and in part, seemingly, to her mother's reputation (most of the children in the family were not fathered by the man Bobbi calls dad). The white boys in the neighborhood pick on the Native children, but the retaliation of the Native children is also one of racist violence. Ten of the Native children "were making faces at Jimmy (Waddel) from around the corner of a house, calling him 'dirty old man,' 'whitey,' 'white boy' and things like that" (27). They chain him to a tree and leave him crying. He is left there all night, with his mother frantic and the police searching for him.

Violence is part and parcel of almost every story, revealing how internalized colonialism can be manifested in family violence. When her overworked mother is seriously ill, Bobbi Lee calmly announces: "I thought it was my dad's fault that she was dying because he wouldn't take her to the hospital. I decided I would shoot him . . . he was just no good, I thought. . . . I knew about death because we had done a lot of duck hunting and fishing. I thought it wouldn't be difficult to shoot dad. . . . You have to understand that I really loved mom, and I hated my dad—especially when I was a young kid" (28–29). Her seemingly unemotional determination to kill her father underscores her own alienation at age seven.

At school, she frequently threatens to kill other kids who have angered her (36–37). She knows she could get along better if she just said yes to everything, but she refuses "to accept any racist crap or be a 'yes girl.' I figured myself to be a fairly intelligent person; more intelligent than most, in fact, I thought white kids didn't know what the hell was going on. The liberal whites with their racist hang-ups made me sick. It was really ugly. Because I am Métis and light skinned, whites were sometimes confused. It happened fairly regularly that one would come up to me and ask 'No offense, but are you Indian?' I would always reply, saying 'Yes I am . . . but no offense, are you white?'" (50). Things reach a point where she is completely ostracized at school and feels contempt for all whites. Refusing to accept their racist attitudes, she finds that the cockier she is, the more their racism comes out (49): "And because I wouldn't kowtow, bow or scrape or be their scapegoat, I got into a lot of fights and was beaten up more than any kid I knew" (50). Bobbi Lee responds both verbally and physically to the repudiation and denigration she encounters. She denies the attempts of others to project their meanings upon her and to decide her place in society. She questions the perceptions of others and challenges the semantic power they attempt to impose upon her. She does not hesitate to intervene in the language of the others—mimicking their question, "no offense, but are you Indian?" with her own "no offense, but are you white?"—wresting the interpretative power away from members of the dominant society. Bobbi Lee's critical consciousness is formed as she acquires the skill of interpretation, as she learns to read the painful experience of negation in school as the ideology of racism.

Paula Gunn Allen argues that Native women are caught in a bicultural bind that has them vacillating between being dependent and strong, self-reliant and powerless, and that they resolve the dilemma in different ways: "some of us party all the time; some of us drink to excess; some of us travel and move around a lot; some of us land good jobs and then quit them; some of us engage in violent exchanges; some of us blow our brains out. We act in these destructive ways because we suffer from the societal conflicts caused by having to identify with two hopelessly opposed cultural definitions of women. . . . Our situation is caused by the exigencies of a history of invasion, conquest, and colonization whose searing marks are probably ineradicable" (*Sacred Hoop*, 48–49). Most of the forms of destructive behavior outlined by Allen are evinced by Bobbi Lee during the period of her life narrated in the text.[3]

At age fifteen, Bobbi starts getting drunk (44). She alternately argues with and ignores her mother, rarely attends school, stays out until 4:00 a.m., hangs around with different guys, is eventually admitted to a hospital for psychiatric care after an episode at school when she throws a desk at her teacher. The doctors tell her she had a nervous breakdown, keep her medicated for three weeks, and prescribe tranquilizers and psychiatry after her release. The entire episode is recounted in the apathetic tone of an impersonal observer, underscoring her complete sense of alienation from her family, her doctors, her self, and her own body: "I rarely took the tranquilizers and never went to see the psychiatrist. At home I just tried to forget the whole thing" (48).

Shortly before her sixteenth birthday, when Bobbi Lee's mother kicks her out of the house, she goes to Visalia, California, to join her older foster sister. Living with Mexican farmworkers, picking grapes and other farm products, she starts to notice and ponder on the racism in a town made up of mostly Mexicans, some whites, a few blacks, and a few Indians: "This was my first experience with really blatant racism. Not that I'd never experienced any racism before—far from it. But here it was so common, so much a part of everyday life, that people never even thought about it" (53). Whites and Mexicans do not speak to each other, will not frequent each other's stores, and would not be served if they did. The Mexicans consider themselves superior to the Indians, which Bobbi Lee thinks is funny since most of them are of Indigenous descent. The African Americans are mistreated by everyone. Her experience in California helps her to realize that there are various forms of racism and that white people are not the only ones with racist attitudes and actions.

Although she only stays in California for four months, she is very struck by the cultural differences. The experience of racism there starts her process of consciousness-raising on issues of both racism and sexism. Returning to Vancouver, she discovers that her brothers have left home, and that one of her fourteen-year-old twin sisters had been raped while the other had been forced to watch.

The middle part of the book, with chapters entitled "Hippie Life-Style 1967," "Toronto: Anti-War Demonstrations and Racism," and "A Real Bad Trip," tell of her experiences in Toronto living as a hippie, doing drugs, and being involved rather marginally in antiwar demonstrations. Her involvement stems from her loose personal connection with people who are active so that she follows along with them, without any clearly developed or committed politics of her own. She works occasionally, sells drugs on the street, drinks a lot, is witness to further violence, but she recounts that violence, even the death of people she knew, in completely impersonal tones. She laments her sense of distance—"The point, though, was that I really didn't care. And what was worse—what I hated the most—was that I had kind of lost all sense of emotion" (99)—but she seems incapable of enacting any change.

Her drug use increases as she becomes more addicted to heroin, coming close to an overdose on more than one occasion. Looking back, she realizes: "I think that unconsciously I wanted to overdose; I really hated my existence. I had taken this path deliberately, not out of ignorance or naiveté, and was just giving up on life. I knew the stuff would eventually kill me, yet I kept on taking it. And in the meantime I started feeling completely dehumanized, like a vegetable. I actually stopped acting like a human being—didn't laugh, didn't cry, didn't find things funny or sad" (105). At age seventeen, Bobbi Lee is so alienated from her self, from any sense of identity, that she no longer feels human, no longer recognizes any value in her own life. Her heavy drug use keeps her from thinking about the social, political, and economic concerns that impact her own place in society.

It is only when she leaves Toronto, and gets off drugs and alcohol, that Bobbi Lee becomes involved with the Native Alliance for Red Power (NARP), participates in a fish-in, organizes demonstrations, and works as part of a street patrol on skid row in Vancouver to help protect First Nations people against police harassment. Her experiences in Vancouver and on the trip back to British Columbia in some ways can be seen as a journey of maturation, one that allows her to begin to explore personal and communal identity formation.

Drawing Useful Lessons from the Life Story

The original version of *Bobbi Lee: Indian Rebel* ends abruptly, with no closure. Bobbi Lee's life story is presented not as one that has achieved full significance but rather one that is still seeking significance and meaning. Western desire for an ending, or at least the sense of an ending, is frustrated. In *Sojourner's Truth and Other Stories*, Maracle talks about Native storytelling traditions, remarking: "Most of our stories don't have orthodox 'conclusions'; that is left to the listeners, who we trust will draw useful lessons from the story—not necessarily the lessons we wish them to draw, but all conclusions are considered valid. The listeners are drawn into the dilemma and are expected at some point in their lives to actively work themselves out of it" (11–12). In the original text, we see Bobbi Lee as a child and young woman who "was always trying to understand things" (33), one who looks at her life, asks questions and makes some attempts to recognize the social forces that, in part, shape her subjectivity and mire her in dilemmas. The process of understanding herself and her position in society is one that continues in the expanded 1990 edition.

In the 1990 edition of the text, Bobbi Lee's story is framed by prefatory material and an epilogue. This more recent edition begins with a piece entitled "Oka Peace Camp—September 9, 1990" in which Lee Maracle writes of the tense situation in Quebec, of preparing herself for death, "preparing to leave my children motherless because it feels like maybe bloodletting is what this country needs. Maybe if we just let the road to Oka run red with the blood of women, someone in this country will see the death and destruction this country has wrought on us" (6). She writes of Canada as a battered country, with the land scarred in the interests of corporate imperialism and with the language battered in the interest of sanctioning that scarring of the land. She speaks out against the building of golf courses on the sites of Native burial grounds and for the need to talk "from a position of wholeness, completeness" (11) in order to build a sustainable movement toward peace and justice. With an opening piece written from Oka, Maracle situates her own life story into the ongoing struggle of Native peoples in Canada, in particular to a struggle over Native lands and sovereignty that gained considerable national press coverage in Canada. Tying her story into the story of the Oka struggle again reminds readers that Maracle's story is "not just a personal story."[4]

At the end of the testimonial work is an epilogue, written years after the original text, in which Maracle mulls over "my misspent youth, the craziness of internalized racism, my own confusion and the holes rent in my memory" (199). She acknowledges whole parts of her life, including people who were important to her, which were not written into the text. She writes of her great-grandmother: "I began to think about how I had erased T'a'ah from my heart, left her out of my book, how I had breathed the ideology and aspirations of Europe into my soul" (228). That great-grandmother is recognized in later interviews as being terribly important in her intellectual and cultural formation: "My great-grandmother also endured the outlaw of her language, her medicine, her capacity for taking care of the family. She is the sole survivor of seventeen brothers and sisters, so she began our whole lineage from 1835 to 1923. . . . She died when I was nine. I spent a great deal of time with her" (Fee and Gunew 209). Maracle learned stories of her family, her clan, and her people from her great-grandmother, stories that she re-creates in her own writings.

Also in the epilogue to *Bobbi Lee*, Maracle acknowledges the rage inside her that led her to beat her own small daughters, explaining that the violence she inflicted on her children "had nothing to do with drunkenness. I was sober and abusive. It had everything to do with racism and self-hate. I thought I hated white people and in fact, I did not love my own. I see this scene over and over again. Me, armed with a wooden spoon and her begging me to love her" (229–30). Bobbi Lee repeated with her own children the abusive situation in which she was raised. In this instance, as in others, her work emphasizes how women's bodies are often the central site on which and through which social violence is produced and reproduced.

In the epilogue, Maracle reveals that, at twenty-five, as her marriage "sunk into a crazy kind of oblivion," she started writing to save her sanity: "Poetry and the comfort of my diaries—my books of madness I called them—where truth rolled out of my inner self, began to re-shape me. . . . In my diary, I faced my womanhood, my indigenous womanhood. I faced my inner hate, my anger and desertion of myself from our way of being. . . . It took twenty-five years to twist me and only ten to unravel the twist" (230). With the appended epilogue, Bobbi Lee's story becomes, as Joy Harjo calls it on the back cover of the 1990 edition, "the charged story of a Native woman who has done more than survive, who despite great odds has burst forth singing a warrior song. . . . You will be changed."

Maracle's impetus in beginning to write—to save her sanity—and Harjo's comment that Maracle's story is a warrior song both evoke Maria Campbell's comments in "Strategies for Survival." In that piece, Campbell discusses her own autobiography, *Halfbreed* (originally published in 1973), which she wrote out of her need to understand herself and her frustration. When criticized for writing about negative aspects of Native life, she responds: "[W]hen you are oppressed, and when you are trying to be born again, when you are trying to reclaim, you have to go through all of the pain. That's the first thing that comes out, and we have to deal with that. That's our first song" (9). Campbell's *Halfbreed* and Maracle's *Bobbi Lee: Indian Rebel* are early songs in that song cycle of Native Canadian literature.

The more conventional (or Western) sense of narrative closure to *Bobbi Lee* comes in the ending of the epilogue, when Maracle addresses the white population of Canada, arguing that if "they don't struggle with racism they will never be able to chart their own path to freedom" (241). Maracle reminds us in an interview that "'Canada' means village or community, and I've taken the spirit of that, the spirit of community, the spirit of Canada to heart" (Kelly 75). Maracle wants Canada to be a community, but she asserts that all Canadians have to work toward that goal: "We, I, we will take on the struggle for self-determination and in so doing, will lay the foundation, the brick that you can build on in undoing the mess we are all in" (241). In these and the ending lines of the epilogue to *Bobbi Lee: Indian Rebel*, she addresses readers directly:

In my life, look for your complicit silence, look for the inequality between yourself and others. . . . Don't wait for me to jump up, put my back to the plough, wherever racism shows itself. You need to get out there and object, all by yourself.

We have worked hard enough for you. (241)

With the mixed use of "we" and "I" in these last two citations, we see Maracle as both an individual woman committed to social change and as a member of a community. Maracle, her Native community, and all of Canada feel the impact of the racism that all must commit to fight.

We see here the witness moved to narrate by the urgency of a situation of oppression, determined both to denounce and to set aright official history. Like Maria Campbell, who writes in her introduction to *Halfbreed*, "I write this for all of you, to tell you what it is like to be a Halfbreed woman in our country" (2), Maracle writes with the activist intention of much testimonial literature. Like Domitila Barrios de Chungara, Maracle demands readers' participation in the struggle for a new, more just society. And like N. Scott Momaday, who argues that "[t]he contemporary white American is willing to assume responsibility for the Indian—he is willing to take on the burdens of oppressed peoples everywhere—but he is decidedly unwilling to divest himself of the false assumptions which impede his good intentions" (72), Maracle critiques the supposed good intentions of white society.

Linda Marley argues that the "autobiographer recognizes that taking stock of one's own subjectivity is a task that must be undertaken from many different points in time and space" (8)—a recognition that is exemplified in the 1990 edition of *Bobbi Lee*. For, "in not abandoning that early representation of her self, in choosing to republish the original autobiography rather than rewriting it, Maracle also implicitly recognizes that no single narrative could ever fully represent or fix her subjectivity" (8). The construction of the 1990 edition of the text itself, where two first person singular voices, representing Maracle at different historical moments, "meet and enter into dialogue, suggests that the autobiographical process is an ongoing one" (Marley 8). That dialogue must also include the readers for, as Maracle states at the end of her introductory essay to the 1990 edition, "The life of Bobbi Lee is about why we must talk" (ii).

The dialogue created in and by *Bobbi Lee* is part of an autobiographical project that "posits the word as a process of knowing, provisional and partial, rather than as revealed knowledge itself, and aims to produce texts . . . that would create truth as interpretation rather than those in the

Western mimetic tradition that reveal truth as pre-established knowledge" (Godard 184). *Bobbi Lee* can be read as "a contestatory discourse that positions itself as a literature of resistance within the conventions, though marginally so, of the dominant discourse" (184). In her preface to *Writing the Circle: Native Women of Western Canada*, Emma LaRocque asserts that "much of Native writing, whether blunt or subtle, is protest literature in that it speaks to the processes of our colonization: dispossession, objectification, marginalization, and that constant struggle for cultural survival expressed in the movement for structural and psychological self-determination" (Perrault and Vance xviii). Certainly much of Maracle's writing speaks to these processes, and *Bobbi Lee* can be read as an act of narrative resistance. *Bobbi Lee* emphasizes Native resistance movements against colonialism, confronts racism, discusses sovereignty and Native nationalism, seeks connections between literature and liberation struggles and roots itself, as a literary text, in land and culture, all elements (as noted earlier) stressed by Craig Womack in *Red on Red*.

Maracle's Literary Acts of Resistance

Lee Maracle has gone on to become an acclaimed writer of fiction, essays, and poetry as well as a noted orator. Her first novel, *Sundogs*, was published in 1992, and her second, *Ravensong*, came out the following year. In 1996, Maracle published a second edition of *I Am Woman: A Native Perspective on Sociology and Feminism* (originally published in 1988 by Write-On Press). In her preface to the 1996 edition, Maracle writes that "*I Am Woman* represents my personal struggle with womanhood, culture, traditional spiritual beliefs and political sovereignty, written during a time when this struggle was not over. . . . My original intention was to empower Native women to take to heart their own personal struggle for Native feminist being" (vii). The second edition contains some revisions to the original, which she explains are "more to fill in gaps than to alter the original" (vii). Maracle's statement that the text "remains my attempt to present a Native woman's sociological perspective on the impacts of colonialism on us, as women, and on myself personally" (vii) shows the continued testimonial nature of her autobiographical work, that intention to use her personal story to address the hegemonic forces of colonialism, racism, sexism, and capitalism that impact the lives of Native women.

Maracle refers to *I Am Woman* as "an inside look at the madness which the colonial process creates" (143), and the preface provides another inside look at her life story. In putting the story of her struggle into the context of her own life story, Maracle begins by addressing the challenges her mother faced, thus self-consciously placing herself into a line of mothers and daughters, grandmothers and granddaughters: "I was born during the 1950s to a mother who struggled relentlessly to feed, clothe and house eight children, instill in them some fundamental principles of culture, educate them in our original sense of logic and story and ensure that they would still be able to function in the larger world. . . . [S]he managed to re-create in me a deep sense of hope for the future, as well as national pride, social conscience, fairness and a tenacious will" (viii). Maracle's description of her own mother's sense of household management reveals the roots of the type of social, economic, and community justice in which Maracle believes: "Our mother insisted that those who eat must work, those who work are entitled to participate in the general management of the family and those who participate must be prepared to make intelligent choices about their lives and family context" (viii). She speaks also of learning important lessons from her great-grandmother, T'a'ah, "whose eyes spoke love, discipline and wisdom when words failed" (ix) and from a host of elders.

While writing in the context of her own life, not every story in the book is her own. She tells the stories of other people she has known (mostly women and children), but the emotions are shared emotions. As she notes: "Through all the stories runs a common thread: for us racism is not an ideology in the abstract, but a very real and practical part of our lives. The pain, the effect, the shame are tangible, measurable and murderous" (4). She takes the stories of her own life and of others' lives "and added some pure fabrications of my imagination, rewriting them as my own" (5). She is forthright in describing her process in creating this autobiographical text: "Rather than distorting the facts, I have altered their presentation. They are presented as I saw them, from my own emotional, spiritual and visual perspective. To be faithful to my view I have put myself as the central figure in all the lives recounted here. If I was not really there, it does not matter. I have eyes and I can see" (5). While telling her own life story, she also includes stories from the lives of others. She acknowledges that the grandmother in the book "is a composite of a number of old Native women I have known" (6). While Stoll criticized Menchú for telling the lives of others through her own eyes, Maracle recognizes, in her forthright description of her autobiographical production, the influence of storytelling traditions. Her "If I was not really there, it does not matter. I have eyes and I can see" is a preemptive strike against critics like Stoll who might challenge her text.

Like many of the Latin American women involved in the production of *testimonios*, Maracle writes in the service of liberation. She recognizes that the path is not an easy one; in fact, she admits she "sometimes feel[s] like a foolish young grandmother armed with a teaspoon, determined to remove three mountains from the path to liberation: the mountain of racism, the mountain of sexism and the mountain of nationalist oppression" (x). She stresses the difficulties of working for change when "we did not create this history, we had no say in any of the conditions into which we were born (nor did our ancestors), yet we are saddled with the responsibility for altering those conditions and re-building our nations" (x). She acknowledges that often "it is difficult to critically examine our current condition while the power to alter or maintain it rests outside ourselves" (xi). Her writings fall into the category of resistance literature, literature that draws attention to itself as a political and politicized activity, literature that affirms Native cultural and political identity over and against the dominant culture.

In *Sojourner's Truth*, as in *Bobbi Lee: Indian Rebel*, Maracle calls on her readers to participate in social, political, and cultural change. At the end of her preface, she explains: "In the writing of these stories I tried very hard to draw the reader into the centre of the story, in just the same way the listener of our oral stories is drawn in. At the same time the reader must remain central to the working out of the drama of life presented. As listener/reader, you become the trickster, the architect of great social transformation at whatever level you choose" (13). Maracle reminds readers of their responsibilities to effect social change. In all of her publications, Maracle strives to express the harsh realities of life for Indigenous people in Canada, to critique Canadian society, and to plant seeds in her readers that she hopes will blossom forth to create a better Canada, a better world.

Maracle takes her responsibilities as a Native writer seriously. She reminds us, in her 2000 interview with Fee and Gunew, that "[w]hen I lay a word down on that page, some tree had to perish and that tree is my relative, and I believe that. . . . Words are sacred, just like that tree. I took a life so that this book could exist" (213–14). Maracle sees herself as standing "between my infinite grandchildren and my infinite grandmothers. The farther . . . backward in time I go, the more grandmothers I have. The farther forward, the more grandchildren. And I am obligated to the whole lineage: this lineage holds up the spirit of all things—trees, flora, fauna, human" (214–15). She writes for her infinite grandchildren and her infinite grandmothers, but also for the rest of the world: "I thought of the whole country as my audience, the whole world as my audience. That the whole word and the whole country doesn't read me is not my problem" (213).

In the same interview, she explains that she and Jeannette Armstrong (Okanagan) "both believe that we must be able to deliver the culture in English as well as in our own languages, that it will take time to recover our languages" (217). Because Maracle is not sure that her people will be successful in recovering their language, she tries to take a traditional story or ceremony, and create "story from it, like a mythmaker, create new myths out of the old myths, directly from the old myths" (218). What she calls her journey is "to master this language and turn it to account to make it work for us" (218).

And in her own work on literature by First Nations women of Canada, Agnes Grant argues that the question we must ask of these texts is precisely that, whether the language "works to good effect, whether it communicates, whether it moves readers, whether it makes them see Canadian society through another person's eyes" (125). Both Maracle's testimonial work *Bobbi Lee: Indian Rebel* and Sterling's autobiographical novel *My Name Is Seepeetza*, like the testimonial works by women in Latin America, meet that challenge and more as they struggle to overcome the violence of epistemological enforcement that has ignored, yet often appropriated, the cultural contributions of First Nations people. As Kateri Damm states, in analyzing autobiographical works by two other authors (Maria Campbell and Beatrice Culleton), these works "present an alterNative perspective of the history of Canada and in so doing, affirm and preserve Native views, Native realities, and Native forms of telling, while actively challenging and redefining dominant concepts of history, truth and fact" ("Dispelling" 95). Just as Ana María Shua and Nélida Piñon propose alternate histories of their nations, Maracle and Sterling present readers with other views of Canadian history, truth, and fact via their powerful autobiographical manifestos or *testimonios*.

6 / "Part of Surviving Is through Remembering":
The Ethics and Politics of Life Narratives about
Indian Residential School Experiences

Shirley Sterling's 1992 *My Name Is Seepeetza* is an autobiographical first
novel that tells the story of an Interior Salish girl in British Columbia
who is sent to an Indian residential school where her name is changed,
all aspects of her Native identity denied. While telling the story of one
young girl, *My Name Is Seepeetza* speaks to the racism and oppression
encountered by Native children taken from their families and communities and sent to Indian boarding schools throughout Canada and the
United States.

Shirley Sterling's autobiographical novel is one that bears out Charlotte
Abbott's claim in a program on National Public Radio about the blurry
line between autobiographical first novels and memoirs. Abbott, the
"Book News" editor at *Publisher's Weekly* who was interviewed for a
May 21, 2006, story called "Flipping through the Pages at Book Expo
America," argues that "[t]hat line between fact and fiction has always
been a little blurry and where before people told their stories through
fiction, now it's more often through sort of fictionalized memoir. So
publishers aren't going to back away from that genre—it's too much in
the grain of our culture." Her claim that autobiographical novels and
memoirs (and other works on that blurry continuum) are too much in
the grain of our culture echoes claims by Smith and Watson about the
everyday nature of autobiography in our contemporary lives.

But while I consider *My Name Is Seepeetza* to be an autobiographical
novel, it is testimonial in many respects. Borrowing again from Yúdice's

definition of testimonial literature, we can see Sterling using "her own experience as representative of a collective memory and identity," as stressed in the dedication to her book: "To all those who went to the residential schools, and those who tried to help, may you weep and be made free. May you laugh and find your child again. May you recover the treasure that has been lost, the name that gives your life meaning, the mythology by which you can pick up and rebuild the shattered pieces of the past" (7).[1] For Sterling, writing—and perhaps for Native readers, reading—the novel is to be cathartic, to recover and release strong emotions buried deep in the psyche. The emotions are felt not as past, but as present ones, as trauma makes itself felt on and through the body long after the original incident has happened. Sterling and others who suffered through abuses (physical, psychological, sexual, and emotional) in the residential schools carry scars that might be recognized and soothed in part through the writing and reading of testimonial works.

A winner of the British Columbia Book Award for Children's Literature that was also short-listed for a Governor General's Award, *My Name Is Seepeetza* has had an impact on readers who are residential school survivors. In an article on her work in a University of British Columbia publication, Sterling recognizes that "[s]ome people who lived in residential schools have the book, but wait two or three years before they have the courage to read it" (Wilson 1), and reports that "[t]he comment I most often hear is 'I thought I was the only one who felt that way.' It opens up feelings that have been silent for 20, 30, or 40 years" (1). We can see how Sterling's presentation of her own experience is received as representative of a collective memory and identity (another aspect of *testimonio*).

Writing the book was a revelatory process for Sterling as well. In "Seepeetza Revisited: An Introduction to Six Voices," Sterling notes that "in many ways, writing the novel was a process of discovery for me. Some of the incidents surprised me as did the new point of view I gained as a result. For instance, I realized that my father, by giving me my real name before the rite of passage would have allowed it, gave me a lasting sense of my cultural identity. It was something that could not be taken from me" (8). Writing the autobiographical text allows Sterling the opportunity, as an adult, to examine her childhood experiences and learn culturally specific lessons about her Native heritage that then enable her to connect her own struggles to those of her community. Writing the life narrative also allowed Sterling to release emotions she was not free to release at the time of the events described. As she notes, "I did the child's weeping for her, calling out, 'Please don't leave,' in front of a computer, decades after hearing Mum's footsteps fading down the long hall" (11). As Diana Taylor reminds us: "Trauma makes evident that memory is stored in the body not just as visual memory or as written input, but also as kinetic function. . . . Trauma makes itself felt live—as embodied and present" (54). In writing the story of herself as a child in the Indian residential school, Sterling feels—as embodied and present—the traumas of those years. But the telling and retelling offer her a way of coping as well. Sterling finds seeds for survival, for herself and for her Nlakapamux people, in the telling of her story. As Sterling explains, "Writing the story of the child Seepeetza was a way to peel back the fetid layers of labels and names and awful experiences imposed on her, and in turn, sometimes created by her, over many years. I discovered that the incarcerated child had something for me, a story and an image and a handshake, a poem even, and a wonderful energy and love I would have not dreamed possible. I admire the way she spoke honestly, holding to her heart the real and lasting treasure of the Nlakapamux way, the way of honouring the family" (11). Sterling's description of what the incarcerated child had for her, the adult woman recalling the experiences of the young girl, includes "a wonderful energy and love I would not have dreamed possible." Sterling's use of love recalls Craig Womack's characterization of love, in another context, as something that "is not trivially universalizing but fully contextualized within an awareness of the colonization process. Love, in Harjo's work [and I would add in Sterling's and in Lee Maracle's], is also an act of resistance. . . . part of the spirit of resistance that has kept Indian people alive these last five hundred years as they have stood against the forces of colonization" (259). The love Sterling and Maracle feel for others, as well as for their younger selves (as they write autobiographical works), is part of that resistance. The ability to cultivate the art of living and loving while in pursuit of change is itself a political act (Braidotti 268).

Writing *My Name Is Seepeetza* is a process of self-discovery for Sterling as well as an opportunity to examine issues of "language, and history, of voice and representation and appropriation, of institutional racism, of re-socialization programs, and genocide" (Sterling, "Seepeetza Revisited" 12). Sterling's autobiographical acts, in writing both *My Name Is Seepeetza* and "Seepeetza Revisited," can be seen as therapeutic interventions, examples of what Suzette Henke refers to as "scriptotherapy." Writing about trauma can be a process through which the author "finds words to give voice to what was previously unspeakable" (Smith and Watson, *Reading* 22). In "Seepeetza Revisited," Sterling directly addresses the therapeutic or cathartic effects of writing about her residential school experiences.

But the writing (or reading) of *My Name Is Seepeetza* is more than catharsis for Sterling (and those of her readers who are also survivors of the residential schools). By tracing back the aspects of colonization that have had a direct impact on her life, Sterling gains insight into both how she has been constructed as a colonized subject of the Canadian state and how she can resist that construction. For as Gloria Bird (Spokane) asserts, "writing remains more than a catharsis; at its liberating best, it is a political act. Through writing we can undo the damaging stereotypes that are continually perpetuated about Native peoples. We can rewrite our history, and we can mobilize our future" (30). Neal McLeod (Cree) also asserts that "part of surviving is through remembrance: when you remember, you know your place in creation" (17). The connection between remembering and surviving is an important aspect of testimonial literature, and highlighting the testimonial aspects of *My Name Is Seepeetza* here helps us to understand the text as a political act, a narrative act of resistance and decolonization. Rosi Braidotti's assertion that "[e]thics includes the acknowledgement of and compassion for pain, as well as the activity of working through it. Any process of change must do some sort of violence to deeply engrained habits and dispositions which got consolidated in time" (267) reminds us that *My Name Is Seepeetza* and other narratives of the Indian residential school experience are ethical works.

The examination of institutional racism and genocide highlights another testimonial aspect of *My Name Is Seepeetza*: its effort to summon truth in the cause of denouncing the situation of exploitation and oppression in the Indian residential schools. From the early days of colonization, European missionaries sought to transform Indian peoples according to their own Christian and European ideals. Roman Catholic missionaries in New France wanted not only to convert the Native peoples they encountered to the Catholic faith, but also to civilize them per the standards of French culture. By the 1630s, they had built a residential school for Huron children at Quebec City (Furniss 17). Church-run schools, many of them day schools, had spread throughout Canada by the mid-1850s. The residential school system started in earnest in the late 1870s, after the passage of the Indian Act in 1876 made Native people wards of the government. Residential schools in Canada operated through a partnership between the state and a variety of churches. The government was to provide core funding, set certain standards, supervise the administration of the schools, and take care of its wards. The churches (a number of Catholic orders as well as Anglican, Methodist, and Presbyterian churches) had more local control of their own schools. From 1920, subsequent to amendments to the Indian Act, Canadian law required that all Native children go to residential schools, where they were to be "civilized," either assimilated into white culture or at least have their own culture stripped from them. Residential schools continued throughout most of the twentieth century, with the last one in British Columbia, the St. Mary's Indian Residential School in Mission, closing in 1985, and the last government-run residential school in Canada closing only in 1996. A look at works written about the residential schools in the United States and Canada—both historical accounts and first-person narrations of individual experiences—shows that children died in great numbers from disease, accidents, and neglect, that the discipline was harsh, the food was usually poor and never sufficient, and that many children suffered cultural, emotional, physical, and sexual abuses.[2] As Seepeetza writes succinctly in her journal: "I don't like school. We have to come here every September and stay until June. My dad doesn't like it either, but he says it's the law. All status Indian kids have to go to residential schools" (13).

Like the titles of some of the more well-known testimonial works by Latin American women mentioned above (most notably *Me llamo Rigoberta Menchú y así me nació la conciencia* but also "*Si me permiten hablar . . .*" *Testimonio de Domitila, una mujer de las minas de Bolivia*),[3] the title of Sterling's text is an affirmation of identity and an assertion of her real name. On the cover of the book *My Name Is Seepeetza*, all the letters of "Seepeetza" are capitalized, making the affirmation even more emphatic. The statement is a reclamation of her own name, the name she was given by her family, by her beloved father, not the unbidden "Martha Stone" she was called in the residential school.[4] Sterling's choice of a title underscores Valery Smith's claim that autobiography "underscores the importance of naming oneself and shaping one's own story" (153). The great-grandmother in Lee Maracle's *Daughters Are Forever* similarly stresses the importance of choosing your own names. In speaking of the white man's language, she asserts: "This language has so many nasty sounds in it. The good part is white men never did wholeheartedly settle on the names they gave life's beings. So they gave them many names. The trick is to choose carefully the names you use" (185). Sterling chooses carefully the name she uses, reclaiming her Native name, her "real name" given to her by her father, the name that gives her "a lasting sense of [her] cultural identity" ("*Seepeetza* Revisited" 8).

"The Work Is 'Fictionalized.' . . . The Voice Is Mine": Seepeetza's Journal

Sterling's autobiographical novel is written in the form of a journal, with dated entries, in the voice of a young schoolgirl. It is not an auto-biography in which an adult self discusses childhood events from the adult perspective, but rather an attempt to re-create or recapture the perspective and the voice of the young girl Seepeetza/Martha Stone, the focalizer throughout the text. The journal is a repository of stories from her childhood that helps the adult Sterling piece together her life and her identity. Like Martha Stone, who attended the fictionalized Kalamak Indian Residential School, Shirley Sterling attended the Kamloops Indian Residential School (which operated from 1893 to 1977). Sterling, in "Seepeetza Revisited," explains: "The work is 'fictionalized' because Martha could not remember exactly what she did on Thursday, October 23, 1958, but the incidents are based on real experiences. The brown parcel is real. Martha Stone is real. The voice is mine" (7). That Sterling claims not just the incidents but the voice as her own is significant to our discussion of voice in testimonial and autobiographical texts.

We learn about Seepeetza through her diary entries but also through the two hand-drawn and hand-lettered maps that precede the first diary entry. One is of the ranch where the protagonist lived with her family prior to being sent away to school, and one is of the school property. The first map is labeled "Joyaska Ranch by Seepeetza"; the second, "School Map by Martha Stone" (8–9; see figures 6 and 7). The labels stress the split identity she experienced: Martha Stone at school, Seepeetza at home on the ranch.

The items drawn in on the maps are those important to the young girl. On the map of the ranch, we see not only "our house," the wood shed, the outhouse, the barn, large corral, small corral, well, granary, and blacksmith, but also "Dad's truck," "trees where the cows have their calves," "Jimmy's secret strawberry patch," "Missy's picnic spot," the "dead calf tree," and "animal graves." There is an intimacy to the draw-ing, a sense that sites of nature are personalized, made special (perhaps almost sacred),[5] by their connections with the occupants of the ranch, both human and animal—"trees where the cows have their calves" or "Missy's picnic spot." The lines of the ranch drawing have more curves: the creek meanders, the trail to the river is not straight, the old fence zigzags, the trees are in bunches.

The school map, by contrast, is more strictly ordered, organized, full of straight lines and carefully lined up items. The map is mostly of buildings and roads; the only representatives of the natural world are the trees unnaturally placed in strict rows in the orchard or the one straight line of maple trees in front of the main school building. Divisions are carefully marked: old classrooms, new classrooms; boys' side, girls' side. While the ranch drawing gives the impression that all of the ranch was open to and celebrated by the children, on the school drawing it is clear that different areas were designated for separate approved activities.[6]

The first diary entry, dated "Thursday, September 11, 1958, Kalamak Indian Residential School," supports the impression created by the maps. Her description of the journal as a class assignment also reflects the split identity:

> Today my teacher Mr. Oiko taught us how to write journals. You have to put the date and the place at the top of the page. Then you write about what happens during the day. I like journals because I love writing whatever I want. Mr. Oiko says a good way to start is to talk about yourself, where you live, your age, grade, what kind of family you have. (11)

The Native children must be taught, by their non-Native teacher, the proper conventions to follow in writing their journals. They are taught the genre and are expected to conform to certain standards of style. Yet Seepeetza senses an opportunity for freedom and resistance in the assignment as well. While she starts by following the suggested form, introducing herself—"My name is Martha Stone. I am twelve years old in grade six at the Kalamak Indian Residential School" [11], she later reveals her plan "to write secret journals for a year. . . . I'll write a short one every day for Mr. Oiko. Then in Thursday library time and on weekends when Sister Theo is busy I'll write this one in a writing tablet titled arithmetic" (12).

Thus from the first entry we know that the diary we read is a secret journal, an act of narrative resistance. Expressing her true feelings has to be a secret activity, an act of transgression, as she lives under a system of censorship. As she explains: "I'll get in trouble if I get caught.

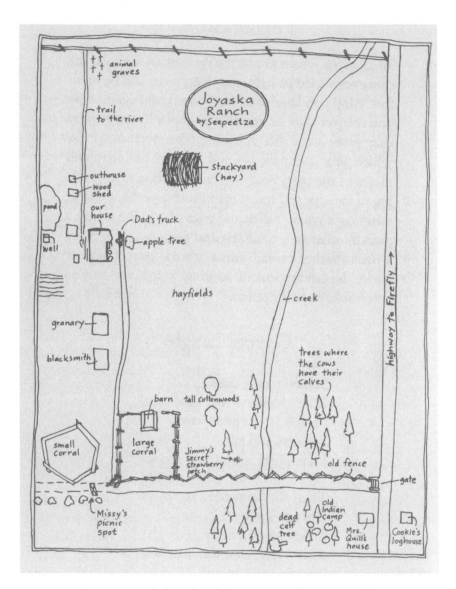

FIGURE 6. Seepeetza includes a hand-drawn map of her beloved home, Joyaska Ranch, in her journal about life in the Indian residential school. *My Name Is Seepeetza*. Copyright © 1992 by Shirley Sterling. First published in Canada by Groundwood Books Ltd. Reprinted by permission of the publisher.

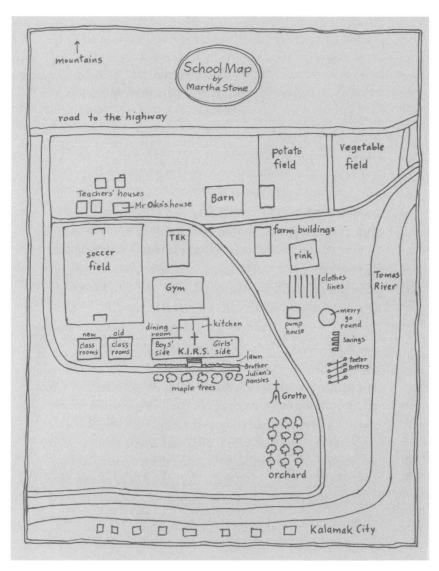

FIGURE 7. In contrast, when she draws the map of the school, she uses not her Native name, Seepeetza, but rather Martha Stone, the name she is given at school. *My Name Is Seepeetza.* Copyright © 1992 by Shirley Sterling. First published in Canada by Groundwood Books Ltd. Reprinted by permission of the publisher.

Sister Theo checks our letters home. We're not allowed to say anything about the school. I might get the strap, or worse. Last year some boys ran away from school because one of the priests was doing something bad to them. The boys were caught and whipped. They had their heads shaved and they had to wear dresses and kneel in the dining room and watch everybody eat. They only had bread and water for a week. Everybody was supposed to laugh at them and make fun of them but nobody did" (12–13). The passage describes the physical and emotional abuse heaped onto boys who had run away to escape what is implied sexual abuse by one of the priests at the school. These various forms of abuse were common in the residential schools.

In addition to introducing herself, Seepeetza describes life in the residential school, detailing the division of the school into grades, into different dormitories and recreation rooms, adding, "We're not allowed to leave our own rec or dorm except for meals" (12). That she explains that dormitories are called "dorms" and recreation rooms are called "recs" emphasizes the foreignness of the residential school culture to the young Nlakapamux girl.

The activities and behaviors of the students are closely monitored, with no allowance for family affection or interaction. Seepeetza's description of supervised meals in the dining hall, with a wall separating the boys' side from the girls' side, is particularly poignant: "One of the Sisters watches us eat, but not when we walk back to our recs. That's when my sisters Dorothy and Missy and I sometimes hold hands as we walk down the hall. It's the happiest part of my day" (12). The age difference between the sisters keeps them apart most of the time, and they must sneak these unsupervised moments of affection and connection in an alienating world.

In the first diary entry, Seepeetza also contrasts life at home, where "we can ride horses, go swimming at the river, run in the hills, climb trees and laugh out loud and holler yahoo anytime we like and we won't get in trouble" (13–14), with life at the residential school, where "we get punished for talking, looking at boys in church, even stepping out of line," and she ends the first diary entry with the bald statement, "I wish I could live at home instead of here" (14).

In the third journal entry, Seepeetza describes when her parents took her to the residential school for the first time. "We drove for a long time" stresses the distance, literally the geographical distance but also the cultural distance, between their ranch and the residential school. When her mother leaves her in the school with the nuns, "I looked at her walking away from me. I heard her footsteps echoing, and I was so scared I felt like I had a giant bee sting over my whole body. Then I stopped feeling anything" (17). The short, stark "Then I stopped feeling anything" carries a powerful emotional punch, with the author using conciseness as a form of understatement.

As it is assumed that all Indian children are dirty, all the new girls are lined up to have coal oil put in their hair "to kill nits and lice, even though we didn't have them" (18), given baths and haircuts ("Sister Theo says long straight hair makes us look like wild Indians" [32]) and dressed in matching smocks, bloomers, and undershirts. Their own clothes and things are taken away from them and locked in a storage room. The zealousness and devastation of the assimilationist policies of the Indian residential school system are revealed throughout Seepeetza's story.

When she is first asked her name by one of the nuns, she answers, "my name is Seepeetza. Then she got really mad like I did something terrible. She said never to say that word again" (18). From then on she is Martha Stone.[7] As part of the assimilationist policies of the Indian residential school system, Native children were not allowed to use their Native names, a proscription that had an impact on the use of those names even in their own homes, with their own families. Seepeetza explains that her father gave her her Indian name, naming her "after an old lady who died a long time ago. My dad laughs sometimes when he says my name, because it means White Skin or Scared Hide. It's a good name for me because I get scared of things, like devils" (77). She also knows the names of her siblings: "Jimmy is Kyep-kin, Coyote Head, because he sings a lot. Dorothy is Qwileen meaning Birch Tree because she worries about trees. Missy is Kekkix meaning Mouse Hands and Benny is Hop-o-lox-kin" (78). But, as Seepeetza explains in her journal: "We don't use our Indian names much. My parents know we would get in trouble at school if we used them there" (78). Sterling's choice to title her novel *My Name Is Seepeetza* (and to claim the Native names of her siblings) is thus a conscious reclamation of her Native name, a rejection of her white name and of the racist ideology of the residential school.

In the residential school, Seepeetza is not only called by a name she does not recognize as her own, but she is given a number, 43, that she had to stitch into all her clothes. Identification by numbers was common practice in the residential school system, underscoring the impersonal and institutionalized aspects of a system established in order to do away with Indigenous lifeways, assimilating Indian children out of "savagery" and into "Christianity" and "civilization," as defined by Euro-Canadians.

The brutality of the system is also revealed in the violence inflicted on Seepeetza and the other children by the nuns in the residential school. When Seepeetza is too frightened by the nuns' stories of devils under her bed to get up at night to use the bathroom, she wets her bed and, in the morning, gets punished: "Sister Superior strapped me. I had to wear a sign to the dining room saying, I am a dirty wetbed" (19). The threat of violence is constant in the residential school. The sister who is supervisor of an older grade "uses judo on the girls to make them obey" (42). Sister Theo gives Seepeetza the strap for forgetting her towel (83): "Sister Superior carries the strap in her sleeve all the time. It looks like a short thick leather belt with a shiny tip. When someone is bad Sister Superior makes them put their hands out, palms up. Then she hits their hands with the strap usually about ten times. When you get used to it, it doesn't hurt that much but your hands sting, and you can't help crying" (18). Seepeetza and the other Indigenous children have to "get used to" the physical violence in the residential school, but she does not forget that "[m]y mum and dad never hit us" (83).

Seepeetza also recalls an incident in which Sister Theo entered her tub room when Seepeetza was preparing to take a bath.

> She told me to get my clothes off and get in the water. I wouldn't. I will not let anyone see me without my clothes on. When she yelled at me to take my bloomers off and get in the tub I looked at the DANGER sign up where the electricity switches are. She saw it too. I was thinking that if she made me do it I would wait till she left, climb up on the pipe, touch the switch and get electrocuted. We stared at each other. Then she opened the door and went out.
>
> I took off my bloomers and climbed in the tub. My hands were shaking for a long time. We're not supposed to look at the Sisters like that. (83)

The psychological violence, the impending sexual violence, and the threatened physical violence of this scene are made even more powerful by the simple language and sentence structure—"We stared at each other. Then she opened the door and went out."

Not to be obscured by the simple language is Seepeetza's strength and courage as a young girl, willing to stand up to the nun's threatened violence, and then again, as an adult willing to face the memories of her trauma. McLeod argues that the survivors of the Indian residential schools "are modern day *okicitawak* (Worthy Men— 'warriors'). Instead of fighting in the world, they fight against the memories of these schools that linger in the landscapes of their souls" (29).[8]

In the residential school, Seepeetza suffers not only at the hands of the nuns, but also in the hands of the bigger girls, particularly a bully named Edna. While the nuns and other teachers look down on her as Indian, the other Native children torment her because she has green eyes, calling her a "dirty shamah" (20). With a paternal great-grandfather who was Irish, she has mixed features, a circumstance that prevents her from having many friends in the residential school (29). The bullying among the schoolchildren might be interpreted as the rage against whites being expressed through violence directed at each other, violence that Seepeetza finds physically and emotionally painful. While Seepeetza writes that she wishes she could hide under the water of the Tomas River and never come out, or travel a million miles into outer space and never come back (20), she resists "the temptation to be pulled under the waters of forgetfulness, to bury the pain under a river of denial" (Womack 228). Writing *My Name Is Seepeetza* and facing the pain of her residential school experiences is a resistant act, a confrontation of the legacy of colonialism.

Always being brought to task by the nuns at her school, Seepeetza wonders why it is that she has to "get into trouble so much. In class I get in trouble for daydreaming. In the rec Edna wants to beat me up because I have green eyes. White people don't like us because our clothes are old. Sister clobbers me for making dancing mistakes. The worst is that I get scared to walk to the bathroom in the dark. In the morning I feel just sick when Sister yells at me and hits me and makes me wear my wet sheet over my head in front of everyone" (84). Readers of Sterling's text can recognize that Seepeetza is punished for things beyond her control (green eyes) or natural in a young child (daydreaming in class, making mistakes in dance, being afraid of the dark when the Sisters have been telling you there are devils under your bed just waiting to drag you into hell), but Seepeetza wonders if it is her fault. The internalization of racist hatred is a nefarious, and often long-lasting, aspect of the residential school system.

Seepeetza frequently mentions being punished by the nuns for daydreaming, but explains that "I can't help it. I can't stop thinking of home. I keep remembering what it's like to go riding horses all summer and help my dad put up the hay" (35). The journal entries are full of contrasts between life at the residential school and life at home. At home, all the family talks ("in Indian," as she says), laughs, and sings while they work; at the school, the girls are not allowed to talk. At home, they have green wool blankets and brightly colored patchwork quilts made by their mother to keep them warm. At school, the blankets are grey and Seepeetza is always cold on winter nights. Each fall when Seepeetza returns to the residential school, she feels something inside of her die: "it's like I get a numb feeling over my whole body and I'm hiding way down inside myself. I don't really hear or see what's going on around me. Just sort of. It's like a buzzing that's far away" (36). In order to survive the cultural alienation of the residential school, she must hide away part of her self.

The buzzing that Seepeetza refers to in the above passage brings to mind the story of Th'ówxeya, Mosquito Woman, as told by Shoysheqelwhet, Gwendolyn Point, included in the introduction to *Stolen from Our Embrace: The Abduction of First Nations Children and the Restoration of Aboriginal Communities*. The story of Th'ówxeya is a traditional Stó:lô tale told by parents to their children, to frighten them into coming home before dark. Mosquito Woman steals small children, cooks them over the fire, and eats them. In the version of the story told in the book, the older children trick Mosquito Woman, push her into the fire, and save the younger children. When she burns in the fire, instead of smoke, mosquitoes come swarming out of her burning body. Although Point was frightened by the story as a child, as an adult, she sees the story as a metaphor for the predatory European society: "Ever since the Europeans first came, our children were stolen from our embrace. . . . First the priests took our children away, to churches, schools, even back to Europe. Then the residential schools took three or four generations away; then the social workers took our children and put them in non-native foster homes" (quoted in Fournier and Crey, 7–8). Point sometimes tells the story to her Stó:lô people, reminding them that "in the evening, when the mosquitoes are the thickest, when you can hear that whine of the Th'ówxeya singing, come back to your people because you never know, there can always be another Th'ówxeya out there. But remember, the children transformed Th'ówxeya into nothing but a cloud of mosquitoes. Mosquitoes we can handle" (9).

The priests and nuns at the residential school sometimes appear as the fierce and devouring creature of the Th'ówxeya story; in fact, the nuns look like witches to the frightened children.[9] But the resistance and self-reliance taught by that traditional story also form a part of Seepeetza's character. Like the children in the story of Mosquito Woman, she has the capacity to transform those fierce characters into mosquitoes, annoying but small creatures that buzz and bite but will not destroy her. She can evade the Th'ówxeyas of the residential school by returning to her people, at least in her thoughts.

Indeed, Seepeetza comes back to her people not only in her daydreams, when she is always thinking about home, family, and the activities taking place on their ranch, but also through her journal. By writing in her secret journal about home and family, about customs, ceremonies, and traditional knowledge of her people, she demonstrates her continuing connection to those traditions and those persons, even in the alienating environment of the residential school. Seepeetza remembers her mother and aunt and grandmother joking, laughing, and telling stories as they clean berries or fish together. The telling of stories shows up repeatedly in the passages about life at home, showing how storytelling is a vital element in the life of her community. Storytelling continues to be a way of maintaining communal identification in spite of the loss and cultural degradation imposed by the residential school system. Seepeetza recalls the story that Yay-yah, her grandmother, tells about spiders, warning them not to kill spiders or there will be a thunderstorm: "She said a long time ago it was Skokki the spider who traveled to the moon and learned from the sky dwellers how to weave. That's why our people have baskets. My mum's grandmother used to make baskets out of cedar roots and chokecherry bark" (79). She notes that her mother does not make baskets, but that she does collect medicine tea from the mountains and that Yay-yah makes moccasins out of buckskin. Seepeetza's stories mark the loss of certain traditions and the continuance of others.

In Seepeetza's family and in her Native culture, we can see how stories act as vehicles of cultural transmission linking one generation to the next (McLeod 31). The residential school system disrupts that transmission, taking children away from the homes in which they were taught by the older generations in a traditional context, in order to place them in an alien environment that worked to destroy their self-esteem. While the residential school system tried to destroy Native traditions, Seepeetza's journal writing can be seen as her own attempt to continue storytelling traditions. When she is home with her family over Christmas, writing in her journal, she sees her grandmother (who is mending a pair of beaded gloves) watching her and tells her grandmother that she is writing a story: "She chuckled and went back to her sewing" (49). Her grandmother's chuckles accept and affirm an activity forbidden in the residential school.

In her forbidden journal, Seepeetza makes reference to various traditional activities, for example, how her mother dries the fish "on little wooden racks in the sun with a small fire underneath to keep bees off" (14–15) or how her parents always take meat to older members of the community when they visit (66). She recounts how her father spears fish in the river (88) or how her mother can make a fish trap out of willow switches and twine, a skill her mother learned from her own grandmother when she was still a child (89). Her memories of her mother, father, grandmother, and other family members provide her with beliefs and values other than those the residential school attempts to instill in her. Seepeetza recalls her mother saying that "her grandmother, Quaslametko, didn't want her and her brothers and sisters to go to school, because school would turn them into white people. They wouldn't be able to hunt or fish or make baskets or anything useful anymore" (30).

Seepeetza also recounts occasional episodes from the residential school in which she and others maintain and enact traditional cultural activities. In her entry of November 20, 1958, she writes of burying a doll in the playground, one of the old dolls that someone in town had donated to the school. Seepeetza buries her doll to keep it safe from the cold. Another girl sees her burying the doll and comes over and tells Seepeetza that she is a grandmother and has stsa-wen: "I was surprised to hear her say that word. It means dried fish. I thought only we knew that word from home. She handed me an old dried piece of pine wood and told me to sit on the ground to eat my stsa-wen" (37–38). Seepeetza recounts that the girl surprised her "by talking Indian. We're not supposed to. She ordered me to eat all my fish just like she was a real grandmother" (38–39). In their short, whispered conversation, the other girl asks Seepeetza if they ate dried salmon as well. When they see the nun coming, they throw away the wood and run back into the school. The two girls pretend to share traditional food—dried salmon—and to act out the familial roles of grandmother and grandchild. Although their traditional practices are forbidden in the residential school, the girls sometimes find moments to enact these traditions in secret, resisting the rules imposed on them in the school. The girls' use of their Native language, as well as Sterling's use of that language intermittently in the journal entries, is another site of resistance. As Neal McLeod (Cree) reminds us, "Every time a story is told, every time one word of an Indigenous language is spoken, we are resisting the destruction of our collective memory" (31).

Although Seepeetza lives and studies in the residential school, she does not always understand the values and judgments of the white society. In speaking of her admiration of her father, who is not just a rancher, but also a court interpreter, Seepeetza remarks: "He speaks lots of Indian languages, but he won't teach us. Mum won't either. She says the nuns and priests will strap us. I wonder why it's bad" (36). While she does not understand the white society imposed on her in the residential school, her journal entries show that she maintains a strong sense of her own Native identity. She explains that the "Indians in the movies are not like anyone I know. Real Indians are just people like anyone else except they love the mountains" (90). She remembers her family's tradition of gathering with other families late in the summer in the mountains at Tekameen Summit to camp, tell stories, pick berries, and hunt for deer. In reflecting on their traditions, she proclaims: "There is something really special about being mountain people. It's a feeling like you know who you are, and you know each other. You belong to the mountains" (91). She values the time spent with the "old people like Yay-yah" who "smile at you and tell you something about the trail you're following or show you how to cover your berries with leaves so they stay fresh" (91). The time spent with her family and the elders has given her the strength of her own traditions, a sense of belonging that sustains her even in the residential school, where her Native identity is not valued.

Seepeetza's experience at the residential school highlights the valorization of certain ethnic identities and the rejection of others. While the ethnicities of the First Nations are not valued, Seepeetza and other classmates are taught to perform Irish dances, in costume ("green kilts with big silver pins, white satin shirts, black sequined boleros, black dance slippers and green hats" [73]), for the entertainment of (presumably white) Canadian audiences. Seepeetza usually does the sailor's hornpipe, the Highland fling, the Irish jig, and the fairy reel, and reports that "Sister makes us smile all the time we are dancing. If we don't she punches us on the back or hits us with the shilayley. That's an Irish walking stick and I don't know how to spell it" (63). The Irish culture is yet another foreign culture imposed on Seepeetza. Older children in her school "do a Ukrainian dance, a garland dance, the tarantella which is an Italian dance, a Mexican dance, a Danish dance, a Spanish dance and other Irish dances" (73). The valorization of European cultures is notable.

Seepeetza comments in her diary that Father Sloane took pictures of them dancing in their costumes at the Irish concert: "It was funny because I was smiling in those pictures. I looked happy. How can I look happy when I am scared all the time?" (36–37; see figure 8). She experiences a sense of dislocation in looking at the pictures, as the pictures present an identity and an emotion she does not recognize as her own.

At the Christmas concert, Seepeetza and her classmates are forced to lip-synch and dance to a record played offstage. Told by their teacher to wear tight skirts and pullover sweaters, they have to pretend to sing "Wake Up Little Suzy. . . . On stage we had to line up in a half circle and snap our fingers like Elvis and dance in place to the music. Half the girls couldn't keep time, and we were all scared to look jazzy. The song seemed to go on and on and on. I could feel the sweat on my face and I didn't know where to look. I never felt so stupid in my whole life" (43). The passage reflects the severe discomfort felt by Seepeetza and the other girls when forced to perform an identity not their own. While the dance concerts are perhaps the most dramatic (and dramatized) example, the entire residential school system imposed a foreign identity on the children on a daily and hourly basis. As we read the diary entries, we are given the opportunity to view Canadian society and, in particular, the residential school system through the eyes of Seepeetza. Her gaze defamiliarizes and denaturalizes the world of adults, especially of white adults. The autobiographical narrative explores the complex processes through which the Salish Nation child is to be turned into a subject of the Canadian state. A careful reading of the text thus serves to reveal how becoming an adult Canadian citizen requires the interiorization and naturalization of a racist ideology.

Seepeetza's last journal entry, August 27, 1959, is written when she is preparing to return to the residential school after a summer at home on her family's ranch. She has decided to leave her secret journal at home and will ask her grandmother to make a beaded buckskin cover for it. Among the First Nations of British Columbia, the making and use of beaded articles serves as an important marker of cultural identity and a commitment to cultural continuity. The giving of beaded gifts reaffirms kinship ties, and often grandmothers bead bags and ceremonial garments for grandchildren (Duncan 106, 109).

The image Seepeetza will ask her grandmother to bead on the buckskin cover of her journal is fireweed. Just before coming to this decision, she had hiked up a mountain with her family: "When we got to the top of the trail we saw thousands of purply-pink flowers all together in the tall grass along the creek. We stopped and looked at it for awhile because it was so pretty. 'Fireweed,' said Dad" (124). She selects the fireweed as a beautiful image from home, one that reminds her of her connection to her mountain people.

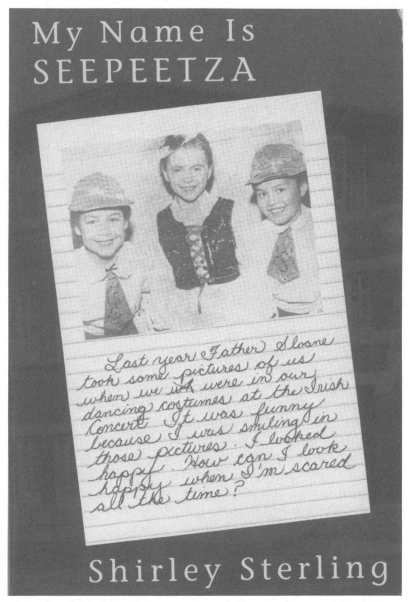

My Name Is
SEEPEETZA

Last year Father Sloane took some pictures of us when we wh were in our dancing costumes at the Irish Concert. It was funny because I was smiling in those pictures. I looked happy. How can I look happy when I'm scared all the time?

Shirley Sterling

FIGURE 8. The cover photo from the book shows Seepeetza in her dancing costume, along with a handwritten entry that includes the poignant question, "How can I look happy when I'm scared all the time?" Seepeetza's photo and her diary entry highlight the split between the exterior and interior of the person. *My Name Is Seepeetza.* Copyright © 1992 by Shirley Sterling. First published in Canada by Groundwood Books Ltd. Reprinted by permission of the publisher.

"A Message the World Needs to Hear"

Deanna Reder has proposed fireweed as an appropriate metaphor to describe Native autobiography and autobiographical fiction in Canada, asserting that "the First Nations autobiography ought to be seen as fireweed, the textual equivalent of the relentlessly enduring perennial that is first to appear in earth, scarred by fire, ironically spreading 'like wildfire'" (277). Describing it as "a striking, scrappy and troublesome weed," she writes that it is an appropriate symbol for Canadian Native autobiography because the genre, like fireweed, "grows out of many different, disturbed landscapes, beautiful and relentlessly enduring," and while the two do not celebrate the destructiveness of the fire, they are "undeniably the result of it" (277). Reder's idea to use fireweed as metaphor for Native autobiography in Canada comes, in part, from her reading of these final pages of *My Name Is Seepeetza*.

Readers of *My Name Is Seepeetza* are left with this vision of the journal written in English by the child sent to boarding school, lovingly encased in a traditional art form practiced by her grandmother. The hybridity highlighted in this final image is characteristic of what many critics have written about the genre of Indian women's autobiography as already hybrid, drawing on both the written tradition of Euro-American autobiography and the traditions of Native orature (Lundgren 71). Gretchen Bataille and Kathleen Sands point out that Indian women's autobiographies commonly convey "the connectedness of all things, of personal life flow, and episodes often are not sequential but linked thematically to establish a pattern of character developing through the response to private experience" (8). The thematic rather than sequential links are common to Seepeetza's narrative, a characteristic apparently at odds with the journal format.

By choosing a format that would seem to require a linear chronology, and then subverting that linear chronology, Sterling presents her readers with a text that can be interpreted as an act of narrative resistance and decolonization. Barbara Godard reminds us that "[n]arrative is a way of exploring history and questioning the historical narratives of the colonizer which have violently interposed themselves in place of the history of the colonized. Experimentation, especially with structures of chronology, is part of this challenge, a radical questioning of historiographical versions of the past as developed in the 'master narratives,' in order to rewrite the historical ending" (198). The breaks from linear chronology, the development by association rather than by chronological sequence, and the often colloquial tone are all elements that link Sterling's autobiographical text to Native oral traditions.

Sterling's text can also be seen as exemplifying what certain Native scholars have written about the importance of stories in Native traditions. As Kimberly Roppolo explains in her article "Towards a Tribal-Centered Reading of Native Literature: Using Indigenous Rhetoric(s) Instead of Literary Analysis," Native peoples "are taught by story, and we explain by story, not by exposition" (268). Marlene Brant Castellano notes that stories traditionally were the "primary medium used to convey aboriginal knowledge. Stories inform and entertain; they hold up models of behaviour; and they sound warnings" (31). Brant Castellano and Roppolo both stress that stories "teach without being intrusive, because the listener can ignore the oblique instruction or apply it to the degree he or she is ready to accept, without offence. Stories of personal experience can be understood either as personal reminiscences or as metaphors to guide moral choices and self-examination" (Brant Castellano 31).

Sterling's autobiographical text can be understood, then, as personal reminiscences—remembering her own life at Joyaska Ranch and at Kamloops Indian Residential School, which she attended from the time she was five and a half years old until her graduation from grade twelve—or it can be read as a metaphor to guide moral choices and self-examination. Part of the self-examination that can be inspired by texts like *My Name Is Seepeetza* is a reflection on the residential school policies of the United States and Canadian governments that worked to sever the connections between Indigenous children and their families, communities, and traditions. The Indian residential school system forms a part of U.S. and Canadian history we have been reluctant to examine critically, but one that demands addressing.

For the survivors of the Indian residential school system, remembering and sharing those experiences, as Sterling does in *My Name Is Seepeetza*, can be painful. In "Seepeetza Revisited," she confesses: "A book about residential school would have been the last thing I would have considered writing. I could not and did not want to remember school, and having written the book I certainly did not want to have it published. It was too close to me. People knowing all those awful things: Welcome to the tub room where a supervisor tries to bully an eight-year-old into undressing completely" (9). Sterling would have rather written something "from that safe storybook place where I live a lot of the time" (9), not something that recalled and reflected a brutal reality.

Sterling goes on to explain that the book grew out of an assignment in a creative writing course in children's literature, when the instructor asked them each to write a journal entry from when they were nine years old. She wrote from her memory of having received a parcel from home. Her instructor was impressed, told her to drop everything else and keep writing. When that instructor later suggested Sterling send the manuscript to a publisher, "I was reluctant to do so because I didn't think any publisher in Canada would take the manuscript and besides I didn't really want this particular work published" (10). Her daughter, who holds a degree in English literature, told her that the manuscript "had a message the world needs to hear" (10). While Sterling was reluctant both to write and to publish the text, she also speaks of the power of seeing the book in print, with two of her names on the front cover, and of thinking that "unborn generations of Nlakapamux children will read this book, and they will know who Yaya was and Baldy and my dad" (10). Sterling feels joy, pride, and hope at seeing her work in print and thinking of the example it can provide for children in the Salish Nation. She is aware of how her text will serve as a vehicle of cultural transmission, passing her stories on to future generations. Sharing her stories is an act of resistance against the policies of a residential school system that made concerted efforts to destroy Native stories and Native languages.

Within the world of the text, the journal written by the young girl is a secret one, as her writing is a forbidden activity for which she would have been punished by her nun-teachers. The text by the adult Seepeetza is written with the encouragement of a teacher and was granted the British Columbia Book Award in 1993. That difference does seem to indicate some degree of change in society, but *My Name Is Seepeetza* leaves many crucial questions still to be addressed. While written in simple language, in the voice of a young schoolgirl, the text highlights vital questions about the residential school system, many of which Sterling enunciates more specifically in "Seepeetza Revisited":

> In a system which separated families, how did a child gain a sense of her cultural identity or family role? How did total, blind obedience prepare a child for a life in any society outside of a military one? . . . The educator asks how such a system is supposed to prepare a child for citizenship in a society from which she is removed? How does a silenced group learn to voice opinion and guard democracy when blind obedience and prison-like conditions prevail? Most importantly, who stands to benefit from the assimilation of First Nations children? How does the present education system

contribute to on-going colonialist initiatives? How can we best combat the type of racist thinking which put together the residential schools? (12–13)

"Seepeetza Revisited" is, as the title implies, a revisiting in an adult, academic, and activist voice of the issues first touched on by the child's voice in My Name Is Seepeetza. Sterling's autobiographical project, her testimonial tendencies, and her acts of narrative resistance can be traced throughout both works.

The Indian residential school system worked to sever the connections between Native children and their homes, their families, their communities, and their cultures, between the children and all that they knew. Autobiographical writings about the Indian residential school experiences have proven to be one way for residential school survivors to reclaim a sense of home. As Neal McLeod (Cree) has said: "'To be home' means to dwell within the landscape of the familiar, a landscape of collective memories. . . . 'Being home' means to be a nation, to have access to land, to be able to raise your own children, and to have political control. It involves having a collective sense of dignity" (17). The residential schools took away the chance to dwell within the landscape of the familiar. The schools also, for many former students, resulted in a loss of access to land, a loss of ability to raise children, to have political control, and to have a collective sense of dignity. That sense of being home can, perhaps, be partially and problematically regained through the writing of testimonial and other life narratives. In this way, the autobiographical writings about the Indian residential school experiences are indeed messages the world needs to hear.

Lee Maracle and Shirley Sterling are examples of Indigenous women in the Americas who "must survive (and write) in the interval between different cultures and languages," to borrow a phrase from Françoise Lionnet (1). Their autobiographical texts explore fundamental issues such as a woman's choice of language, a woman's presentation of self in society (or societies), a woman's claiming of her own history. In their autobiographical acts, their childhood selves come alive again through the aesthetic evocation of memory. The painful parts of their pasts are felt again; as adult Indigenous women, they face that pain and locate its causes in the racist, colonialist, and patriarchal systems in which they were raised. They face, and resist, "the temptation to be pulled under the waters of forgetfulness, to bury the pain under a river of denial" (Womack 228). Their autobiographical acts are important steps in decolonizing their minds.

I read their autobiographical texts here as forms of resistance literature in which the Native women, seen as subalterns in Canadian society, take up political positions. Their autobiographical texts uncover mechanisms of oppression and discover means of resistance and survival. Maracle and Sterling offer textual inscriptions of the immersion of the self into a struggle for the people (DiNova 74).

Jeannette Armstrong has written that "[t]he dispelling of lies and the telling of what really happened until *everyone*, including our own people, understands that this condition did not happen through choice or some cultural defect on our part, is important" ("The Disempowerment" 209). The autobiographical works discussed in these chapters work to dispel lies about Native peoples in general, and Native women more particularly, by telling the stories of what really happened in the lives of the authors as young women. Both texts demonstrate a developing double consciousness on the part of the autobiographical protagonist, the double consciousness that is developed in members of a marginalized group who participate both in a dominant culture and in their own culture. As Deborah Cohn describes it: "Double consciousness is the liminality of someone who looks into the mainstream from outside and sees the ideals that the center claims to uphold but experiences instead a harsher reality. It is also the urge to self-definition against the norms by which others measure it" (40). Neither Lee Maracle nor Shirley Sterling is willing to be defined by the norms of white Canadian society; both insist on their own self-definitions in part through their autobiographical writings. Their texts reveal how they have been subject to an education that would make them subjects in the colonizers' language, beliefs, and values, while repressing their own Indigenous languages, beliefs, and values. Moving between their individual stories and the broader political and social realities in which they live, the authors show how racism affects not only individuals but society as a whole.

Craig Womack, in *Red on Red*, asserts that the tribal writer "has the moral responsibility to use writing in whatever ways possible to build that society, to strengthen the tribal nation" (258). Sterling and Maracle take that responsibility seriously in all their autobiographical writings. Their autobiographical acts of resistance give witness to their defiance of colonial oppression and to the continuing strength they draw from their Native cultures. In their writings, they recognize and value the beauty and strength of Native peoples. Their words are important because, as Jeannette Armstrong remarks, "it *is* through words, it *is* through the ability to communicate to another person, to communicate to your children the thinking of your people in the past, their history, that you *are* a people" ("Words" 25–26). Maracle and Sterling use autobiographical genres as tools to undo the process of colonization and to communicate to their children and to others their lives, their thinking, their continued existence and strength as Native peoples.

Conclusion

When we tell or write about our own lives, our stories establish our identities both as content—I am the person who did these things—and as act—I am someone with a story to tell. And we do something even more fundamental—we establish ourselves as persons: I am someone, someone who has lived a valuable life, a value affirmed precisely by any life story's implicit claim that it is worth telling and hearing.
—PAUL JOHN EAKIN, *THE ETHICS OF LIFE WRITING*

Stuart Hall has argued that identity is "a 'production' which is never complete, always in process, and always constituted within, not outside, representation" (222). In exploring identity as a production constituted within autobiographical representation, the authors discussed in this study interrogate how it is that identities and bodies perform race, gender, sexuality, ethnicity, and nationality. Their works investigate how it is that bodies might both possess and perform identities. These works encourage us to delve into questions as to how, when, and whether texts perform autobiography and how it is that readers are encouraged or discouraged to read certain texts as autobiographies. The texts I have presented in this study are not autobiographies in the most traditional sense. I have referred to these narratives variously as autobiographical fiction, fictional autobiography, autobiographical novels, semi-autobiographical novels, memoirs, and *testimonios*. But they are all texts that perform autobiography, simultaneously encouraging and discouraging us to read them as autobiographies.

These works perform autobiography in creative ways and for specific purposes. In *Cultural Agency in the Americas*, Doris Sommer affirms that culture produces agency, noting that "[w]here structures or conditions can seem intractable, creative practices add dangerous supplements that add angles for intervention and locate room for maneuver" (3). Thus, the family sagas by Ana María Shua and Nélida Piñon show us how, when the South American conditions of dictatorship seemed intractable, citizens and authors found creative practices that allowed them to add angles for intervention and locate room for maneuver. Not only were authors able to insert political commentary and critique in literary works in ways that escaped the notice of censors, but their works became some of the most telling representations of the lives lived under dictatorship. As a narrator in *The Book of Memories* reminds us, "at times a short story or a novel can help to understand or to imagine more easily a period in time than a list of names and dates that ends up forgotten or confused with the truth of what happened to the people involved" (92).

Indeed, the autobiographical genres and texts studied here can all be seen as cultural practices that constitute vehicles for change. These authors challenge the dominant discourses at work in their societies and resist the identities those discourses would seek to impose upon them. Lee Maracle and Shirley Sterling use their autobiographical works to uncover mechanisms of oppression and to promote social, political, educational, and economic change for Native peoples in Canada; Shua and Piñon propose alternative histories of their nations that signal a change from the official histories offered by dictatorial regimes of Argentina and Brazil. All four of those authors, through their very different life narratives, show how nationhood itself is a concept that promotes and preserves certain forms of injustices. Their works offer critical insights that then serve as springboards for change.

In other chapters, we have seen how Helena Parente Cunha and Luisa Futoransky challenge the discourses of gender, race, and ethnicity of their countries at the same time that they challenge the restrictive conventions of traditional autobiography. Their autobiographical metafictions highlight their struggles against "the old symbolic order with its inbuilt taboos and restrictions" (Braidotti 264). They resist concepts of identity that involve "a narrowing down of the internal complexities of a subject for the sake of social conventions" (Braidotti 266). The protagonists they inscribe in their autobiographical metafictions are examples of nonunitary subjectivity, complexity, and multiplicity.

Braidotti asserts that it is "the task of critical theory to track down . . . shifting locations and account for them through adequate figurations in politically informed cartographies that combine accountability with the quest for possible sites for resistance" (264). My readings of contemporary life narratives by women of the Americas highlight how these women use their writings to strive for more adequate figurations of the female self in politically informed cartographies that demonstrate resistance and demand accountability. My efforts in this book have been to show how their autobiographical acts of storytelling can be read as acts of narrative resistance *and* can enable acts of political resistance, in their lives, in our lives, and in our teaching.

Notes

Introduction

1. For example, Craig Womack asserts, in *Red on Red*, that the formulation of new ways of seeing and imagining are "as important a part of resistance to genocide as physical struggle" (251). There are many works by Indigenous authors who are formulating new ways of seeing and imagining in their autobiographical texts as part of their resistance to colonial oppression and genocide. Teaching these works as resisting genres can be a useful way of engaging students with a variety of issues both literary and extraliterary.

2. "Mosaic" is a term used in Canada to refer to the combination of ethnic groups, languages, and cultures that make up Canadian society. It is intended to support the idea of multiculturalism and can be opposed to the rhetoric of the melting pot in the United States, which would seem to represent assimilation. The problematic aspects of both terms are beyond the scope of my discussion here.

3. By citing Fischer on "ethnic autobiographies," I do not mean to affirm that all the authors studied here are writing what are often termed "ethnic autobiographies." As Elizabeth Cook-Lynn forcefully reminds us, "Indians . . . are not 'ethnics' in American society; rather, they are indigenous populations with a particular political, cultural, and historical status different from any other population in the United States. They have signed treaties, reserved lands and rights and resources."

1 / The Mirrored Self

1. Personal conversation with Parente Cunha.

2. In the discussion of Shirley Sterling's text in chapter 6, we shall also see how naming is an act of narrative and political resistance as Seepeetza refuses the dominant society's regime of names and the identities it compels. By entitling her autobiographical novel *My Name Is Seepeetza*, she reclaims her Native name and identity and rejects the ideology behind the Indian residential school system and the identities it seeks to compel.

3. "Se eu depende da mulher que me escreve, a autora depende de mim. Sem mim, não haverá este livro. Sem a mulher que me escreve, eu não me incorporo. E a autora não será, sem uma sem outra. A interdependência dos planos. Tudo depende de tudo" (72).

4. The slave trade in Brazil was outlawed in 1850; slavery itself was not made illegal until 1888.

5. *Candomblé* is a religion that grew out of Yoruba beliefs brought to Brazil by African slaves. *Candomblé* includes the celebration of various *orixás*, male and female, each with his/her own characteristics, favorite foods, and colors. The *orixá* referred to most often in the text is Xangô, the *orixá* of thunder and war, associated both with the black boy, the son of the cook next door in the protagonist's childhood, and with the handsome black man dressed in white with whom the adult protagonist enters into a relationship later in the text. That one of Xangô's lovers, Oxum (*orixá* of streams and rivers), carries a mirror in *candomblé* ceremonies also resonates with *Woman between Mirrors*. Recurrent references to mirrors, wind, water, thunder, lightning, cowry shells (thrown in the *jogo de búzios* to divine one's future), mango trees, lavender, basil, dance, and drums all have connections to Afro-Brazilian culture.

6. In Clarice Lispector's *Uma Aprendizagem ou O livro dos Prazeres*, the protagonist, Loreley, must also learn to touch herself before she can touch the other, or touch the world ("Mas antes precisava tocar em si própria, antes precisava tocar no mundo" [67]).

7. "Continuarei a criar a minha realidade de independência da mesma forma que inventei a minha submissão" (111).

8. "De um certo modo, sabemos o que eu vou fazer, mas não sabemos como, pois precisamos de um mínimo de coerência e verossimilhança. A minha autora nao é mais verossímil nem mais coerente do que eu" (110).

9. She is narcissistic in the sense used by Linda Hutcheon in her work *Narcissistic Narrative*.

10. The names recall the famous ballad "Frankie and Johnny." There are different versions of the ballad, its title, and its origins, but in most the woman shoots her man "'cause he was doing her wrong."

11. In Patrick White's novel *The Twyborn Affair*, writing in a diary is compared to masturbating.

12. Carlos Fuentes's *La muerte de Artemio Cruz* is also narrated in three voices (first, second, and third persons), but the three voices are not presented on each page at the same time.

13. If *Women between Mirrors* borrows from the image of Alice through the looking glass, this title for the preface of *As doze cores do vermelho* must evoke Dorothy's song "Somewhere over the Rainbow" in *The Wizard of Oz*. Parente Cunha seems to have a penchant for providing feminist re-visions of fairy tales.

14. "A campainha tocando. . . . Seu marido vai abrir a port. Quem é? Ninguém. Foi engano. Sorvetinho. Cafezinho. Pela janela você vê lá embaixo sua amiga negra entrando no carro branco" (37).

15. Tierney-Tello discusses Diamela Eltit's use of linguistic experimentalism in *Por la patria* in similar terms (95–101).

16. Gilmore discusses this phenomenon for women writers in *Autobiographics*, affirming that the autobiographical subject is not a singular unity but a web of differences

within which the subject is inscribed. She explains that the autobiographical subject is distributed between the historical self and the textual self, both of which are versions of the self who writes (85).

2 / The Self in Exile

1. All translations from Futoransky's novels, interviews, and speeches are mine.

2. Benstock's description of the experience of women in patriarchy can be extended to discussions of Native literatures. Although Native peoples may live on the land of their ancestors, their experience of colonization can also be "internalized, experienced as an exclusion imposed from the outside and lived from the inside" (20).

3. See Schwartz review in *Hispamérica*.

4. For an excellent discussion of how Kaplansky uses images of Paris "to coordinate and make coherent China's unusual and often obscured reality," see chapter 5 in Schwartz's *Writing Paris*.

5. I borrow these words from Ashcroft, Griffiths, and Tiffin's discussion of a Kipling poem (5).

6. "Los japoneses y los chinos tienen palabras ofensivas para llamar a los que no son chinos o japoneses respectivamente: henna gaijin extranjero loco en Japón y 'diablo de extranjero' en China" (21).

7. Kaplansky derives from the German *Kaplan*, an occupational name for a chaplain or curate. As a Jewish name, Kaplan was used as a translation of Cohen. Not all Jews bearing this last name are descended from the priestly caste, but are more likely to have ancestors who changed their names to Kaplan in an attempt to gain an exemption from military service at a time in the Russian empire when all other Jewish males were required to serve for twenty-five years (Hanks and Hodges, *Surnames* 289). Kaplansky is a Jewish derivative of Kaplan, with the addition of a variant of the common Polish suffix -ski, a standard adjective ending in Polish, which was very widely used in forming surnames. Thus the surname that Futoransky chooses for her protagonist is one that carries with it a history of exile and translation as well as links to a priestly status. Taking on the surname Kaplan in order to avoid military service also resonates with the Derridean reading of the surname. For these Jews, it was necessary to rename, to take on a new surname, when the name lacked the ability to exempt them from the service.

8. Berenice is a feminine name in both English and Italian, derived from the Greek name Berenike, which seems to have originated in the royal house of Macedon. Berenike is considered a Macedonian dialectal form of the Greek name Pherenike, meaning "victory bringer" (Hanks and Hodges, *First Names* 40). Berenice is also a biblical name, appearing in the New Testament as the name of the daughter of Herod Agrippa I, first married to her uncle Herod, king of Chalcis. Berenice thus carries high-status connotations of royalty and victory.

9. Beatriz is the Spanish cognate of Beatrice, itself the Italian and French form of Beatrix, an English and German form derived from a late Latin personal name, borne by a saint executed in Rome in the early fourth century. The name is believed to have come from Viatrix, a feminine version of Viator, "voyager (through life)." Viatrix was then altered by association with the Latin Beatus, "blessed," as *via-* and *bea-* were pronounced quite similarly in late Latin (Hanks and Hodges, *First Names* 37).

10. The transgression echoes that of Miguel de Unamuno's *Niebla*, in which the

protagonist traveled to Salamanca in order to discuss his future with Unamuno. The mutual recognition of character and author also reproduces Parente Cunha's *Women between Mirrors*.

11. In the paragraphs on the back cover, the protagonist is mentioned first as Laura Kaplansky and then as Luisa Kaplansky as though the identity is merging or evolving into the two references to Luisa Futoransky, writer, that follow.

12. Although not noted in Futoransky's text, the Hebrew word *Abraxas* most closely resembles in Spanish *abrazo*, hug, or perhaps *abrasar*, to burn.

13. For more on the Tower of Babel and its relationship to names, identity, and psychiatry, see Shmueli.

14. Vita Sackville-West, in a letter written to Virginia Woolf from Egypt, similarly employs the alphabet to deal with that foreign country. We will also see how Shirley Sterling and Lee Maracle frequently found it difficult to understand the cultural codes of the Anglo-Canadians living around them.

15. The gallo is cross-culturally significant as both one of the twelve animals in the Chinese horoscope and the symbol of France. In *Son cuentos chinos*, Laura Kaplansky equates herself with an old chicken: "Como en el picante de gallina. . . . China es el ají y la gallina vieja son mis cuarenta años" (36; Like the spicy chicken. . . . China is the chili pepper and at forty I am the old hen).

16. See Zivin's "Sick Jews" on the relationship between Jewishness, illness, and language.

17. See the first chapter of Le Gallez's *The Rhys Woman*. See also chapter 1 of Hite's *The Other Side of the Story*.

Part II / From Self to Family to Nation

1. When Sommer refers to nineteenth-century novels of the nation as "romances," she means "a cross between the contemporary use of the word as a love story and a nineteenth-century use that distinguished romance as more boldly allegorical than the novel" (*Foundational Fictions* 75).

2. The dictatorship in Argentina, called the "Process of National Reorganization" by the military regime, lasted from 1976 to 1983. Brazil lived under a military regime from 1964 to 1985.

3 / Re-membering the Nation by Remembering the Family

1. See Foster 134. Besides Rimetka being an intensely Argentine last name, the passion for soccer on the part of the Rimetka children (28–40) can be seen as very Argentine.

2. *Babuela* is a combination of the words *abuela*, in Spanish, and *bobbe*, in Yiddish. The richness of the term *babuela* is lost in the unfortunate choice of "Granny" for the English translation.

3. In *How the García Girls Lost Their Accents*, Julia Alvarez similarly writes of the mother who always mixed up the proverbs in English.

4. David William Foster notes, "As a synecdoche of the European tradition of forcing Jews beyond the pale, Jews, though they could live in Buenos Aires, could not be buried within the city limits" (*Buenos Aires* 138).

5. Personal correspondence with the author, May 2006.

6. Ibid.

7. In his introduction to *King David's Harp*, Sadow asserts that from 1976 to 1983, "Jews were arrested in numbers that far exceeded their tiny percentage of the population. When abducted, they were treated more harshly than non-Jews" (xxii).

8. Patrick O'Connell also discusses this aspect of the novel in his article. For a discussion of women's writing under dictatorship that addresses other texts, see Tierney-Tello.

9. See Tierney-Tello's chapter on Piñon's *A casa de paixão*.

4 / The Autobiographical Text as Memory Box

1. See my article "Consuming Passions" for more on the relationship between food and sex in *Caetana*.

2. The original phrase is "verdadeiras caixas acústicas da memória" (204); *caixas* are boxes in Portuguese.

3. See Renan's "What Is a Nation?" in Bhabha.

Part III / Bearing Witness to the Self and the Community

1. A clarification of terms is useful here, particularly for readers not familiar with the Canadian context. In Canada, "Indian" is a legal term for people defined by the Indian Act of 1876, which states: "The term 'Indian' means *First*. Any male person of Indian blood reputed to belong to a particular band; *Secondly*. Any child of such person; *Thirdly*. Any woman who is or was lawfully married to such person." (Note that Indian women who married non-Indian men lost their legal status as Indians.) "First Nation" is a self-designation used by Native peoples in Canada as a sovereignty-affirming term. While tribes in the United States determine who their members are, in Canada, the Canadian government determines who is recognized as of "Indian status." As Kateri Damm notes, in "Says Who": "This has led to a rather complicated and confusing number of definitions of Native identity, all of which have political, geographic, social, emotional, and legal implications. There are status Indians, non-status Indians, Metis, Dene, Treaty Indians, urban Indians, on reserve Indians, off-reserve Indians; there are Indians who are Band members and Indians who are not Band members. There are First Nations peoples, descendants of First Nations, Natives, Indigenous peoples, Aboriginal peoples, mixed-bloods, mixed-breeds, half-breeds, enfranchised Indians, Bill C-31 Indians" (12).

2. The Casa de las Americas was founded in Cuba in 1959 to investigate, publish, and award the work of writers, artists and musicians. See www.casa.cult.cu/.

3. A quick search on the MLA Bibliography via First Search revealed 364 entries under the keyword "testimonio" and 529 entries for the keywords "testimonial literature."

4. Smith and Watson also discuss the varying reception of Harriet Jacobs's *Incidents in the Life of a Slave Girl: Written by Herself* and its "veracity." Their discussion of that example "suggests how narratives, and the authority of experience asserted in them, enter a public arena where issues of verifiability and authenticity are fiercely contested by interested groups and where changing norms of the 'truth' of experience lead to reevaluation" (50). *I, Rigoberta Menchú, An Indian Woman in Guatemala* also entered a public arena where issues of verifiability and authenticity were fiercely contested by interested groups.

5. Defined on the inside front cover as "a theoretical and scholarly journal for

discussion and debate on the political economy of capitalism, imperialism, and socialism in the Americas."

6. It is interesting to note that when I requested this first version via my university's Inter-Library Loan (ILL) program (I had the Siglo XXI edition as my own copy), the book listed Elisabeth Burgos as the author while the blue paper slip put over an ILL book was marked "Author: Menchú, Rigoberta.; Burgos-Debr." Presumably the computer did not allow enough space for the complete version of Elisabeth Burgos-Debray to appear, but the discrepancy of attribution of authorship between the book itself and the ILL slip shows that the issue of who is the author of this testimonial is an ongoing one.

7. See DiNova, 35–39, 41–47, 55–58, 175–78 for a sense of these debates.

8. Krupat makes a distinction between the Indian autobiography, which he argues is defined by "the principle of *original bicultural composite composition*" (*For Those Who Came After*, 31, emphasis in the original), and the autobiographies made by "civilized" or christianized Indians, whose texts originated with them and contained a bicultural element but were not compositely produced. Krupat "would class the many 'as-told-to' autobiographies of Indians which have appeared in the twentieth century among autobiographies-by-Indians rather than Indian autobiographies because their subjects' competence in written English allows them to take responsibility for the form of the work to a degree impossible for most Native American subjects of Indian autobiography: but this is, to be sure, a judgment in degree, not kind" (31). Many critics find Krupat's distinctions problematic. DiNova asserts that Krupat's "argument for the universal right to knowledge, if accepted, can be extended to justify any and all acts of cultural appropriation. More important, his challenge to American Indian identity not only devalues identity as a recurring theme in Native literary works; the dismissal of artistic and critical distinctiveness also undermines the validity of tribal sovereignty claims. For if there is no *Indian*, there can be no Indian land, culture, literature, or anything else" (35).

9. For more, see the articles by Godard and Young-Ing.

10. Brian Swann's introduction to his work on translation of Native American literatures begins bluntly: "The fact that Indians were human took some time to sink in. The fact that their languages had value took longer" (xiii).

5 / "The Life of Bobbi Lee Is about Why We Must Talk"

1. I thank Deborah Miranda for sharing her e-mailed letter to Jan Warner and Warner's response with the Association for the Study of American Indian Literatures (ASAIL) Listserv, and for her permission to use the example here. The Web site for the "Resilience of the Human Spirit" conference was accessed at www.blueflowerarts.com/guthriecenter.html.

2. G. Thomas Couser writes that all collaborative autobiography "speaks with a cloven tongue . . . because it conflates two consciousnesses . . . in one undifferentiated voice" (*Altered* 208). Maracle is aware of the problematics of this rhetorical feature.

3. Allen and Maracle's comments also evoke Paul Tennant's definition of the notion of internal colonialism as "the continued subjugation of an indigenous people in a post-colonial independent nation state. Subjugation will in every case involve restriction of land and resources as well as varying degrees of administrative supervision,

social discrimination, suppression of cultural and denial of political and other rights and freedoms" (3–4, quoted in Emberley 131).

4. Oka is a small town in Quebec whose townspeople wanted to enlarge their golf course by appropriating land claimed by the Mohawk people. The Mohawks protested the taking of their lands, put a barricade across the road, and were joined by Native peoples from other nations.

6 / "Part of Surviving Is through Remembering"

1. Dedications of other works by those who lived in the residential schools are quite similar. *Residential Schools: The Stolen Years*, edited by Linda Jaine, is dedicated "to those who attended residential school, to those who are still experiencing the effects of it, and to those who still need to share their story" (iii). Basil Johnston dedicates his *Indian School Days* "to all the boys who preceded us and bequeathed their maroon sweaters to us, to all of my colleagues with whom I endured the hurts and shared the laughter, to those who inherited our maroon sweaters and wore them every Sunday until Garnier was closed in 1958, and to all the prefects and priests and teachers who tried to instruct us and made possible the events herein recorded" (11). He dedicates the work specifically to one friend, Boozo, who "is probably now regaling St. Peter with tales from Spanish" (11). In *From Our Mother's Arms: The Intergenerational Impact of Residential Schools in Saskatchewan*, Constance Dieter notes that her "deepest gratitude goes to the men and women who shared their stories for this book. Their courage and generosity of spirit are steps towards healing in our community" (n.p.).

2. To list just some examples, see Brant Castellano, Davis, and Lahache's *Aboriginal Education: Fulfilling the Promise*; Wallace's *Education for Extinction: American Indians and the Boarding School Experience, 1875–1928*; Archuleta, Child, and Lomawaima's *Away from Home: American Indian Boarding School Experiences, 1870–2000*; Child's *Boarding School Seasons: American Indian Families, 1900–1940*; Chrisjohn and Young's *The Circle Game: Shadows and Substance in the Indian Residential School Experience in Canada*; Fournier and Crey's *Stolen from Our Embrace: The Abduction of First Nations Children and the Restoration of Aboriginal Communities*; Furniss's *Victims of Benevolence: The Dark Legacy of the Williams Lake Residential School*; Haig-Brown's *Resistance and Renewal: Surviving the Indian Residential School*; Johnston's *Indian School Days*; Lomawaima's *They Called It Prairie Light: The Story of the Chilocco Indian School*; Mihesuah's *Cultivating the Rosebuds: The Education of Women at the Cherokee Female Seminary, 1851–1909*; and Miller's *Shingwauk's Vision: A History of Native Residential Schools*.

3. Smith and Watson point out how often life narratives announce particular identities. They give a variety of examples (34–35), but the English version of Menchú's text, *I, Rigoberta Menchú, an Indian Woman from Guatemala*, and *Let me speak!: Testimony of Domitila, a Woman of the Bolivian Mines* are additional examples that mark out identities and nationalities for the women telling their life stories in those texts.

4. Gerald Vizenor notes that the word "Indian" is an invented name that does not come from any Native language or reveal the experiences of the diverse Native peoples grouped under that imposed noun: "The name is unbidden, and the native heirs must bear an unnatural burden to be so christened in their own land" (xiii). Just so is the unbidden name Martha Stone an unnatural burden for Seepeetza.

5. Paula Gunn Allen makes the connection between the term "sacred" and the term "sacrifice," defining the latter term as "'to make sacred.' What is made sacred is empowered" (28). The sites on the ranch are empowering sites for Seepeetza.

6. In her article on N. Scott Momaday's *The Way to Rainy Mountain*, Arlene A. Elder argues that the paintings in that text serve "to demonstrate this written work's interpretation of the 'unity of the arts,' a performance value intrinsic to orature" (273). She quotes Momaday's comment that drawing is a type of storytelling: "writing is drawing, and so the image and the word cannot be divided" (Coltelli 96, quoted in Elder 273). While the paintings done by Momaday's father to illustrate the Kiowa myths and legends are more closely linked to Native artistic traditions than may be the maps in Sterling's text, Elder's reflection on the performance value intrinsic to orature is significant for Sterling's text.

7. Luther Standing Bear (Lakota), in his *My People, the Sioux*, writes of his own experience going to the federal boarding school in Carlisle, Pennsylvania, in 1879, and the imposition of Anglo names:

> One day . . . there was a lot of writing on one of the blackboards. We did not know what it meant, but our interpreter came into the room and said, "Do you see all these marks on the blacksboard? Well, each word is a white man's name. They are going to give each one of you one of these names by which you will hereafter be known." (36)

8. Discussing the Indian residential school experience or reading about the schools may trigger an incident in which the memories recalled are too powerful and too painful. In Canada, the National Indian Residential School Crisis Line has been set up to provide support for former residential school students where they can access emotional and crisis referral services and get information on the Health Canada Indian Residential Schools Resolution Health Support Program at 1–866–925–4419.

9. "Sister Theo looks just like the wicked witch in the Wizard of Oz. She wears a black dress down to her shoes. Her shoes are black too. She doesn't have a witch hat but a black veil with a white thing around the edge. You can't see her hair. She had a big nose and small shiny eyes and thin lips. . . . All the sisters dress like that" (51).

WORKS CITED

Ackerman, Lillian A., ed. *A Song to the Creator: Traditional Arts of Native American Women of the Plateau.* Norman and London: University of Oklahoma Press, 1996.

Adams, David Wallace. *Education for Extinction: American Indians and the Boarding School Experience, 1875–1928.* Lawrence: University of Kansas Press, 1995.

Adams, Timothy Dow. *Light Writing and Life Writing: Photography in Autobiography.* Chapel Hill and London: University of North Carolina Press, 2000.

Agosín, Marjorie. *Passion, Memory, and Identity.* Albuquerque: University of New Mexico Press, 1999.

Aizenberg. Edna. "How a Samovar Helped Me Theorize Latin American Jewish Writing." *Shofar* 19, no. 3 (Spring 2001): 33–40.

Aldama, Arturo J. "Tayo's Journey Home: Crossblood Agency, Resistance, and Transformation in *Ceremony* by Leslie Marmon Silko." In *Cross-Addressing: Resistance Literature and Cultural Borders,* edited by John C. Hawley, 157–80. Albany: State University of New York Press, 1996.

Allen, Chadwick. "Blood as Narrative/Narrative as Blood: Declaring a Fourth World." *Narrative* 6, no. 3 (October 1998): 236–55.

Allen, Paula Gunn. *The Sacred Hoop: Recovering the Feminine in American Indian Tradition.* Boston: Beacon Press, 1986.

———. *Studies in American Indian Literatures: Critical Essays and Course Designs.* New York: Modern Language Association, 1983.

Alonso, Carlos J. *The Burden of Modernity: The Rhetoric of Cultural Discourse in Spanish America.* New York: Oxford University Press, 1998.

Alvarez, Julia. *How the García Girls Lost Their Accents.* 1991. New York: Penguin, 1992.

Andrews, Molly. *Shaping History: Narratives of Political Change.* Cambridge: Cambridge University Press, 2007.

Arias, Arturo, ed. *The Rigoberta Menchú Controversy.* Minneapolis: University of Minnesota Press, 2001.

Archuleta, Margaret L., Brenda J. Child, and Tsianina Lomawaima, eds. *Away from Home: American Indian Boarding School Experiences, 1870–2000.* Phoenix: Heard Museum, 2000.

Armstrong, Jeannette. "The Disempowerment of First North American Native Peoples and Empowerment through Their Writing." In *An Anthology of Native Canadian Writing in English,* edited by Daniel David Moses and Terry Goldie, 207–11. Oxford: Oxford University Press, 1992.

———. "Land Speaking." In *Speaking for the Generations: Native Writers on Writing,* edited by Simon Ortiz, 175–94. Tucson: University of Arizona Press, 1998.

———, ed. *Looking at the Worlds of Our People: First Nations Analysis of Literature.* Penticton, British Columbia: Theytus Books, 1993.

———. "Words." In *Telling It: Women and Language across Cultures,* edited by Sky Lee, Lee Maracle, Daphne Marlatt, and Betsy Warland, 23–29. Vancouver: Press Gang, 1990.

Ashcroft, Bill, Gareth Griffiths, and Helen Tiffin. *The Empire Writes Back: Theory and Practise in Post-colonial Literatures.* London: Routledge, 1989.

Ashley, Kathleen, Leigh Gilmore, and Gerald Peters, eds. *Autobiography and Postmodernism.* Amherst: University of Massachusetts Press, 1994.

Awiakta, Marilou. *Selu: Seeking the Corn Mother's Wisdom.* Golden, Colo.: Fulcrum, 1993.

Ballón, José. *Autonomía cultural de América: Emerson y Martí.* Madrid: Pliegos, 1986.

Barrios de Chungara, Domitila. *Let Me Speak! Testimony of Domitila, a Woman of the Bolivian Mines.* Translated by Victoria Ortiz. New York: Monthly Review Press, 1978.

———. *"Si me permiten hablar . . . ": Testimonio de Domitila, una mujer de las minas de Bolivia.* With Moema Viezzer. Mexico City: Siglo XXI, 1978.

Barthes, Roland. *The Pleasure of the Text.* New York: Hill and Wang, 1975.

———. *Roland Barthes par Roland Barthes.* New York: Hill and Wang, 1977.

Bartow, Joanna R. *Subject to Change: The Lessons of Latin American Women's Testimonio for Truth, Fiction, and Theory.* Chapel Hill: University of North Carolina Press, 2005.

Bartowski, Frances. *Travelers, Immigrants, Inmates: Essays in Estrangement.* Minneapolis: University of Minnesota Press, 1995.

Baskin, Judith R., ed. *Women of the Word: Jewish Women and Jewish Writing.* Detroit: Wayne State University Press, 1994.

Bataille, Gretchen, ed. *Native American Representations: First Encounters, Dis-*

torted Images, and Literary Appropriations. Lincoln: University of Nebraska Press, 2001.

Bataille, Gretchen M., and Kathleen Mullen Sands. *American Indian Women, Telling Their Lives*. Lincoln: University of Nebraska Press, 1984.

Beard, Laura J. "A is for Alphabet, K is for Kabbalah: The Babelic Metatext of Luisa Futoransky." *Intertexts* 1:1 (1997): 25–39.

———. "Consuming Passions in *A doce canção de Caetana*." *Monographic Review/Revista Monográfica* 21 (2005): 104–16.

———. "'Contar la vida de una familia también es contar la historia de un país': *El libro de los recuerdos* de Ana María Shua." *Hispanófila* 148 (Fall 2006): 45–57.

———. "Giving Voice: Testimonial/Autobiographical Works by First Nations Women of British Columbia." *Studies in American Indian Literatures* 12, no. 3 (Fall 2000): 64–83.

———. "The Mirrored Self: Helena Parente Cunha's *Mulher no espelho*." *College Literature* 22, no. 1 (1995): 103–18.

———. "Navigating the Metafictional Text: Julieta Campos' *Tiene los cabellos rojizos y se llama Sabina*." *Hispanófila* 129 (2000): 45–58.

———. "La sujetividad femenina en la metaficción feminista latinoamericana." *Revista iberoamericana* 64, no. 182–83 (1998): 299–311.

Benhabib, Seyla, and Drucilla Cornell. "Introduction: Beyond Politics and Gender." In *Feminism as Critique: On the Politics of Gender*, edited by Benhabib and Cornell, 1–15. Minneapolis: University of Minnesota Press, 1987.

Benstock, Shari. "Expatriate Modernism: Writing on the Cultural Rim." In *Women's Writing in Exile*, edited by Mary Lynn Broe and Angela Ingram, 19–40. Chapel Hill: University of North Carolina Press, 1989.

Bergland, Betty. "Postmodernism and the Autobiographical Subject: Reconstructing the 'Other.'" In *Autobiography and Postmodernism*, edited by Kathleen Ashley, Leigh Gilmore, and Gerald Peters, 130–66. Amherst: University of Massachusetts Press, 1994.

Beverley, John. "The Margin at the Center." In *The Real Thing: Testimonial Discourse and Latin America*, edited by Georg M. Gugelberger, 23–41. Durham: Duke University Press, 1996.

Bhabha, Homi K., ed. *Nation and Narration*. London and New York: Routledge, 1990.

Bird, Gloria. "Breaking the Silence: Writing as Witness." In *Speaking for the Generations: Native Writers on Writing*, edited by Simon Ortiz, 26–49. Tucson: University of Arizona Press, 1998.

Blaeser, Kimberly M. "Native Literature: Seeking a Critical Center." In Armstrong, *Looking at the Words of Our People*, 51–62.

Borges, Jorge Luis. *Ficciones*. Buenos Aires: Emecé, 1956.

Braidotti, Rosi. *Transpositions: On Nomadic Ethics*. Cambridge: Polity Press, 2006.

Brant Castellano, Marlene. "Updating Aboriginal Traditions of Knowledge." In *Indigenous Knowledges in Global Contexts: Multiple Readings of Our World*, edited by George J. Sefa Dei, Budd L. Hall, and Dorothy Goldin Rosenberg, 21–36. Toronto: University of Toronto Press, 2000.

Brant Castellano, Marlene, Lynne Davis, and Louise Lahache, eds. *Aboriginal Education: Fulfilling the Promise*. Vancouver: University of British Columbia Press, 2000.

Brodzki, Bella, and Celeste Schenck, eds. *Life/Lines: Theorizing Women's Autobiography*. Ithaca: Cornell University Press, 1988.

Broe, Mary Lynn, and Angela Ingram, eds. *Women's Writing in Exile*. Chapel Hill: University of North Carolina Press, 1989.

Buchanan, Rhonda Dahl, ed. *El río de los sueños: Aproximaciones críticas a la obra de Ana María Shua*. Colleción Interamer/Interamer Collection 70. Washington, D.C.: Organización de Estados Americanos, 2001.

———. "Entrevista a Ana María Shua." In Buchanan, *El río de los sueños*, 305–26.

———. "Narrating Argentina's 'Epoca del Miedo' in Ana María Shua's *El libro de los recuerdos*." *Confluencia* 13, no. 2 (Spring 1998): 84–91.

Butler, Judith. *Bodies That Matter: On The Discursive Limits of "Sex."* New York: Routledge, 1993.

———. *Gender Trouble: Feminism and the Subversion of Identity*. New York: Routledge, 1990.

Campbell, Maria. *Halfbreed*. 1973. Halifax: Goodread Biographies, 1983.

———. "Strategies for Survival." In *Give Back: First Nations Perspectives on Cultural Practice*, edited by Maria Campbell et al., 5–14. North Vancouver: Gallerie, 1992.

Campos, Julieta. *Tiene los cabellos rojizos y se llama Sabina*. Mexico City, Mexico: Joaquín Mortiz, 1978.

———. *She Has Reddish Hair and Her Name Is Sabina*. Translated by Leland H. Chambers. Athens: University of Georgia Press, 1993.

Castillo, Debra A. *Talking Back: Toward A Latin American Feminist Literary Criticism*. Ithaca: Cornell University Press, 1992.

Castro-Klarén, Sara. *Narrativa femenina en América Latina: Prácticas y perspectivas teóricas/Latin American Women's Narrative: Practices and Theoretical Perspectives*. Madrid: Iberoamericana; and Frankfurt: Vervuert, 2003.

Castro-Klarén, Sara, Sylvia Molloy, and Beatriz Sarlo. *Women's Writing in Latin America*. Boulder, Colo.: Westview Press, 1991.

Chaves Tesser, Carmen. "Post-Structuralist Theory Mirrored in Helena Parente Cunha's *Woman between Mirrors*." *Hispania* 74, no. 3 (September 1991): 594–97.

Chevigny, Bell Gale, and Gari Laguardia, eds. *Reinventing the Americas: Comparative Readings of Literature of the United States and Spanish America*. Cambridge: Cambridge University Press, 1987.

Child, Brenda. *Boarding School Seasons: American Indian Families, 1900–1940*. Lincoln: University of Nebraska Press, 1998.

Chrisjohn, Roland, and Sherri Young. *The Circle Game: Shadows and Substance in the Indian Residential School Experience in Canada*. With Michael Maraun. Penicton, British Columbia: Theytus Books, 1997.

Ciplijauskaité, Biruté. *La novela femenina contemporánea*. Barcelona: Anthropos, 1988.

Cohn, Deborah. *History and Memory in the Two Souths: Recent Southern and Spanish American Fiction*. Nashville: Vanderbilt University Press, 1999.

Collette, Marianella. *Conversación al sur: Entrevistas con escritoras argentinas*. Buenos Aires: Simurg, 2003.

Coltelli, Laura. *Winged Words: American Indian Writers Speak*. Lincoln: University of Nebraska Press, 1990.

Cook-Lynn, Elizabeth. "Lesson of Churchill Fiasco: Indian Studies Need Clear Standards." *Indian Country*, July 7, 2006. www.indiancountrytoday.com/archive/28209314.html.

Cornell, Drucilla, and Adam Thurschwell. "Feminism, Negativity, Intersubjectivity." In *Feminism as Critique: On the Politics of Gender*, edited by Seyla Benhabib and Drucilla Cornell, 143–62. Minneapolis: University of Minnesota Press, 1987.

Cortázar, Julio. *Rayuela*. Caracas: Biblioteca Ayacucho, 1980.

———. *62: Modelo para armar*. Buenos Aires: Sudamericana, 1968.

———. *Último round*. Mexico: Siglo Veintiuno, 1969.

Couser, G. Thomas. *Altered Egos: Authority in American Autobiography*. New York: Oxford University Press, 1989.

Cox, Harvey. *The Secular City: Secularization and Urbanization in Theological Perspective*. London: SCM Press, 1966.

Cunha, Eneida Leal. Introductory remarks for Helena Parente Cunha. In *Com a palavra o Escritor*, edited by Carlos Ribeiro, 154–56. Salvador, Bahia, Brazil: Fundação Casa de Jorge Amado, 2002.

Currie, Mark, ed. *Metafiction*. London and New York: Longman, 1995.

Damm, Kateri. "Dispelling and Telling. Speaking Native Realities in Maria Campbell's *Halfbreed* and Beatrice Culleton's *In Search of April Raintree*." In Armstrong, *Looking at the Worlds of Our People*, 93–112.

———. "Says Who: Colonialism, Identity and Defining Indigenous Literature." In Armstrong, *Looking at the Worlds of Our People*, 9–25.

de Lauretis, Teresa. *Technologies of Gender: Essays on Theory, Film, and Fiction*. Bloomington: Indiana University Press, 1987.

Deloria, Vine, Jr. *God Is Red*. New York: Dell, 1973.

———. "Sacred Lands and Religious Freedom." *American Indian Religions* 1, no. 1 (Winter 1994): 75–76.

Derrida, Jacques. "Des Tours de Babel." In *Difference in Translation*, edited by Joseph F. Graham, 81–101. Ithaca: Cornell University Press, 1985.

———. *On the Name.* Edited by Thomas Dutoit. Stanford: Stanford University Press, 1995.

Dieter, Constance. *From Our Mothers' Arms: The Intergenerational Impact of Residential Schools in Saskatchewan.* Toronto: United Church Publishing House, 1999.

DiNova, Joanne R. *Spiralling Webs of Relation: Movements toward an Indigenous Criticism.* New York and London: Routledge, 2005.

Druxes, Helga. *Resisting Bodies: The Negotiation of Female Agency in Twentieth-Century Women's Fiction.* Detroit: Wayne State University Press, 1996.

Duncan, Kate. "Beadwork and Cultural Identity on the Plateau." In Ackerman, *A Song to the Creator,* 106–11.

DuPlessis, Rachel Blau. *Writing beyond the Ending.* Bloomington: Indiana University Press, 1985.

Eakin, John Paul. *How Our Lives Become Stories: Making Selves.* Ithaca and London: Cornell University Press, 1999.

———. *Touching the World: Reference in Autobiography.* Princeton: Princeton University Press, 1992.

Egan, Susanna. *Mirror Talk: Genres of Crisis in Contemporary Autobiography.* Chapel Hill: University of North Carolina Press, 1999.

Eigenbrod, Renate, and Jo-Ann Episkenew, eds. *Creating Community: A Roundtable on Canadian Aboriginal Literature.* Penticton, British Columbia: Theytus Books; Brandon, Manitoba: Bearpaw, 2002.

Elder, Arlene A. "'Dancing the Page': Orature in N. Scott Momaday's *The Way to Rainy Mountain.*" *Narrative* 7, no. 3 (October 1999): 272–88.

Eltit, Diamela. *Por la patria.* 1986. Santiago: Cuarto Propio, 1995.

Emberley, Julia. *Thresholds of Difference: Feminist Critique, Native Women's Writings, Postcolonial Theory.* Toronto: University of Toronto Press, 1993.

Espadas, Elizabeth. "Destination Brazil: Immigration in Works of Nélida Piñon and Karen Tei Yamashita." *MACLAS* (1998): 51–61.

Evangelista, Liria. *Voices of the Survivors: Testimony, Mourning, and Memory in Post-Dictatorship Argentina (1983–1995).* Translated by Renzo Llorente. New York and London: Garland, 1998.

Fee, Margery, and Sneja Gunew. "From Discomfort to Enlightenment: An Interview with Lee Maracle." *Essays on Canadian Writing.* 83 (Fall 2004): 206–21.

Felman, Shoshana, and Dori Laub. *Testimony: Crises of Witnessing in Literature, Psychoanalysis, and History.* New York: Routledge, 1992.

Fischer, Michael. "Ethnicity and the Post-modern Arts of Memory." In *Writing Culture: The Poetics and Politics of Ethnography,* edited by James Clifford and George E. Marcus, 194–233. Berkeley and Los Angeles: University of California Press, 1986.

Fitz, Earl E. *Brazilian Narrative Traditions in a Comparative Context.* New York: Modern Language Association, 2005.

Fitz, Earl E., and Sophia A. McClennan, eds. *Comparative Cultural Studies and Latin America*. West Lafayette, Ind.: Purdue University Press, 2004.

Flax, Jane. *Thinking Fragments*. Berkeley and Los Angeles: University of California Press, 1990.

"Flipping through the Pages at Book Expo America." *Sunday Edition*. National Public Radio. May 21, 2006. Archived at www.npr.org/templates/story/story.php?storyId=5420695.

Foster, David William. "Ana María Shua: Yiddish and Cultural Memory." In Buchanan, *El río de los sueños*, 83–87.

———. *Buenos Aires: Perspectives on the City and Cultural Production*. Gainesville: University Press of Florida, 1998.

———. "Recent Argentine Women Writers of Jewish Descent." In Agosín, *Passion, Memory, Identity*, 35–57.

Foucault, Michel. "Language to Infinity." In *Language, Counter-Memory, Practice: Selected Essays and Interviews*, 53–67. Ithaca: Cornell University Press, 1977.

Fournier, Suzanne, and Ernie Crey. *Stolen from Our Embrace: The Abduction of First Nations Children and the Restoration of Aboriginal Communities*. Vancouver and Toronto: Douglas and McIntyre, 1997.

Friedman, Ellen G. "Where Are the Missing Contents?: (Post)Modernism, Gender and the Canon." *PMLA* 108, no. 2 (1993): 240–52.

Friedman, Ellen, and Miriam Fuchs, eds. *Breaking the Sequence: Women's Experimental Fiction*. Princeton: Princeton University Press, 1989.

Fuchs, Miriam. *The Text Is Myself: Women's Life Writing and Catastrophe*. Madison: University of Wisconsin Press, 2004.

Fuentes, Carlos. *La muerte de Artemio Cruz*. Mexico City, Mexico: Fondo de Cultura Económica, 1962.

Furniss, Elizabeth. *Victims of Benevolence: The Dark Legacy of the Williams Lake Residential School*. Vancouver: Arsenal Pulp Press, 2000.

Futoransky, Luisa. *De Pe a Pa (o de Pekín a París)*. Barcelona: Anagrama, 1986.

———. Lecture presented for Women's History Month at Johns Hopkins University, Baltimore, Md. March 1993.

———. *Son cuentos chinos*. Montevideo: Trilce, 1986.

———. *Urracas*. Buenos Aires: Planeta, 1992.

García Márquez, Gabriel. *Cien años de soledad*. Buenos Aires: Sudamericana, 1969.

Gattai, Zélia, and Carlos Ribeira. *Com a palavra o Escritor*. Salvador: Fundação Casa de Jorge Amado, 2002.

Gilbert, Sandra M., and Susan Gubar. *The Madwoman in the Attic*. New Haven: Yale University Press, 1979.

Gilmore, Leigh. "An Anatomy of Absence: *Written on the Body*, *The Lesbian Body*, and Autobiography without Names." In *The Gay '90s: Disciplinary and Interdisciplinary Formations in Queer Studies*, edited by Thomas Foster,

Carol Siegel, and Ellen E. Berry, 224–51. New York and London: New York University Press, 1997.

––––––. *Autobiographics: A Feminist Theory of Women's Self-Representation.* Ithaca: Cornell University Press, 1994.

––––––. *The Limits of Autobiography: Trauma and Testimony.* Ithaca and London: Cornell University Press, 2001.

Glickman, Nora. "Jewish Women Writers in Latin America." In *Women of the Word: Jewish Women and Jewish Writing,* edited by Judith R. Baskin, 299–322 . Detroit: Wayne State University Press, 1994.

Godard, Barbara. "The Politics of Representation: Some Native Canadian Writers." *Canadian Literature* 124–25 (Spring–Summer 1990): 183–225.

González Echevarría, Roberto. *The Voice of the Masters: Writing and Authority in Modern Latin American Literature.* Austin: University of Texas Press, 1985.

Grant, Agnes. "Contemporary Native Women's Voices in Literature." *Canadian Literature* 124–25 (Spring–Summer 1990): 124–32.

Grosz, Elizabeth. "Bodies—Cities." In *Sexuality and Space,* edited by Beatriz Colomina, 241–53. New York: Princeton Architectural Press, 1992.

Gugelberger, Georg, ed. *The Real Thing: Testimonial Discourse and Latin America.* Durham and London: Duke University Press, 1996.

Gugelberger, Georg, and Michael Kearney. "Voices for the Voiceless: Testimonial Literature in Latin America." *Latin American Perspectives,* 18, no. 3 (Summer 1991): 3–14.

Hafen, P. Jane. "More Than Intellectual Exploration." *Paradoxa,* 6, no. 15 (2001): 280.

Haig-Brown, Celia. *Resistance and Renewal: Surviving the Indian Residential School.* Vancouver: Arsenal Pulp Press, 1988.

Hall, Stuart. "Cultural Identity and Diaspora." In *Identity: Community, Culture, Difference.* Edited by Jonathan Rutherford. London: Lawrence and Wishart, 1990: 222–37.

Hallett, Nicky. *Lesbian Lives: Identity and Auto/biography in the Twentieth Century.* London, and Sterling, Va: Pluto Press, 1999.

Hanks, Patricia, and Flavia Hodges. *A Dictionary of First Names.* Oxford: Oxford University Press, 1990.

––––––. *A Dictionary of Surnames.* Oxford: Oxford University Press, 1988.

Harlow, Barbara. *Resistance Literature.* New York: Methuen, 1987.

Henke, Suzette A. *Shattered Subjects: Trauma and Testimony in Women's Life-Writing.* New York: St. Martin's Press, 1998.

Higonnet, Margaret R. *Borderwork: Feminist Engagements with Comparative Literature.* Ithaca and London: Cornell University Press, 1994.

Hirsch, Marianne. *Family Frames: Photography, Narrative and Postmemory.* Cambridge: Harvard University Press, 1997.

Hite, Molly. *The Other Side of the Story.* Ithaca: Cornell University Press, 1989.

hooks, bell. "Essentialism and Experience." *American Literary History* 25, no. 1 (1991): 172–83.

Hutcheon, Linda. *Narcissistic Narrative: The Metafictional Paradox*. Waterloo, Ontario: Wilfrid Laurier University Press, 1980.

———. *The Politics of Postmodernism*. London and New York: Routledge, 1989.

Indigenous Knowledges in Global Contexts: Multiple Readings of Our World. Edited by George J. Sefa Dei, Budd L. Hall, and Dorothy Goldin Rosenberg. Toronto: University of Toronto Press, 2000.

Irigaray, Luce. *This Sex Which Is Not One*. Ithaca: Cornell University Press, 1985.

Jacobs, Harriet A. *Incidents in the Life of a Slave Girl: Written by Herself*. Edited by Lydia Maria Child and Jean Fagan Yellin. Cambridge: Harvard University Press, 1987.

Jaine, Linda, ed. *Residential Schools: The Stolen Years*. Saskatoon: Extension Division Press, University of Saskatchewan, 1993.

Johnston, Basil H. *Indian School Days*. Toronto: Key Porter Books, 1988.

Kaminsky, Amy K. *After Exile: Writing the Latin American Diaspora*. Minneapolis: University of Minnesota Press, 1999.

Kantaris, Elia Geoffrey. *The Subversive Psyche: Contemporary Women's Narrative from Argentina and Uruguay*. Oxford: Clarendon Press, 1995.

Kelly, Jennifer. "Coming out of the House: A Conversation with Lee Maracle." *Ariel* 25, no. 1 (January 1994): 73–88.

Klein, Laura F., and Lillian Ackerman, eds. *Women and Power in Native North America*. Norman: University of Oklahoma Press, 1995.

Kolmar, Wendy K., and Frances Bartkowski, eds. *Feminist Theory: A Reader*. 2nd ed. Boston: McGraw-Hill, 2005.

Kristeva, Julia. *Desire in Language*. New York: Columbia University Press, 1980.

Krupat, Arnold. *For Those Who Came After: A Study of Native American Autobiography*. Berkeley and Los Angeles: University of California Press, 1985.

———. *The Voice in the Margin: Native American Literature and the Canon*. Berkeley and Los Angeles: University of California Press, 1989.

Kuokkanen, Rauna. "'Survivance' in Sami and First Nations Boarding School Narrative: Reading Novels by Kerttu Vuolab and Shirley Sterling." *American Indian Quarterly* 27, nos. 3 and 4 (Summer and Fall 2003): 697–727.

Kutzinski, Vera. *Against the American Grain: Myth and History in William Carlos Williams, Jay Wright, and Nicolás Guillén*. Baltimore: Johns Hopkins University Press, 1987.

La Belle, Jenijoy. *Herself Beheld: The Literature of the Looking Glass*. Ithaca: Cornell University Press, 1988.

Le Gallez, Paula. *The Rhys Woman*. London: Macmillan, 1990.

Lejeune, Phillipe. "The Autobiographical Pact." In *On Autobiography*, edited and with a foreword by Paul John Eakin; translated by Katherine Leary, 3–30. Minneapolis: University of Minnesota Press, 1989.

———. *On Autobiography*. Minneapolis: University of Minnesota Press, 1989.

Lentricchia, Frank, and Thomas McLaughlin, eds. *Critical Terms for Literary Study*. Chicago: University of Chicago Press, 1990.

Lionnet, Françoise. *Autobiographical Voices: Race, Gender, Self-Portraiture*. Ithaca: Cornell University Press, 1989.

Lispector, Clarice. *An Apprenticeship or The Book of Delights*. Translated by Richard A. Mazzara and Lorri A. Parris. Austin: University of Texas Press, 1986.

———. *Uma aprendizagem; ou, O livro dos prazeres, romance*. Rio de Janeiro: Francisco Alves, 1991.

Lockhart, Darrell B. Introduction to *Jewish Writers of Latin America: A Dictionary*. New York: Garland, 1997.

Lomawaima, Tsianina. *They Called It Prairie Light: The Story of the Chilocco Indian School*. Lincoln: University of Nebraska Press, 1994.

Lundgren, Jodi. "'Being a Half-breed': Discourses of Race and Cultural Syncreticity in the Works of Three Metis Women Writers." *Canadian Literature* 144 (Spring 1995): 62–77.

MacAdam, Alfred. *Textual Confrontations: Comparative Readings in Latin American Literature*. Chicago: University of Chicago Press, 1987.

Maier, Linda. *Woman as Witness: Essays in Testimonial Literature by Latin American Women*. New York: Peter Lang, 2004.

Mankiller, Wilma, and Micheal Wallis. *Mankiller: A Chief and Her People*. New York: St. Martin's Press, 1993.

Maracle, Lee. *Bobbi Lee: Indian Rebel*. Toronto: Women's Press, 1990.

———. *Daughters Are Forever*. Vancouver: Polestar, 2002.

———. *I Am Woman: A Native Perspective on Sociology and Feminism*. North Vancouver: Write-On Press, 1988.

———. *Ravensong*. Vancouver: Press Gang, 1993.

———. *Sojourner's Truth and Other Stories*. Vancouver: Press Gang, 1990.

———. *Sundogs*. Penticton, British Columbia: Theytus Books, 1992.

Marín, Lynda. "Speaking Out Together: Testimonials of Latin American Women." *Latin American Perspectives*, 18:3 (Summer 1991): 41–68.

Marinho, Beatriz. "Ilusão, Matéria-Prima Fundamental." In *Cultura—O Estado de São Paulo*, 7:551.

Marley, Linda. "Reviewing Past and Future: Postcolonial Canadian Autobiography and Lee Maracle's *Bobbi Lee: Indian Rebel*." *Essays in Canadian Writing* 60 (Winter 1996): 59–77.

Martínez-Richter, Marily, ed. *La caja de la escritura*. Frankfurt: Vervuert, 1997; Madrid: Iberoamericana, 1997.

Masiello, Francine. "In Search of the Nomad's Shadow." In *Luisa Futoransky y su palabra itinerante*, edited by Ester Gimbernat González, 41–55. Montevideo: Hermes Criollo, 2005.

McLeod, Neal. "Coming Home through Stories." In *Addressing Our Words: Aboriginal Perspectives on Aboriginal Literatures*, edited by Armand Garnet Ruffo, 17–36. Penticton, British Columbia: Theytus Books, 2001.

McMaster, Gerald, ed. *Reservation X: The Power of Place in Aboriginal Contemporary Art*. Seattle: University of Washington Press, 1998.

Menchú, Rigoberta. *I, Rigoberta Menchú, An Indian Woman in Guatemala*. Edited and introduced by Elisabeth Burgos-Debray. Translated by Ann Wright. 1984. London and New York: Verso, 1993.

———. *Me llamo Rigoberta Menchú y así me nació la conciencia*. Havana: Casa de las Américas, 1983.

Mihesuah, Devon A. *Cultivating the Rosebuds: The Education of Women at the Cherokee Female Seminary, 1851–1909*. Urbana: University of Illinois Press, 1993.

Miller, J. R. *Shingwauk's Vision: A History of Native Residential Schools*. Toronto: University of Toronto Press, 1996.

Miller, Nancy K. "Facts, Pacts, Acts." *Profession* 92 (1993): 10–14.

Milloy, John S. *A National Crime: The Canadian Government and the Residential School System, 1879–1986*. Winnipeg: University of Manitoba Press, 1999.

Moi, Toril. *Sexual/textual Politics: Feminist Literary Theory*. Routledge: London, 1988.

Molloy, Sylvia. *At Face Value: Autobiographical Writing in Spanish America*. Cambridge: Cambridge University Press, 1991.

———. *En breve cárcel*. Barcelona: Seix Barral, 1981.

Momaday, N. Scott. *The Way to Rainy Mountain*. Albuquerque: University of New Mexico Press, 1969.

Moniz, Naomi Hoki. *As viagens de Nélida, a escritora*. Campinas, S. P., Brazil: Editoria Unicamp, 1993.

Moore, David L. "Return of the Buffalo: Cultural Representation as Cultural Property." In Bataille, *Native American Representations*: 52–78.

———. "Rough Knowledge and Radical Understanding: Sacred Silence in American Indian Literatures." *American Indian Quarterly* 21, no. 4 (Fall 1997): 633–62.

Morrison, Toni. *Beloved*. New York: Knopf, 1987.

Narayan, Uma. "Contesting Cultures: 'Westernization,' Respect for Cultures, and Third-World Feminists." In Kolmar and Bartowski, *Feminist Theory*, 542–50.

Native American Representations: First Encounters, Distorted Images, and Literary Appropriations. Edited by Gretchen M. Bataille. Lincoln: University of Nebraska Press, 2001.

Nussbaum, Martha C. *Poetic Justice: The Literary Imagination and Public Life.* Boston: Beacon Press, 1995.

O'Connell, Patrick L. "Individual and Collective Identity through Memory in Three Novels of Argentina's 'El Proceso.'" *Hispania* 81, no. 1 (March 1998): 3–41.

Ortiz, Simon. "Towards a National Indian Literature: Cultural Authenticity in Nationalism." *Melus* 8, no. 2 (Summer 1981): 7–12.

——, ed. *Speaking for the Generations: Native Writers on Writing.* Tucson: University of Arizona Press, 1998.

Parente Cunha, Helena. *As doze cores do vermelho.* Rio de Janeiro: Editora Espaço e Tempo, 1988.

——. *Mulher no espelho.* São Paulo: Art Editora, 1985.

——. Untitled chapter. In *Com a palavra o Escritor*, edited by Carlos Ribeiro, 157–63. Salvador, Bahia: Fundação Casa de Jorge Amado, 2002.

——. *Woman between Mirrors.* Translated by Fred P. Ellison and Naomi Lindstrom. Austin: University of Texas Press, 1989.

Pease, Donald E. "Author." In Lentricchia and McLaughlin, *Critical Terms for Literary Study*: 105–17.

Pérez Firmat, Gustavo. *Do the Americas Have a Common Literature?* Durham and London: Duke University Press, 1990.

Perreault, Jeanne, and Sylvia Vance, eds. *Writing the Circle: Native Women of Western Canada.* Edmonton: NeWest, 1993.

Pfeiffer, Erna. *Exiliadas, emigrantes, viajeras: Encuentros con diez escritoras latinoamericanas.* Frankfurt: Vervuert, 1995.

Piñon, Nélida. *A doce canção de Caetana.* Rio de Janeiro: Editora Guanabara, 1987.

——. *A força do destino.* Rio de Janeiro: Francisco Alves, 1978.

——. *A república dos sonhos.* Rio de Janeiro: Francisco Alves, 1984.

——. *The Republic of Dreams.* Translated by Helen Lane. New York: Knopf, 1989.

——. *Caetana's Sweet Song.* Translated by Helen Lane. New York: Knopf, 1992..

Pollack, Beth. "Scribe of Time and Memory: [Con]Textualizing the Jewish Experience in Ana María Shua." In Buchanan, *El río de los sueños*, 117–27.

Posadas, Claudia. "'Yo soy una memoria . . . ': Entrevista con la brasileña Nélida Piñon." www.librusa.com/entrevista_nelida_pinon.htm.

Pratt, Mary Louise. *Imperial Eyes: Travel Writing and Transculturation.* London: Routledge, 1992.

Proust, Marcel. *Du côté de chez Swann.* Paris: Gallimard, 1954.

Prucha, Francis Paul, S.J., ed. *Americanizing the American Indians: Writings by the "Friends of the Indian," 1880-1900.* Cambridge: Harvard University Press, 1973.

Ragland-Sullivan, Ellie. "The Magnetism between Reader and Text: Prolegomena to a Lacanian Poetics." *Poetics* 13 (1984): 381–406.

Rand, Richard. "o'er-brimm'd." In *Difference in Translation*, edited by Joseph F. Graham, 81–101. Ithaca: Cornell University Press, 1985.

The Real Thing: Testimonial Discourse and Latin America. Edited by Georg Gugelberger. Durham and London: Duke University Press, 1996.

Reder, Deanna. "Stories of Destruction and Renewal: Images of Fireweed in Autobiographical Fiction by Shirley Sterling and Tomson Highway." In Eigenbrod and Episkenew, *Creating Community*, 275–94.

Renan, Ernest. "What Is a Nation?" Translated by Martin Thom. In *Nation and Narration*, edited by Homi K. Bhabha, 8–22. London and New York: Routledge, 1990.

Rhys, Jean. *Left Bank and Other Stories.* Freeport, N.Y.: Books for Libraries Press, 1970.

———. *Wide Sargasso Sea.* London: Deutsch, 1966.

Riera, Carme. "Entrevista con Nélida Piñon: La vida es la literatura." *Quimera: Revista de literatura* 54–55: 44–49.

Roppolo, Kimberly. "Towards a Tribal-Centered Reading of Native Literature: Using Indigenous Rhetoric(s) Instead of Literary Analysis." In "Native American Literatures: Boundaries & Sovereignties." Special issue, *Paradoxa: Studies in World Literary Genres* 15 (2001): 263–74.

Rosenthal, Debra J. *Race Mixture in Nineteenth-Century U.S. and Spanish American Fictions: Gender, Culture and Nation Building.* Chapel Hill and London: University of North Carolina Press, 2004.

Rowbotham, Sheila. *Woman's Consciousness, Man's World.* London: Penguin, 1973.

Sackville-West, Vita. *The Letters of Vita Sackville-West to Virginia Woolf.* Edited by Mitchell Leaska and Louise DeSalvo. New York: William Morrow, 1984.

Sadow, Steven A. *King David's Harp: Autobiographical Essays by Jewish Latin American Writers.* Albuquerque: University of New Mexico Press, 1999.

Sáenz de Tejada, Cristina. "Representaciones de la negritude brasileña en *Mulher no espelho* y *As Mulheres de Tijucopapo.*" *Afro-Hispanic Review* 16, no. 1 (Spring 1997): 47–52.

Sands, Kathleen M. "American Indian Autobiography." In Allen, *Studies in American Indian Literatures*, 55–65.

———. "Cooperation and Resistance: Native American Collaborative Personal Narrative." In *Native American Representations*, 134–49.

Sarlo, Beatriz. "Política, ideología y figuración literaria." In *Ficción y política: La narrativa argentina durante el proceso militar*, edited by René Jara y Hernán Vidal, 30–59. Minneapolis: Institute for the Study of Ideologies and Literature, 1987.

Schaffer, Kay, and Sidonie Smith. "Conjunctions: Life Narratives in the Field of Human Rights." *Biography* 27, no. 1 (Winter 2004): 1–24.

Schwartz, Marcy. "Paris under Her Skin: Luisa Futoransky's Urban Inscriptions of Exile." In *Luisa Futoranksy y su palabra itinerante*, edited by Ester Gimbernat González, 171–201. Montevideo: Hermes Criollo, 2005.

———. Review of *Urracas*, by Luisa Futoransky. *Hispamérica* 69 (December 1994): 114–17.

———. *Writing Paris: Urban Topographies of Desire in Contemporary Latin American Fiction.* Albany: State University of New York Press, 1999.

Scott, Nina M. "Inter-American Literature: An Antidote to the Arrogance of Culture." *College English* 41, no. 6 (February 1980): 635–43.

Sewell, Anna Marie. "Natives on Native Literature: What Do We Rightly Write? OR: Shot Headfirst from the Canon." In Eigenbrod and Episkenew, *Creating Community*, 19–31.

Shanley, Kathryn W. "'Born from the Need to Say': Boundaries and Sovereignties in Native American Literary and Cultural Studies." *Paradoxa* 6, no. 15 (2001): 3–26.

Shua, Ana María. *Los amores de Laurita.* Buenos Aires: Sudamericana, 1984.

———. *The Book of Memories.* Translated by Dick Gerdes. Albuquerque: University of New Mexico Press, 1998.

———. *Los días de pesca.* Buenos Aires: Corregidor, 1981.

———. *El libro de los recuerdos.* Buenos Aires: Sudamericana, 1994.

———. *El marido argentino promedio.* Buenos Aires: Sudamericana, 1991.

———. *El sol y yo.* Buenos Aires: 1967.

———. *La muerte como efecto secundario.* Buenos Aires: Sudamericana, 1997.

———. *Soy paciente.* Buenos Aires: Sudamericana, 1996.

———. *Viajando se conoce gente.* Buenos Aires: Sudamericana, 1988.

Shmueli, Ali. *The Tower of Babel: Identity and Sanity.* Atlantic Highlands, N.J.: Humanities Press, 1978.

Siskind, Mariano. "Tradición y reescritura: La construcción de una identidad judía." In Buchanan, *El río de los sueños*, 89–102.

Sklodowska, Elzbieta. "The Poetics of Remembering, the Politics of Forgetting: Rereading *I, Rigoberta Menchú*." In Arias, *The Rigoberta Menchú Controversy*, 198–218.

Smith, Paul Chaat. "The Meaning of Life." In McMaster, *Reservation X*, 31–40.

Smith, Sidonie. "The Autobiographical Manifesto: Identities, Temporalities, Politics." In *Autobiography and Questions of Gender*, edited by Shirley Neuman, 186–212. London: Frank Cass, 1991.

———. *Moving Lives: 20th Century Women's Travel Writing.* Minneapolis: University of Minnesota Press, 2001.

———. *A Poetics of Women's Autobiography.* Bloomington: Indiana University Press, 1987.

———. *Subjectivity, Identity, and the Body: Women's Autobiographical Practices in the Twentieth Century.* Bloomington and Indianapolis: Indiana University Press, 1993.

Smith, Sidonie, and Julia Watson. *Reading Autobiography: A Guide for Interpreting Life Narratives*. Minneapolis: University of Minnesota Press, 2001.

———, eds. *Getting a Life: Everyday Uses of Autobiography*. Minneapolis: University of Minnesota Press, 1996.

———, eds. *Women, Autobiography, Theory: A Reader*. Madison: University of Wisconsin Press, 1998.

Smith, Valery. *Self-Discovery and Authority in Afro-American Narrative*. Cambridge: Harvard University Press, 1987.

Sneed, Paul M. "An Interview with Nélida Piñon." *World Literature Today* 29, no. 1 (2005): 18–21.

Sobral, Patricia Isabel. "Entre fronteiras: A condição do migrante n' *A república dos sonhos*." *Portuguese Literary & Cultural Studies* 1 (Fall 1998): 67–87.

Sommer, Doris, ed. *Cultural Agency in the Americas*. Durham and London: Duke University Press, 2006.

———. *Foundational Fictions: The National Romances of Latin America*. Berkeley and Los Angeles: University of California Press, 1991.

———. "Irresistible Romance: The Foundational Fictions of Latin America." In *Nation and Narration*, edited by Homi K. Bhabha, 71–98. London and New York: Routledge, 1990.

———. "No Secrets." In *The Real Thing: Testimonial Discourse and Latin America*, edited by Georg Gugelberger, 130–57. Durham and London: Duke University Press, 1996.

———. "'Not Just a Personal Story': Women's *Testimonios* and the Plural Self." In Brodzki and Schenck, *Life/Lines*, 107–30.

———. *Proceed with Caution, When Engaged by Minority Writing in the Americas*. Cambridge and London: Harvard University Press, 1999.

———. "Resisting the Heat: Menchú, Morrison, and Incompetent Readers." In *Cultures of United States Imperialism*, edited by Amy Kaplan and Donald E. Pease, 407–32. Durham and London: Duke University Press, 1993.

Spengemann, William C. "What Is American Literature?" *Centennial Review* 22 (1978): 119–38.

Spitzer, Leo. "Rootless Nostalgia: Vienna in La Paz, La Paz in Elsewhere." *Shofar* 19, no. 3 (Spring 2001): 6–17.

Standing Bear, Luther. Selections from *My People, the Sioux*. In Vizenor, ed., *Native American Literature*, 32–44.

Stavans, Ilan. "Ana María Shua: Memory and Myth." In Buchanan, *El río de los sueños*, 79–82.

Sterling, Shirley. *My Name Is Seepeetza*. Toronto: Groundwood Books, 1992.

———. "Seepeetza Revisited: An Introduction to Six Voices." Centre for the Study of Curriculum and Instruction, UBC. http://ccfi.educ.ubc.ca/publication/insights/online/v03n01/sterling.html.

Stern, Steven J. *Remembering Pinochet's Chile*. Durham and London: Duke University Press, 2004.

Stoll, David. *Rigoberta Menchú and the Story of All Poor Guatemalans.* Boulder, Colo.: Westview Press, 1999.

Sukenick, Lynn. *The Authority of Experience: Essays in Feminist Criticism.* Amherst: University of Massachusetts Press, 1977.

Swann, Brian, ed. *On the Translation of Native American Literatures.* Washington and London: Smithsonian Institution Press, 1992.

Taylor, Diana. "DNA of Performance: Political Hauntology." In *Cultural Agency in the Americas,* edited by Doris Sommer, 52 – 81. Durham and London: Duke University Press, 2006.

Teixeira, Vera Regina. "Nélida, the Dreamweaver." *World Literature Today* 79 (January–April 2005): 23–26.

Tennant, Paul. "Native Indian Political Organization in British Columbia, 1900–1969: A Response to Internal Colonialism," *BC Studies* 55 (Autumn 1982): 3–49.

Tierney-Tello, Mary Beth. *Allegories of Transgression and Transformation: Experimental Writing by Women Living Under Dictatorship.* Albany: State University of New York, 1996.

Unamuno, Miquel de. *Niebla.* Barcelona: Plaza and Janés, 1985.

Valente, Luis Fernando. Review of *Woman between Mirrors,* by Helena Parente Cunha. *Hispania* 74, no. 3 (September 1991): 697–98.

Vieira, Nelson H. "Editor's Introduction: The Jewish Diaspora of Latin America." *Shofar* 19, no. 3 (Spring 2001): 1–5.

Vizenor, Gerald, ed. *Native American Literature.* New York: Harper Collins, 1995.

Warrior, Robert. *The People and the World: Reading Native Non-Fiction.* Minneapolis: University of Minnesota Press, 2005.

Watson, Julia. "Ordering the Family: Genealogy as Autobiographical Pedigree." In Smith and Watson, *Getting a Life: Everyday Uses of Autobiography*: 297–323.

Weaver, Jace, ed. *Defending Mother Earth: Native American Perspectives on Environmental Justice.* Maryknoll, N.Y.: Orbis Books, 1996.

White, Patrick. *The Twyborn Affair.* 1979. New York: Viking, 1980.

Whitlock, Gillian. *The Intimate Empire: Reading Women's Autobiography.* London and New York: Cassell, 2000.

Williams, Raymond Leslie. "Power Relations." Review of *Woman between Mirrors,* by Helena Parente Cunha. *American Book Review* 13, no. 1 (1991): 15.

Wilson, Gavin. "Grad Reveals Wisdom in Elders' Storytelling." www.publicaffairs.ubc.ca/ubcreports/1997/97nov13/gradgw.html.

Womack, Craig. *Red on Red: Native American Literary Separatism.* Minneapolis: University of Minnesota Press, 1999.

Wong, Hertha Dawn. *Sending My Heart Back across the Years: Tradition and Innovation in Native American Autobiography.* New York and Oxford: Oxford University Press, 1992.

Young-Ing, Greg. "Aboriginal Peoples' Estrangement: Marginalization in the Publishing Industry." In Armstrong, *Looking at the Worlds of Our People*, 177–87.

Yúdice, George. "*Testimonio* and Postmodernism." *Latin American Perspectives* 18, no. 3 (Summer 1991): 15–31.

Zamora, Lois Parkinson. *Contemporary American Women Writers: Gender, Class, Ethnicity.* London and New York: Longman, 1998.

———. "The Usable Past: The Idea of History in Modern U.S. and Latin American Fiction." In Pérez Firmat, *Do the Americas Have a Common Literature?*: 7–41.

———. *Writing the Apocalypse: Historical Vision in Contemporary U. S. and Latin American Fiction.* Cambridge: Cambridge University Press, 1989.

Zivin, Erin Graff. "Sick Jews: Disease and Deformity in Luisa Futoransky's *De Pe a Pa: De Pekín a París* and Margo Glantz's 'Zapatos: andante con variaciones.'" In *Luisa Futoransky y su palabra itinerante*, edited by Ester Gimbernat González, 121–32. Montevideo: Hermes Criollo, 2005.

Index